SPANISH BALLADS

(ROMANCES ESCOGIDOS)

EDITED WITH

INTRODUCTION, NOTES, AND VOCABULARY

BY

S. GRISWOLD MORLEY, Ph.D.

Professor of Spanish in the University of California

GREENWOOD PRESS, PUBLISHERS
WESTPORT, CONNECTICUT

Library of Congress Cataloging in Publication Data

Morley, Sylvanus Griswold, 1878-   ed.
    Spanish ballads (romances escogidos)

    Reprint of the ed. published by H. Holt, New
York.
    Bibliography: p.
    Includes index.
    1. Ballads, Spanish--Texts.   I.   Title.
PQ6196.M7   1976   861'.04   78-137068
ISBN 0-8371-5531-2

Originally published in 1938 by Henry Holt and Company,
New York

Reprinted in 1977 by Greenwood Press, Inc.

Library of Congress catalog card number 78-137068

ISBN 0-8371-5531-2

Printed in the United States of America

PREFACE

THE popular ballads of Spain may be said to constitute the most important single body of poetry (leaving aside the drama) known to the history of Spanish literature. The medieval epic, the courtly lyric of the fifteenth and sixteenth centuries, the highly meritorious narrative and lyric productions of the nineteenth, interest each a group of scholars or students of literature, but the ballad has made a wide appeal to the general reading public of many countries. To the critic it represents the perfection of popular poetry; the layman finds it interesting because it combines dramatic directness with lyric charm.

Such poems would seem to be ideal material for the use of college classes. The one drawback which tells against their wide availability is the somewhat archaic nature of the language, both in words and grammar. This difficulty the editor has tried to overcome as much as possible by a vocabulary which distinguishes carefully between archaic and modern words and meanings, and by grammatical notes which call attention to every important variation from modern usage. The language of the *romances* is not hard to understand, and the sentences are not involved; but, as in dealing with the French seventeenth-century drama, the

iii

student should guard against conferring new meanings on old words, and against accepting obsolete constructions as modern.

The present collection is intended to be representative of Spanish popular ballads (*romances viejos populares, juglarescos, tradicionales modernos*), and to this end by far the greater part of the text is given to the popular poems. A very few of the more artificial classes (*rs. eruditos, artísticos, vulgares*) are included as specimens of the further development of the *romance*. If, in addition to an acquaintance with the Spanish ballad, the student obtains some notion of the epic poetry of Spain in the Middle Ages, that will be an incidental advantage, but not the one primarily aimed at by the editor.

Neither did it enter into the editor's plan to give comparative references covering all the countries where similar folk-themes may be found. It is intended to specify relationships within the Iberian Peninsula, and to refer to easily accessible works where fuller details are given. In other words, the editor wishes to point the way to further research, without overloading the notes with more erudition than is necessary.

As to the choice of poems, there will always be differences of opinion concerning the most desirable selection, and many will recall favorite ballads which they will not find here. The exigencies of class use have compelled the omission of some of the best, but it is believed that none of the popular class are included which have not real literary value, and that all the important divisions of subject-matter are represented.

The texts of the old poems are those of Wolf, or of Durán and Menéndez y Pelayo in the case of poems that do not appear in the *Primavera y Flor de Romances*. Wolf's texts were modernized somewhat in spelling; the only further change which the present editor has made is to bring the accents up to date. A few variants given by Wolf have been incorporated in the text, but no arbitrary changes are made. The poems are printed entire, with two exceptions, viz. one line in no. XII, and three in no. XXXVI. Wolf suppressed all the paragogic *e*'s, in accordance with a theory which has since been overthrown. In no. XLIII the *e*'s have been restored after the text of the *Silva de Varios Romances*, 1602 (Ticknor Library), to serve as an example.

An exact reproduction of the earliest printed texts would hardly be desirable for general class use, and it certainly would have been attended by considerable difficulty, as the *Cancionero de romances* "sin año," that of 1550, and the *Silva de Varios Romances* of 1550 are among the rarest books known to bibliographers.

The *romances* are here classified primarily according to character instead of subject, possibly for the first time in the history of collections of *romances*. Such a classification is attended by many difficulties, since there are always some poems which fall in the border regions, but it is necessary if the student is to gain an idea of the historical development of the ballad. If there were any doubt as to the advantage of this arrangement, it would be set at rest by the recommendations of A. Morel-Fatio (*Romania*, I, 125) and R. Menéndez Pidal (*Notas para el romancero de Fernán González*, p. 504), who both advocate it as the only satisfactory one. Scholars may take exception to placing the *rs. juglarescos* under the general heading *rs. populares*. But the particular juglaresque ballads in this collection were so widely known in the sixteenth century and so popular in the looser sense, that the license does not appear open to severe criticism.

The editor makes grateful acknowledgment of aid and support from several sources. Prof. J. D. M. Ford of Harvard, without whose encouragement the book would never have been published, has made many valuable suggestions. Prof. Ramón Menéndez Pidal of Madrid very kindly answered a long list of queries with regard to special difficulties. Prof. C. Carroll Marden of the Johns Hopkins University read the Notes in manuscript, and Prof. E. C. Hills of Colorado College read the second proof of the entire book. Other material favors were received from Sig. Benedetto Croce of Naples and Dr. Arthur F. Whittem of Harvard. Those who know the pressure of work which accompanies the daily life of all these scholars will appreciate the value of the favors received from them.

S. G. M.

May, 1911.

CONTENTS

vii

ABBREVIATIONS

Catál.	*Catálogo del romancero judío-español*
cf.	compare
Crón. gen.	*Primera crónica general de España*, publicada por Ramón Menéndez Pidal
D.	Agustin Durán, *Romancero general*
ed.	edition
Ép. cast.	*l'Épopée castillane à travers la littérature espagnole*
JMP	Juan Menéndez Pidal, *Colección de los viejos romances*, etc.
l.	line
MF	Milá y Fontanals, *De la poesía heroico-popular castellana*
mod.	modern
MP	Menéndez y Pelayo, *Antología de poetas líricos castellanos*
n.	note
p.	page
r., rs.	*romance, romances*
RMP	Ramón Menéndez Pidal
Rom. geral	Th. Braga, *Romanceiro geral portuguez, segunda edição ampliada*
Rs. trads.	*Los romances tradicionales en América*
Sp.	Spanish
W.	Wolf and Hofmann, *Primavera y Flor de romances*

N.B. *Titles* in the text not between brackets are found in the earliest Spanish editions; the others have been supplied by later editors.

INTRODUCTION

I. MEANING OF THE WORD *ROMANCE*

THE word *romance* is used in modern Castilian to designate a short form of epico-lyric poetry, that called in English the *popular ballad;* and thence any poem written in the same meter as such a ballad. Originally *romance* or *romanz* (Lat. *romanicĕ*) was a term applied to the vulgar tongues of Latin-speaking countries, that is, to Provençal, French, Spanish, etc., when these began to be recognized as speeches separate from Latin. In Spain, any writing in the local language, whether verse or prose, was early designated by this term, and it was only when Latin as a vehicle of literary expression was fading well into the distance that the meaning of the word *romance* narrowed down, first to any sort of poetry, and later to the short ballad. About 1450 we first find *romance* used as a synonym of *cantar* where ballads are certainly referred to. Later on the term came into the commonest use, and was applied not only to all verse written in the characteristic ballad meter, but even to the meter itself.

II. ORIGIN OF THE SPANISH POPULAR BALLAD

At about the same time with the allusion to them by name the ballads themselves appear in literary history. Although not published in large numbers till a

century later, isolated poems in ballad meter are not
wanting before 1450. References to specific *romances,*
often qualified as "viejos," become more frequent in
the works of literary men toward the close of the fifteenth century. By 1500 the *romance* meter is used
by cultured rimers for all kinds of matter.

Whence came these remarkable poems, without
known author, and called "old" when they first appear to view? The question was long answered by
more or less ingenious guesses, without solid foundation of knowledge, and the ballads were supposed to
be hoary with age, perhaps a relic of the very earliest
compositions in Castilian, which were the nucleus of
the long epics. But recent investigations of the medieval epics and chronicles in Spain have served both
to limit the age of the earliest *romances* and to shed
light on their origin.

The popular ballads of Spain represent a stage in
the development of epic poetry, — of the narrative
Early epic poe- heroic poem. The twelfth, thirteenth
try in Spain and fourteenth centuries produced in
Spain, just as in Northern France, though in far less
number, long epics, partly historical, partly fictitious,
with the origin of which we are fortunately not here
concerned, for it is still warmly debated. They were
written doubtless mostly by professional minstrels, or
juglares, men whose business it was to entertain the
fighters of those rude times in their hours of idleness.
The epics consisted of some thousand long lines each
(see below under *Meter*), arranged in *laisses* or series

of varying length, within which the assonance does not change. Rime was not employed.

By a combination of causes peculiar to Spain the greater number of these epics have been lost; in fact, only three have been preserved in verse (*Poema del Cid, Infantes de Lara, Crónica rimada*), and all these in a more or less fragmentary state. Educated persons were perhaps rarer in Christian Spain during the Middle Ages than in any other Latin nation; few copies were written and those few not cared for. Hence the treasure of legend mingled with history, as well as the admirable poetry, which the Spanish epics undoubtedly contained, has in large part disappeared.

A surprising amount of such material, however, which up to within a short time was thought lost, has been discovered in prose form in the early histories of Spain. The Spanish people have always been fond of their own history, though none too careful of accuracy as to detail provided the national vanity was flattered. Beginning with the Latin chronicles of monks, medieval legends were set down as facts, with or without a saving proviso of doubt. The first important history in Castilian (the *Primera crónica general*, compiled under the direction of Alfonso X, and not yet finished in 1289) incorporates all available material, whether Latin prose or Castilian verse, and often refers directly to epic poems (*cantares*) as its source. The numerous later versions of the *Crónica general*, each more padded and fabulous than the one before, likewise made use of whatever poems were in vogue in their day, and we thus have in the Chronicles a kind of running summary of lost epics, coming down to 1500 and later. Some of these Chronicles followed their poetic sources so closely that it is possible to pick out of the prose page assonating lines, and so roughly to reconstruct the original verse. It is not hard, therefore, to trace the development of the poems from the rugged dignity of the twelfth century to the romantic vagaries of the fourteenth. In this way we know that beside the epics preserved in verse, others existed on many national subjects, such as Bernardo del Carpio, Fernán González, Garci Fernández, Sancho García, the Infante D. García, the division of the Christian kingdoms at the death of Fernando I°, and the Siege of Zamora[1]; and on one theme based on a French legend, the Mainet or Youth of Charlemagne. The *1ª crónica general* is very important for the early poems of which it contains traces; the *Segunda crónica* (*Crónica de* 1344), as yet unpublished, is of great interest for the later versions, and contains the first allusions to the poem on the Youth of the Cid, or *Rodrigo*.

III. THE *ROMANCES;* THEIR DIFFERENT CLASSES

The underground river of epic creation comes to the surface in the fifteenth century in the shape of the early

Romances viejos

romances. They fall into various classes, according to their style and matter. Such as deal with the early epic cycles, Bernardo del

[1] Possibly on Roderick the Goth; cf. note to nos. XXXIV–XXXV.

Carpio, Fernán González, the Infantes de Lara, the
Cid, are probably mere relics of the lost poems, —
fragments, striking passages remembered by the people and handed down orally from one generation to
another, but with the many changes incident to such
a method of transmission. The popular mind tends
always to warp its traditional morsel to its own view-
point, — hence no two versions are ever quite alike, —
and also to prune away useless words and leave only
the boldest outline, the very kernel of the story. The
extant ballads appear to have been drawn from the
later epics rather than the early ones, and hence it is
likely that the process of disintegration did not begin
until the fourteenth century. None of the *romances* we
have can be much older than 1400 in their present form,
however old the original tradition which they represent.[1]

Slightly different in origin, but similar in style, are
the ballads that deal with events more nearly at hand,
such as the reign of Pedro el Cruel (1350–1369) and the
frontier wars between the Granadine Moors and Christians (*romances fronterizos*). In these cases the poems
were short from the first, and very likely composed
soon after the events, but their inspiration is the same;
there is the same free handling, the same large heroic

[1] The oldest in form of all the popular ballads is thought to
be the fragment from the Infantes de Lara cycle, "Yo me estaba
en Barbadillo" (included in W. 19). The oldest frontier ballad
to which a date can be assigned is "Cercada tiene á Baeza"
(MP, IX, 196), which refers to an obscure event in the year 1368,
and must have been composed soon after (cf. MP, XII, 169–174).

spirit. Of comparatively late origin are probably the *romances* describing dramatic scenes from daily life (*novelescos sueltos*), which, by the way, are almost the only ballads left in oral tradition to-day.

Here it is not out of place to warn against the notion that a "popular ballad" is literally the product of a **Meaning of** people, not an individual. It is called **"popular bal-** popular only "by antonomasia," as Me-**lad"** néndez y Pelayo is fond of saying. Though greatly altered in passing through many hands, until it represents the spirit of a whole nation as well as any poetry can do, *some one composed* the ballad originally, and some other individuals wrought the changes in it. It is well to remember the Spaniard's facility of improvisation, so great that to-day a couplet may be tossed off by a laborer and become current, whilst the author disappears at once from view.

> "Estos romances, señora,
> Nacen al sembrar los trigos"

said Lope de Vega (*Con su pan se lo coma*, quoted by Depping). "Popular ballads" are anonymous, but not because a dancing chorus broke forth into heroic verse spontaneously and responsively. They did not spring mysteriously out of the ground. The facts are well expressed in these words of Joaquín Costa (*Poesía popular española y Mitología y literatura celto-hispanas*, Madrid, 1888, pp. 14–15), which, however, apply rather to the *romances* of isolated subject-matter than to those belonging to the old epic cycles:

". . . Los monumentos de la poesía popular son casi siempre anónimos: el poeta no se considera, por lo común, sino como órgano accidental del pueblo; su inspiración es casi siempre pasagera y fugitiva; escucha el dictado de éste, cuando no canta sus propias aventuras, interprétalo en fáciles y sencillas cadencias, comunica al público ansioso de recogerlo el verso ó versos en que ha cortado su pensamiento, y se abisma de nuevo en la masa como átomo indiferenciado; y cuando las generaciones que reciben ese legado inquieren el nombre del autor, apenas puede contestar la crítica otra cosa que esto: 'se llama *Pueblo*'; respuesta figurada, donde se da á entender el órgano por el todo social á quien sirve y se subordina, el representante por lo representado, la parte por el todo."

The second class of *romances* that are really old consists in those called *romances juglarescos*. They contrast with the first by their length, verbosity ánd use of rime-formulae. They may be regarded as representing a last degenerate stage of the long epic, but they were designed for the ears of the people in the public square, instead of a few nobles of leisure, and hence are shorter than the early epics, and more romantic than historical. It is probable that the *juglares* who composed them kept the reciting largely in their own hands, for the people's memory would soon have mended their prolixity.[1]

Romances juglarescos

---

[1] It did, in fact, in many cases. The same process occurred as with the older historical epics, and the *rs.* of Durandarte, Belerma

The subjects they treat belong chiefly to the cycle of Carolingian chivalry, and are therefore foreign to the Spanish soil. Yet many of the juglaresque ballads are interesting for their frankness, and the characters of Gaiferos, Calaínos and the Marquis of Mantua became so dear to the people that the poems about them may well be called popular. Some, like the first two of Gaiferos (nos. XL and XLI), appear quite old; others, like the famous story of Count Alarcos (no. XLIV), are skilful compositions of a true poet.

The subsequent history of the popular ballad in Spain is not so glorious. The golden age of the *romance* **Decadence of** terminated with the cessation of the age-**the popular** long struggle against the Moors, as if a **ballad** truly national enterprise and spirit were necessary for their formation. The later wars of conquest in Europe left the people cold. After the fifteenth century the true epic vein was exhausted, or diverted into the channel of the drama. The profound changes in the government affected the character of the nation. As the monarchs rose in power, the people sank, and from a nearly homogeneous race of warriors appeared a ruling class and a subject class. The gulf widened, and though the drama for a time still appealed to both classes alike, in other branches each must have its own literature, adapted to its needs, instead of one, embodying the aspirations of all.

(no. XLII), Rosaflorida, etc., are popular fragments reduced from longer juglaresque poems.

Worthy creation in the pure popular epic ceased, but interest in the popular poetry as a branch of literature increased through the sixteenth century, so that several publishers made collections of the ballads most in vogue, but for which fact our knowledge of them would be scant indeed.[1]

From about 1600 on, the poetic taste of the people was satisfied by the cheap poems well named *romances* *Romances* *vulgares*, printed on loose sheets for sale, *vulgares* and sung by beggars in the streets. The authors are without education, and their names often appear with their work, which is rude in form and matter. This sort of production still continues, and is concerned with all kinds of legends, fantastic tales and adventures of the dime-novel type, as well as contemporary events ("bulletin-ballads").

[1] Spain was the first European country to preserve its popular ballads in print. A few *rs. viejos* are included in the *Cancionero general* of Castillo (1511), as in the previous similar lyric *Cancionero* of Constantina (date unknown). At about the same time or soon after, they began to be published in separate sheets (*pliegos sueltos*, English "broadsides"), which have continued to the present day. The first collections devoted exclusively to *rs.* were the *Cancionero de romances* "sin año" (published at Antwerp shortly before 1550), the *Cancionero de romances* "de 1550" (at the same place), and the *Silva de varios romances* (in three parts, Saragossa, 1550 and 1551). These three books and *pliegos sueltos* contain the great majority of the old ballads which we possess, though some appear first in later collections of *rs.* For the complete bibliography see Durán, *Rom. gen.*, I, LXVII–XCVI, and II, 678–695; Wolf, *Studien*, 310–400; and MP, IX, 281 ff.

Parallel with this vulgar current in the popular life ran that of the old ballads which still remained in oral *Romances* tradition. While the former sufficed to *tradicionales* amuse the lower classes in the cities, *modernos* the latter endured in the rural districts. The ballads, borne on the wings of the melodies to which they were sung, were not only preserved by the country-folk of Spain, but spread wonderfully. Catalonia and Portugal adopted the form (if it was not native there) and many Castilian subjects. The *romances* were carried to the eastern end of the Mediterranean by the exiled Jews (see note to no. LVIII, l. 70), and to all the lands explored and settled by the Spanish and Portuguese *conquistadores*. Fragments of them have been found not only in the Iberian peninsula, but in the Azores, Madeira, Morocco, Salonika and South America. It is since the middle of the nineteenth century that folklorists have begun systematically to collect such poems from the lips of peasants, and the yield has been full of interest. The old stories of national heroes seem to have died out, and it is very rarely that one meets the name of Bernardo or the Cid. Stories of domestic life are far more common, but some of them are of early origin.[1]

[1] Most of the traditional ballads in Castilian discovered up to 1900 may be found united, with lists of sources, in MP, X. New ones are constantly being published. (See *Bibliography*.) Prior to that date it was thought that the central regions of Spain were almost barren of traditional ballads, but closer. investigation, initiated by RMP, has produced remarkable results in Cas-

Going back to the point of separation between popular and artistic poetry, we take up the latter branch. The *romances* and medieval epics were despised as vulgar products by the courtier poets of the early fifteenth century, dazzled by the recent discovery of the Latin and Italian literatures. The Marquis of Santillana (1388–1458) put them in the lowest of his three categories of poetic productions: "Infimos poetas son aquellos que facen estos romances é cantares de que la gente baja é de servil condición se alegra" (*Carta al Condestable de Portugal*, ca. 1450). The first signs of interest in the popular productions *Romances trovadorescos* appear toward the close of the century. Queen Isabella is said to have listened to *romances* with pleasure. Some of the amorous poets of the cour-

tile and other provinces. The majority of the versions are as yet unpublished. RMP declares that he possesses over 1500 such (*Romancero español*, p. 103). He proposes to collate all the available material, ancient and modern, and form critical texts as the basis for a new *Romancero general*. As nearly as one can judge from extant data, such a publication will add interesting details to our knowledge of the Spanish ballad, and will resuscitate a few old *rs.* which did not find their way into the sixteenth century collections, but will hardly change our estimate of the genre as a whole. RMP himself says that "la versión individual es hoy muy inferior á la del siglo XVI," so that the only future advantage consists in the ability to compare many versions. Search in Portugal and Catalonia seems nearly to have ceased, and tradition in those countries may be considered adequately represented in the printed collections of Braga and Milá. The astonishing vitality of tradition among the Spanish Jews is demonstrated by RMP in his *Catálogo del romancero judío-español*.

tier school, such as Tapia, Quirós and Lope de Sosa,
deigned to expand with their glosses some *romances viejos*, and to compose poems of their own in the *romance*
meter, sometimes very prettily, in the lyrical "trouba-
douresque" style.[1]

A later development was the *romance erudito*, wholly
different in nature. It was devised probably by Alonso
Romances de Fuentes (*Quarenta cantos*, 1550),
eruditos and continued by Lorenzo de Sepúlveda
(*Romances nuevamente sacados de historias antiguas de
la crónica de España*, 1551) and others. These men
were actuated by didactic and moral motives. They
saw that the popular ballads contained more false-
hoods than history, and undertook to perform an edu-
cational work by composing poems which should
embody facts and supplant the fiction. Unfortunately
for the scheme, the verses they wrote are so bad as
poetry that they could hardly replace the old ballads,
and as history are very little better than the former
versions. Fuentes and his successors merely turned
into rime with the least possible effort the prose of

[1] The earliest ballads by a cultured poet are probably those
of Carvajal, published in the *Cancionero de Stúñiga*, one of which
(W. 100) internal evidence shows to have been written in 1442.
They are rivaled by certain *rs.* ascribed to Juan Rodríguez del
Padrón, a Galician poet who flourished in the first half of the
fifteenth century. (See *Bibliography* under Rennert; and MP,
XI, 10.) It is doubtful if they are really his, and in any case they
are merely variants of well-known *rs. viejos* (W. 153, 154 and
179), and thus present a totally different character from that of
Carvajal's compositions.

the *Crónica general* (usually the edition published by Ocampo in 1541), and that, although they did not know it, was itself compiled in part from legendary poems.

The *romance* meter has been used continually by cultured poets from the appearance of the earliest col-
Romances lections of ballads to the present day.
artísticos The *romances artísticos* which they produced include every variety of matter, erotic, satiric, lyric, narrative, descriptive; and some possess high merit. What is very exceptional among them is the real epic spirit. A perfect flood of *romances artísticos* appeared toward the end of the sixteenth century. Prosy historical narratives were composed by Lucas Rodríguez, G. Laso de la Vega, Juan de la Cueva and others. Freer poems were written by such well-known men as Gregorio Silvestre, Vicente Espinel, Castillejo, López de Maldonado (*Cancionero*, 1586) and hosts of anonymous authors; Lope de Vega, Góngora and Quevedo gave final perfection to the form. The principal repository for these poems is the *Romancero general* (1600, 1604; *Segunda parte*, 1605). The *romance* meter was employed with success for religious themes (José de Valdivielso, *Romancero espiritual*, 1612; Lope de Vega, *Romancero espiritual*, 1622). In later centuries classicists (N. F. de Moratín) and romanticists (duque de Rivas, Zorrilla) alike have used it. (Cf. below § V.) [1]

---

[1] It appeared best not to complicate this book with minute divisions, and I have employed a classification corresponding to the most obvious distinctions only. Durán divided the *romances* into eight classes, some purely arbitrary. RMP (*Notas para el*

IV. THE LITERARY VALUE OF THE *ROMANCES*

Since modern criticism first became interested in popular poetry the old Spanish *romances* have been famous as embodying its most desirable qualities. Spontaneity, freshness, the substitution of dialogue for narrative, boldness of psychology, are characteristics which they possess in common with the best folk-songs of other lands. The beauties peculiar to themselves may be summed up as laconic realism and unfailing dignity. The *romance* is always close to life. It knows nothing of the elves and fairies so intimately associated with the folk-lore of northern peoples, nor of hammer-hurling gods quarreling among themselves and intervening in the affairs of men; and it is equally innocent of the melancholy yearning expressed in the plaintive refrains of the *Folkeviser*. On the other side, the *romance* never falls into the commonplace, as do so many French popular songs, children of a later and less heroic age. Its closest parallel is the English and Scottish ballad, which resembles it in freedom and

rom. de Fern. Gonz.) recognizes six classes, exclusive of the modern types: 1°, *Rs. viejos populares;* 2°, *Rs. juglarescos;* 3°, *Rs. semi-populares* (old ballads recast by later artistic poets); 4°, *Rs. semi-eruditos* (ballads by artistic poets who take their subjects partly from written sources, as chronicles earlier than that of 1541); 5°, *Rs. eruditos* (versified by Sepúlveda et al. from the Chronicle of 1541); 6°, *Rs. artísticos.* In this work so subtle a subdivision would not be fitting, and it goes without saying that there are many poems that are hard to place, and about whose character authorities differ.

spirit, with the addition of greater flexibility and variety. The *romance* tells in vigorous clear-cut phrases a story stripped of ornament and unnecessary verbiage; it begins and ends abruptly, and leaves behind the impression of a single episode perfectly outlined. It is never trivial and seldom humorous, except with a grim humor not far removed from tragedy. Direct, dramatic and earnest, the Spanish ballads have called forth enthusiastic praise from critics of many nations. The following passage from Hegel's *Esthetics* may serve as an example:

"The *romances* are a necklace of pearls; each scene is finished and complete in itself, and at the same time these poems taken together form a harmonious whole. They are conceived in the feeling and spirit of chivalry, but interpreted according to the national genius of the Spaniards. The subject-matter is rich and full of interest. The poetic motives are taken from love, marriage, pride of lineage, honor, and the glory of the kings gained in the struggles of Christians and Moors. All this . . . forms such a beautiful and charming poetic wreath that we moderns can boldly match it against the finest produced by classical antiquity."[1]

---

[1] *Vorlesungen über die Aesthetik.* Dritter Theil; Dritter Abschnitt; Drittes Kapitel; III; A; 3, c: *Das romantische Epos.* Quoted by MP, XI, 367–368. Hegel probably knew only the ballads of the Cid, and them only through Herder's translation. Herder in turn made most of his German poetic versions from a French prose translation. Cf. A. S. Voegelin: *Herder's Cid, die französische und die spanische Quelle,* Heilbronn, 1879.

The only out and out adverse opinion on the *romances* seems

V. INFLUENCE OF *ROMANCES* IN SPANISH LITERATURE

The *romances viejos*, with the closely allied forms, the medieval epics and chronicles, are so intimately bound up with national spirit and so near to the heart of the people, that their influence appears in most of the literature which is the genuine expression of Spanish character. Spanish literature has never been more successful than when it has adhered to the old epic sources of inspiration.

After the production of *romances viejos* ceased, the immediate and most important outlet for the epic spirit was, as has been stated, the drama of the *siglo de oro*. "La parte más característica y genuinamente nacional," says R. Menén-

Drama

to be Southey's. Speaking of the Cid ballads, he says (Preface to *Chronicle of the Cid*, London, 1808) "very few of them appear to me to bear any marks of antiquity, and the greater part are utterly worthless. Indeed, the heroic ballads of the Spaniards have been over-rated in this country; they are infinitely and in every way inferior to our own. There are some spirited ones in the *Guerras civiles de Granada*, from which the rest have been estimated; but excepting these, I know none of any value among the many hundreds which I have perused." Longfellow comments on this dictum (*Ancient Spanish Ballads*, in *Outre-mer*), and agrees that as a body the English ballads are superior; no *r.* is so good as *Patrick Spence* or Drayton's *Battle of Agincourt*. But D. 646 (translated by Lockhart as "The March of Bernardo del Carpio") equals Chevy Chase, and *Conde Alarcos* "has no peer in all English balladry, — it is superior to Edem o' Gordon."

dez Pidal, speaking of the drama of this period, "está
sacada de dos inagotables fuentes: de los Romances
que suministraban á nuestros poetas, no solamente los
asuntos, sino los más frescos y singulares adornos para
sus dramas; y de las Crónicas populares, donde se en-
cerraban los tesoros de la muerta poesía heroica."[1]
The drama of the late sixteenth and seventeenth centuries not only drew its subjects, its rapidity of movement, its free form, from epic traditions, but frequently
incorporated within itself whole *romances* or fragments
of them. Gil Vicente, the Portuguese dramatist
(1470?-1540?), a great lover of popular poetry, often
quotes lines from Castilian *romances* before they had
appeared in any collection. He mentions nos. XXXIX
and XLI, as well as "Yo me estaba allá en Coímbra"
(W. 104), "Mal me quieren en Castilla" (from W. 19),
"La bella mal maridada" (W. 142) and "Guay Valencia" (cf. no. XII and W. 129). Later Portuguese
playwrights mention many other *romances*.[2]

---

[1] *Leyenda de los Infantes de Lara*, p. 119.

[2] The subject of references to *rs. viejos* in Portuguese authors
from 1450 to 1649 has been investigated to exhaustion by
C. Michaëlis de Vasconcellos in her *Estudos sobre o romanceiro
peninsular* in *Cultura española* (see *Bibliography*). In about 500
Portuguese authors she has found 200 passages with references to
more than 80 *rs.*, mostly existing in the old Castilian collections.
She expands an interesting theory of Braga, that, just as Castilian
poets at an earlier period used Galician as a medium for lyric
poetry, Portuguese writers may have composed *rs.* in Castilian,
and contributed to the common stock of epic poetry. There are
advantages in considering Castilian as the epic language of the

Juan de la Cueva (1550?–1609?) was the first to bring subjects from old epics on the Spanish stage. In 1579 he produced three plays of this style, *La muerte del rey don Sancho*, which quotes from no. VIII, *La libertad de España por Bernardo del Carpio*, and *Los siete Infantes de Lara*. He was the pioneer in the field, and his example was followed by subsequent dramatists so extensively that it is impossible even to indicate the names of all the writers. The great Lope de Vega (1562–1635) was the most skilful of all, and only a few of his plays on epic themes can be mentioned. *El casamiento en la muerte* incorporates a version of no. XXI: *El conde Fernán González*, of nos. II and LIV; *El primer Fajardo*, of no. XVII, etc. Other plays of Lope connected with *romance* subjects are *El bastardo Mudarra* (Infantes de Lara), *Las Almenas de Toro* (W. 54), *El más galán portugués* (W. 107), *El marqués de Mantua* (W. 165, 166, 167) and *La fuerza lastimosa* (no. XLIV). Lope also gave the ballad meter a prominent place in his system of dramatic versification, which had not been done before. Of lesser dramatists who followed the initiative of Lope and Cueva may be mentioned Guillén de Castro, whose two *comedias* of *Las mocedades del Cid* (imitated by Corneille) and *Las hazañas del Cid* are based on many *romances*, including nos. XXXVI and LV; Luis Vélez de Guevara, in *Reinar después de morir* (W. 104 and no. XXXII) and *Los hijos de la bar-*

whole Peninsula, but certain proof of it is lacking. The only popular *romance* which surely originated in Portugal is probably that of St. Irene (*Rom. geral*, II, 507–530).

buda (W. 190 and no. XXXI); A. Hurtado Velarde, in *Los siete Infantes de Lara* (on this theme numerous other plays were composed); and Mira de Amescua, in *El conde Alarcos*, which was treated also by Guillén de Castro and Juan Pérez de Montalbán.

The second generation of playwrights, among whom Calderón was chief, drifted into a more artificial and specious conception of the drama, and consequently drew little inspiration from the Chronicles or *romances viejos*. In remodeling the earlier plays they deliberately rejected any popular elements they found there.[1]

It was to be expected that Cervantes, who created the character of Sancho Panzo, him of the many *re-franes*, would take delight in *romances* as well, and in fact the Quijote is filled with examples of these two kinds of popular Spanish expression. Since the book deals with chivalric novels, references to ballads of the Carolingian cycle predominate. The marquis of Mantua (W. 165) is mentioned several times (I, 5; I, 10; II, 23). The whole episode of the Cave of Montesinos (II, 22, 23) is based on no. XLII,[2] to which indeed Cervantes has given undue fame, for it is not a specially fine specimen of ballad. The puppet-show episode (II, 26), gave notoriety to the third *romance* of Gaiferos (W. 173), mentioned

Cervantes

[1] On the drama see MP, IX, 259–279, and RMP, *Ép. cast.*, chap. VI.

[2] On the topography of the Cave of Montesinos one may consult, beside the notes of Pellicer and Clemencín, MP, XII, 411–413.

again in II, 64. Other allusions to ballads of chivalry
are the "Media noche era por filo" (from *Conde Claros*,
W. 190) that opens chapter 9 of the second part; the
mention of Calaínos (W. 193) and the Almirante Gua-
rinos (W. 186) in the same chapter; the numerous references to Lancelot (W. 148) in I, 2, 13, and II, 23;
and the quotations from no. XLIII in I, 2. Historical *romances* are alluded to and in some cases
quoted, as follows: two of King Roderick, no. XXXV
in II, 26, and W. 7 in II, 33; one of Bernardo (no. I)
in II, 10; one of the Infantes de Lara (no. VI) in II,
60; the ballad of the Cid at Rome (W. 34) in I, 19;
Por el val de las estacas (no. XI) in I, 17; and the challenge of Diego Ordóñez at the siege of Zamora (no.
IX) in II, 27. Finally Cervantes quotes from two
romances apparently old, which have not come down
to us. In II, 34, Sancho remarks: "yo me acuerdo
haber oído cantar un romance antiguo, que dice

> "De los osos seas comido,
> Como Favila el nombrado."[1]

And at the very end (II, 74) the author warns those
who might attempt to continue his work, by quoting

---

[1] Favila was the son of Pelayo, first king of Asturias after the
fall of Roderick. He rashly attempted to kill a bear in a hand-
to-hand encounter, and was slain (in 739). See *Crón. gen.*, p. 330.

There is a *r. erudito* by Sepúlveda on the subject (D. 612).
Both the sense and assonance of the words quoted by Sancho
indicate that the context might be found in the threats made
by the Cid to Alfonso VI in Santa Gadea de Burgos (no.
XXXVIII).

> "Tate, tate, folloncicos,
> De ninguno sea tocada [la pluma],
> Porque esta empresa, buen rey,
> Para mí estaba guardada."

Which seems to be an extract from some *romance ca-balleresco.*[1]

The eighteenth century, in either of its two opposed phases, degenerate Gongorism or French pseudo-classi-

Later writers cism, was far from the right epic spirit.
Many poets employed the *romance* meter for artificial verse. In a barren age one may note the *romances* of the elder Moratín, and his famous *quintillas, Fiesta de toros en Madrid,* which are quite in

---

[1] The allusions to *romances* in the Quijote have been given at some length, because they do not seem to have been brought together before. Cervantes' other works also contain plenty of examples. In the *Viaje al parnaso,* cap. I, he mentions *La mal-maridada* (W. 142), and in cap. IV speaks of himself having written *rs.*:

> "Yo he compuesto *Romances* infinitos,
> Y el de los Zelos es aquel que estimo,
> Entre otros que los tengo por malditos."

Cervantes' *Romance de los Zelos* is thought by some to be D. 1522. In one *comedia* (*El rufián dichoso,* Jornada 1ª) he deigns to burlesque a *r. vulgar* of the ruffianly type; and in another (*La entretenida,* Jorn. 3ª), he quotes lines from three well-known *rs.* (no. XVIII, W. 190 and D. 571). An *entremés* (*Los dos habladores*) mentions the *reto de Zamora* (no. IX); and *El hospital de los podridos* quotes a purposely garbled version of Fajardo and the Moorish king (no. XVII).

the spirit of the *romances moriscos* of nearly two centuries before.[1]

The romantic school of the nineteenth century renewed interest in the drama of the *siglo de oro* and in *romances viejos*. Scholars and men of letters in England and Germany led the fight in behalf of these two branches of literature; at home Agustín Durán contributed greatly to the knowledge of them. The moderns who have worked the epic vein most successfully are Ángel Saavedra, duque de Rivas (1791–1865), with *El moro expósito*, a narrative poem based on the Infantes de Lara story; and José Zorrilla (1817–1893), who utilized the legends of Garci Fernández, Sancho García, the Cid and King Roderick in some of his dramas, *Leyendas* and *Vigilias del Estío*.[2]

VI. ENGLISH TRANSLATIONS OF *ROMANCES*

For English readers a word should be said of the *romance* in English literature. There are scattered translations by numerous authors,[3] but Thomas Rodd

---

[1] Moratín's *r.*, *Don Sancho en Zamora*, is a curious weaving together of most of the old ballads on the Siege of Zamora (nos. VII, VIII, IX and LV; and W. 46), and works in many of the best known lines from them.

[2] For the nineteenth century see RMP, *Ép. cast.*, chap. VII, *La matière épique dans la poésie moderne*.

[3] Bishop Percy (*Reliques*, 1765) translated two *rs*. "Gentle River, Gentle River" is from two versions of "Río-Verde, Río-Verde" (W. 96*a*, 96*b*). "Alcanzor and Zayda" is freely after D. 53. "Monk" Lewis (1775–1818) made three translations of

seems to have been the first to enter the field seriously (1812). He worked almost exclusively upon juglaresque ballads of the Carolingian class, and his twenty-three metrical versions are spirited, but too literal to reach great merit.[1] The *Ancient Spanish Ballads* of John Gibson Lockhart (1823), however, have become accepted as classics in the English language, and have been admired by thousands who knew no word of Spanish. Translation is hardly a fit term for Lockhart's ballads, which are rather free imitations or paraphrases of the originals. This Scotchman did not hesitate to cut down his models, piece them out with passages of his own invention, or even fuse two poems

rs., "Alatar," "The Loss of Alhama" (no. XVIII) and "Zayde and Zayda" (*The Life and Correspondence of M. G. Lewis, with many pieces in prose and verse never before published*, London, 1839; vol. II, pp. 338, 341, 353). Ticknor (chap. VII, note 3) says that Lewis also translated no. XLII. Lord Byron's translation of no. XVIII is well known; he fused with it parts of W. 84*a*. Ticknor in treating of the *rs.* in his *History of Spanish Literature* found occasion to translate several (nos. XXVII and XXXI, W. 115 and 62). Lastly, Longfellow, whose catholic taste and sure poetic feeling led him over a vast range of literature, versified parts of no. LIII, D. 646 and W. 96*b* ("Río-Verde") in *Outremer*. In *The Seaside and the Fireside* he bore testimony to the haunting magic of "Conde Alarcos" (no. XXX) and rendered it into English with the freedom and charm of genius. Mrs. Felicia Hemans often drew material from *rs.*, but never translated (cf. notes on *Bernardo del Carpio*, and on no. XIX, l. 14).

[1] See *Bibliography* for full titles of the works of Rodd and others.

into one. The fifty-six in his collection include some *ro-mances viejos*, but more are of the artistic period. Lock-hart is at his best in spirited martial pieces, and it is certainly true that in rendering some of the artistic *romances* he has improved upon the originals, showing genius in his omissions. Such masterpieces as *Bavieca*, *Garci Perez de Vargas* and *The Lord of Butrago* are made from mediocre Spanish poems. In dealing with the finer models, he could not be so successful. Of the present collection nos. VI, XIV, XXIII, XXIX, XXX, XXXII, XXXV, XXXVII, XXXIX, XL, XLIV and LVI were used by Lockhart, and the student is urged to compare his versions.

A year later John Bowring entered the same field. His collection is intended to exhibit the lyric rather than the ballad, and indeed it conveys to a foreigner a more adequate idea of the beauties of Castilian lyric poetry than any native collection, so sure is the edi-tor's taste in selection. The thirty-one *romances* all tend to the lyric in quality, and Bowring, much more literal than Lockhart, is often as successful in this style as was the other in martial pieces. Bowring has versions of nos. XXVI, XXVII, XXIX, XXX, XXXI, XXXII, XXXIII, XLIV and LVI of the present volume.

After a long interval a scholarly Englishman, James Young Gibson, devoted much time to translations of *romances* (1887). Eighty-three are from the *Roman-cero del Cid*, and are therefore mostly late poems; twenty-eight are of miscellaneous character, and in-clude some of the best. Gibson's work is always careful and never in bad taste, and his selection is superior to Lockhart's.

It is unnecessary to do more than mention the translations of Epiphanius Wilson, as they deal entirely with *romances moriscos*. He seems still to have harbored the delusion that there is something really Moorish in their origin and character. (See *Notes*, p. 173 and n. 1.)

VII. THE *ROMANCE* METER

The *romance* verse, the most characteristic and distinctive of all Spanish meters, consists of lines, containing each, as printed in this book, from 14 to 16 syllables, the last words of each line assonating. The lines vary in number of syllables according as the half-lines end in words accented on the last or next-to-last syllable (*palabras agudas ó graves*). Thus when both hemistichs end in oxytones (a very uncommon case) the line is of 14 syllables, as:

Hijo soy de un labrador, — que el cavar es su vivir.

When one ends in an oxytone and the other in a paroxytone, of 15, as:

Callases tú, doña Sancha, — que tienes por qué callar;
or *En los tiempos que me vi — más alegre y placentero.*

When both end in a paroxytone, of 16, as:

Ay Dios qué buen caballero — fué don Rodrigo de Lara.

According to the Spanish system of nomenclature the verses are classified according to the major number of syllables which they may contain, hence the *romance* line is called a 16-syllable one.

In the early editions final oxytones are sometimes printed with an added *e*, called a *paragogic e*, particularly when the vowel of the final syllable is *a*. Thus an assonance in *a–e* is formed, and *olvidare* or *ciudade* stands in the same series with *padre* and *grande*. This sort of mute *e* is not, however, to be regarded as an artificial device to aid the failing invention of a rimer, but as a result of the music to which the words were sung, and which required always the same number of syllables to match the notes, alike for each half-line.

The earliest and rudest *romances* exhibit many irregularities of meter. Through the carelessness either of the poet or of the copyist, some lines deviate from the prescribed length, and hemistichs of 7, 9 and even 10 syllables can be found (cf. no. VII, 2; XXXIX, 29; XXXVIII, 21). The assonances *á* and *a–a* sometimes stand in the same series, as they did in the *Poema del Cid* and the *Crónica rimada*. (See no. XL, *estaba, pesar,* etc.; and cf. RMP, *Infantes de Lara,* p. 82, note 2.)

The only fixed accent in the *romance* hemistich falls on the seventh syllable. The commonest arrangement shows accents upon syllables 1, 3, 5 and 7; other frequent combinations are 2, 4 and 7; and 2, 5 and 7; rarely, 1, 4 and 7. Frequently, but not always, the poems are divided into couplets (quatrains, when printed with short lines). This usage became the rule with the later artistic poets, except in the drama.

In general the same assonance is preserved throughout each poem. The early *romances* exhibit frequent changes of assonance, mingled with rime, and the final words are often oxytones. A feature of the *romances juglarescos* is the assonance in *á* (*mitad, callar,* etc.) kept through hundreds of lines. The artistic writers of the fifteenth century regarded assonance as merely careless rime, and used perfect rimes instead, but Fuentes and the other *eruditos* of 1550 sq., while not averse to consonantal rime, admitted assonance in imitation of the old poems, and later artistic poets took care to avoid perfect rime entirely, and favored paroxytones as finals.

The antecedents of the present *romance* meter need not detain us. It is certainly derived from the long epic poems of the Middle Ages, which employed, as far as we can tell from those preserved, a long and nebulous line, varying from 12 to 16 syllables in length. Its structure was very likely not clearly defined even to those who wrote it, and its historical derivation is still a matter of controversy. Its sources have been sought in late Latin rhythmical meters, and in French epic verse. A Latin classical line (the acatalectic trochaic tetrameter) has even been pointed out as corresponding closely to the *romance* hemistich, but without any attempt to prove an historical connection between them. Leaving aside uncertainties, it is now clear that the crude meter of the old epics, taking shape and

definiteness with the advancing development of the
language, gave the characteristic *romance* line, with its
fixed length and division into halves by a cesura.[1]

Up to within a few years the *romances* have nearly
always been printed in short lines of eight syllables each,
thus making the assonating words occur in alternate
lines only. This is a distinction more important than
that of mere typesetting, for the quick rhythm of the
short lines makes a different impression on the mind
from that of the more stately long ones. The division
into two octosyllables was made by the fifteenth century *trovadores* in imitation of their lyric verses. The
early collections of the sixteenth century, the great
poets and dramatists of the seventeenth, the classicists
of the eighteenth, the romanticists and the great collectors Depping, Durán and Wolf, of the nineteenth,
all wrote and printed the *romance* as consisting of
short lines. Jakob Grimm (*Silva de Romances viejos*,
1815) used the long line from a vague feeling that it

---

[1] The nature of the meter used in the old Castilian epic poems
is still open to discussion. The opinion expressed by the editor
is that which has received its most brilliant support from RMP,
Cantar de Mio Cid, pp. 83–103. For a history of the controversy
concerning the meter, mainly between the rival supporters of the
French alexandrine and the 16-syllable, see *ibid.*, pp. 76–83.

Concerning the origin of the epic meter, one should add the
plausible suggestion of Menéndez y Pelayo (*Antología*, II, Prólogo, p. xix) that it may be derived from the rimed prose of
the medieval Latin chronicles. This idea is not new (cf. Ros-
seeuw Saint-Hilaire, *Études sur l'origine de la langue et des romances espagnoles*, Paris, 1838, pp. 12–13).

was better adapted to epic verse than the short.[1]   F. Diez (*Altspanische Romanzen*, 1819) maintained the same idea, but it has remained for the most recent investigators, Menéndez y Pelayo and R. Menéndez Pidal, to establish definitely the historical form and adopt it in their collections.   The long line is used in this book, both from regard to the exigencies of space, which is economized by this means, and from respect to the original form; but, though the historical basis of the long line may now be regarded as proved, the fact remains that four centuries of writers have employed the other for the expression of their thought, and that it is an 8-syllable verse with alternating assonance which the Spanish people cherishes to-day as its most national verse-form.

The *romance*, among the people, is always sung. Collectors have been strangely neglectful of the melodies that carry the words, and have **Music** turned all their attention to the latter. Milá, in the *Romancerillo catalán*, publishes forty-six popular tunes which accompany Catalan poems, but there is not even so much for Castilian.   Very recently an effort is being made to fill the gap.   The music is given for one "romance de la muerte del príncipe don Juan" collected by doña María Goyri de Menéndez Pidal (*Bulletin hispanique*, 1904, p. 31), and one of "la

[1] The *rs.* in the *Cancionero* (1508) of Ambrosio Montesino, the religious poet, are printed in long lines; and Antonio de Nebrija (*Gramática sobre la lengua castellana*, 1492) employed that system in quoting three lines from W. 147.

dama y el rústico pastor" in RMP, *Rs. trads.*, p. 94.
The rich folk-song collections of Olmeda and Ledesma
contain the music of about fifteen *romances*. The *Cancionero musical de los siglos XV y XVI* (Madrid, 1890)
of Asenjo Barbieri contains music for a number of *romances*, three of which are in the present collection
(nos. XXI, XXXI and LVI), but it is of the learned
contrapuntal type, written in three or four parts, and
probably has no connection with the popular melodies.
The musical theorists of the Renaissance were more interested than modern musicians in the tunes of the *romances* (cf. RMP, *Ép. cast.*, p. 185). According to some,
the melodies suffer less alteration in the course of time
than the words. The music of the *romances* both old
and new is now being studied by D. Manuel Manrique
de Lara (see RMP, *Rs. trads.*, p. 94).

VIII. BIBLIOGRAPHY

The fundamental sources of material for the *Introduction* and *Notes* are the *Poesía heroico-popular castellana*
of Milá y Fontanals, the various writings of R. Menéndez Pidal, and the *Tratado de los romances viejos* of Menéndez y Pelayo. The latter, by devoting five volumes
of his *Antología* to the *romances*, has made it easy for the
student to reach the most necessary texts and criticism.
The small collection of J. Ducamin, intended for class
use in France, is especially useful with respect to
grammatical points, but the editor's taste in selection
of poems can hardly be commended. The appended

bibliography is not intended to be complete; it names only the indispensable tools provided by modern research. For the bibliography of the early editions of texts, see note, p. xix; for a survey of the critical literature of the subject from the earliest times to 1874, Milá, *Poesía heroico-pop.*, pp. 5–106, should be consulted. Prior to 1874, therefore, only the most important critical works and collections of texts are here named. Other Peninsular dialects are not treated with the same fulness as Castilian.

I. TEXTS

ALONSO A. CORTÉS, NARCISO: *Romances populares de Castilla.* Valladolid, 1906. [Reviewed by María Goyri de Menéndez Pidal in *Cultura española*, 1907, p. 200.]

[ANON.]: *Otra versión del romance del Convidado de Piedra* (in *Cultura española*, 1906, 767–8).

ASENJO BARBIERI, F.: *Cancionero musical de los siglos XV y XVI.* Madrid, 1890.

BAYO, CIRO: *Cantos populares americanos; el romance en América* (in *Revue hispanique*, XV [1906], 796–809).

—— ——: *La poesía popular en la América del Sur* (in *Revista de Archivos*, VI [1902], 43–49).

Boletín Folk-lórico español, El (periodical). Sevilla, 1885.

BONILLA Y SAN MARTÍN, ADOLFO: *Romances antiguos* (in *Anales de la literatura española.* Madrid, 1904. Pp. 29–46).

BRAGA, THEOPHILO: *Romanceiro geral portuguez, segunda edição ampliada.* Lisboa, 1906–7. 2 vols. [A compilation, purporting to contain all previously published Portuguese *rs.*, but defective. On the previous collections, cf. the review of this book by S. G. Morley, in *Mod. Lang. Notes*, 1908, 227–9, and MP, X, 20–22, and 235–240; the bibliography in the *Rom. geral*, I, pp. vii–viii; and below under Leite de Vasconcellos. There are also *Folk-lore trasmontano*, 1905–6, by

José Augusto Tavares Teixeira; and *Folk-lore beirão, toada para os romances populares*, 1906, by Pedro Fernandez Thomaz.]

CHILD, FRANCIS J.: *The English and Scottish Popular Ballads*, edited by . . . Boston, 1882–1898. 10 vols. paged as 5.

DANON, A.: *Recueil de romances judéo-espagnoles chantées en Turquie* (in *Revue des études juives*, XXXII [1896], 102–123; 263–275; XXXIII, 122–139; 255–268).

DURÁN, AGUSTÍN: *Romancero general, ó Colección de romances castellanos anteriores al siglo XVIII, recogidos, ordenados, clasificados y anotados por* . . . Madrid, 1849–51. 2 vols. (10 and 16 of *Bibl. de Aut. Esp.*).

FERNÁNDEZ DURO, CESÁREO: *Romancero de Zamora*. Madrid, 1880.

Folk-lore andaluz, El (periodical). Sevilla, 1882.

Folk-lore bético-extremeño, El (periodical). Sevilla, 1883–4.

FOUCHÉ-DELBOSC, R.: *Fragment d'un romance inconnu* (in *Revue hispanique*, XIII, 256).

[———— ————]: *XV Romances. Ordenólos R. Fouché-Delbosc*. Barcelona, 1907.

———— ————: *Un romance retrouvé* (in *Revue hispanique*, V, 251–254). [The *r*. is reprinted in MP, IX, 184.]

GALANTE, A.: *Quatorze romances judéo-espagnoles, recueillies par M*. . . . (in *Revue hispanique*, X, [1903], 594–606).

GINER ARIVAU, L.: *Folk-lore de Proaza* (in vol. VIII of the *Biblioteca de las tradiciones populares españolas*, Madrid, 1886. *Romances*, pp. 147–168).

GOYRI DE MENÉNDEZ PIDAL, MARÍA: *Romance de la muerte del príncipe D. Juan* (1497) (in *Bulletin hispanique*, VI, 29–37). [The *rs*. are reprinted in MP, XII, 546–9.]

LEDESMA, DÁMASO: *Cancionero salmantino*. Madrid, 1907.

LEITE DE VASCONCELLOS, J.: *Versão portugueza do romance popular de Jean Renaud* (in *Romania*, XI [1882], pp. 585–586).

MENÉNDEZ Y PELAYO, M.: *Apéndices á la Primavera y Flor de Romances* (in *Antología de poetas líricos castellanos*, vol. IX, Madrid, 1899; *Apéndice I, Romances procedentes de manuscritos, de pliegos sueltos ó de colecciones antiguas; Apéndice II,*

Romances que se han conservado por medio del teatro; Apéndice III, Bibliografía y variantes de los primitivos romanceros).

—— ——: *Romances populares recogidos de la tradición oral, con notas y observaciones de . . .* (vol. X of *Antología de poetas líricos castellanos,* Madrid, 1900). [A compilation from many sources. The Asturian *rs.* are nearly all from J. Menéndez Pidal's *Colección;* the Andalusian and Extremaduran *rs.* from numerous books and periodicals (cf. pp. 155-9) and from a private collection of Fr. Rodríguez Marín; the Catalan *rs.* from Milá's *Romancerillo;* and the Jewish *rs.* mostly from Danon, with a few from MS of Carlos Coello. The *Apéndice* contains some curiosities, not traditional.]

MENÉNDEZ PIDAL, JUAN: *Colección de los viejos romances que se cantan por los asturianos en la danza prima, esfoyazas y filandones, recogidos directamente de boca del pueblo, anotados y precedidos de un prólogo por . . .* Madrid, 1885.

MENÉNDEZ PIDAL, R.: *Un nuevo romance fronterizo* (in *Homenaje á Almeida-Garrett,* Génova, 1900). [The *r.* is reprinted in MP, X, 359.]

—— ——: *Primera crónica general, publicada por . . .* Madrid, 1906.

MICHAËLIS DE VASCONCELLOS, C.: *Romancero del Cid.* Leipzig, 1871.

MICRÓFILO [J. A. Torre]: *Un capítulo de Folk-lore guadalcanalense.* Sevilla, 1891.

MILÁ Y FONTANALS, M.: *Nachricht von einem handschriftlichen Romancero der Bibliothek von Barcelona* (in *Jahrbuch für romanische und englische Literatur,* III [1861], 163-172).

—— ——: *Romancerillo catalán; Segunda edición refundida y aumentada* (vol. VIII of *Obras completas,* Barcelona, 1896). [This is the most important of the collections of Catalan *rs.* Others are *Cansons de la terra,* by F. Pelayo Briz, 1866-1877, 5 vols.; *Romancer popular de la terra catalana,* by Aguiló y Fuster, 1893, etc. Cf. MP, X, 23-25.]

MUNTHE, ÅKE W: SON: *Folkpoesi från Asturien.* Upsala, 1888.

—— ——: *Romance de la tierra; chanson populaire asturienne* (in

Recueil de mémoires philologiques, à G. Paris; Stockholm, 1889, pp. 57–62).

OLMEDA, FEDERICO: *Folk-lore de Castilla, ó Cancionero popular de Burgos.* Sevilla, 1904.

PARIS, GASTON: *Une romance espagnole écrite en France au XV* siècle (in *Romania*, I, 373–378). [The *r.* is reprinted in MP, IX, 204.]

PÉREZ BALLESTEROS, JOSÉ: *Cancionero popular gallego, y en particular de la provincia de La Coruña.* Con un Prólogo de Th. Braga, *Sobre a poesia popular da Galliza.* Madrid, 1885–6. 3 vols. [On the Galician *rs.* cf. MP, X, 203–8; Milá y Fontanals, *De la poesía popular gallega* (in *Romania*, VI, 47–75); F. A. Coelho, *Romances galiciennes* (in *Romania*, II, 259–260); Victor Said Armesto, *Romancero de Galicia* (unpublished?).]

RENNERT, HUGO: *Lieder des Juan Rodríguez del Padrón* (in *Zt. für rom. Phil.*, XVII, 544–558).

RÍOS, JOSÉ AMADOR DE LOS: *Romanzen Asturiens aus dem Volksmunde zum ersten Mal gesammelt und herausgegeben* (in *Jahrbuch für romanische und englische Literatur*, III [1861], 268–291).

SÁNCHEZ MOGUEL, ANTONIO: [?] (in *Boletín de la Real Academia de la Historia*, June, 1890; see MP, X, 298).

STIEFEL, LUDWIG: *Unbekannte spanische Romanze* (in *Revue hispanique*, XV [1906], 766–770).

WIENER, LEO: *Songs of the Spanish Jews in the Balkan Peninsula* (in *Modern Philology*, I, 205–216 and 259–274).

WOLF, F. J., and HOFMANN, C.: *Primavera y Flor de Romances, publicada con una introducción y notas por* . . . Berlin, 1856. [Reprinted with *Apéndices* in MP, VIII and IX, Madrid, 1899.]

WOLF, F. J.: *Ueber eine Sammlung spanischer Romanzen in fliegenden Blättern auf der Universitäts-Bibliothek zu Prag*, etc. Wien, 1850.

II. TRANSLATIONS[1]

BERCHET, G.: *Vecchie romanze spagnuole recate in italiano.* Brussele, 1837.

BOWRING, JOHN: *Ancient Poetry and Romances of Spain.* London, 1824.

DAMAS HINARD: *Romancero espagnol, ou Recueil des Chants populaires de l'Espagne, romances historiques, chevaleresques et moresques, traduction complète avec une introduction et des notes.* Paris, 1844. 2 vols. [Prose translations of 275 *rs.* See under *Puymaigre.*]

GIBSON, JAMES YOUNG: *The Cid Ballads and other poems and translations from Spanish and German, by the late . . .* Edited by Margaret D. Gibson, with memoir by Agnes Smith. London, 1887. 2 vols.

HERDER, J. G. V.: *Der Cid nach spanischen Romanzen besungen durch . . .* 1805. [Verse translations, mostly made not from the originals, but from a French prose translation. Cf. *Herder's Cid, die französische und die spanische Quelle. Zusammengestellt von* A. S. Voegelin. Heilbronn, 1879.]

HUGO, ABEL: *Romances historiques.* 1822. [Some 70 translations, by the brother of Victor Hugo.]

LEWIS, M. G.: *The Life and Correspondence of, with many pieces in prose and verse never before published.* London, 1839. 2 vols. [Translations of *rs.* in vol. II, pp. 338, 341 and 353.]

LOCKHART, JOHN GIBSON: *Ancient Spanish Ballads, historical and romantic.* London, 1823.

MONTI, PIETRO: *Romancero del Cid, traduzione dallo spagnuolo, con illustrazioni.* Milano, 1838.

—— ——: *Romanze storiche e moresche, e poesie scelte spagnuole tradotte in versi italiani. Con prefazioni e note.* Milano, 1850.

PUYMAIGRE, LE CONTE DE: *Petit Romancero. Choix de vieux chants espagnols, traduits et annotés par . . .* Paris, 1878. [Prose translations of 58 of the best *rs.* This and the collection of

[1] Except for English, only a few important translations are given. There have been many in French and German. See also *Introduction*, p. xxxii, note 3.

Damas Hinard are the only serious aids to the present-day translator.]

RODD, THOMAS: *History of Charles the Great and Orlando, ascribed to Archbishop Turpin, . . . together with the most celebrated ancient Spanish Ballads relating to the Twelve Peers of France, mentioned in Don Quixote; with English metrical versions.* London, 1812. 2 vols.

WILSON, EPIPHANIUS: *Moorish Ballads* [translated] (in *The World's Great Classics.* New York. No date).

III. CRITICISM

ALLEN, PHILIP S.: *Turteltaube* (in *Mod. Lang. Notes*, XIX [1904], 175–7).

BAIST, G.: *Die spanische Literatur* (in *Gröber's Grundriss der romanischen Philologie*, II. Band, 2. *Abteilung*, Strassburg, 1897. Pp. 430–4, and 453–5).

BASSET, RENÉ: *Les Alixares de Grenade et le château de Khaouarnaq.* Algiers, 1906. [Reviewed by RMP in *Cultura española*, IV (1906), p. 1109.]

BRAGA, THEOPHILO: *Historia da poesia popular portugueza, 3ª edição reescripta.* Lisboa, 1902–5. 2 vols.

COSTA, JOAQUÍN: *Poesia popular española y Mitología y Literatura celto-hispanas.* Madrid, 1888.

DONCIEUX, GEORGE: *La Chanson du Roi Renaud*, etc. (in *Romania*, XXIX [1900], 219–256).

—— ——: *Le Romancéro populaire de la France.* Paris, 1904.

ESPINOSA, AURELIO M.: *The Spanish Language in New Mexico and Colorado.* Santa Fe, N. M., May, 1911. [Pp. 29–32.]

EVERS, HÉLÈNE M.: *Two traces of the Cycle of Guillaume d'Orange in the old Spanish romances* (in *The Romanic Review*, I [1910], pp. 140–148).

FITZMAURICE-KELLY, J.: *Chapters on Spanish Literature.* London, 1908. (Chapter IV, The *Rómancero*.)

—— ——: *Littérature espagnole*, Paris, 1904. [Pp. 115–125.]

FORD, RICHARD: *Preliminary essay on the origin, antiquity, char-*

acter and influence of the ancient ballads of Spain (in *Edinburgh Review*, 1841, pp. 1–34).

GOYRI DE MENÉNDEZ PIDAL, MARÍA: *Romances que deben buscarse en la tradición oral* (in *Revista de Archivos*, XV [1906], 374–386; XVI [1907], 24–36).

HUBER, VICTOR AIMÉ: *Chronica del famoso cavallero Cid Ruy diez Campeador. Nueva edición con una introducción histórico-literaria por* ... Stuttgart, 1853.

—— ——: *De primitiva cantilenarum popularium epicarum (vulgo romances) apud Hispanos forma.* Berlin, 1844.

—— ——: *Ueber G. B. Depping's Romancero castellano* (in *Blätter für literarische Unterhaltung*, 16. 17. 18. and 19. November 1845).

JOHNSTON, OLIVER M.: *Sources of the Spanish ballad on D. García* (in *Revue hispanique*, XII [1905], 281–298).

JULIUS, N. H.: *Ueber F. Wolf's Sammlung spanischer Romanzen* (in *Blätter für literarische Unterhaltung*, 1851, pp. 625–6).

LEITE DE VASCONCELLOS, J.: *A rola viuva na poesia popular portuguesa* (in *Mod. Lang. Notes*, XXI [1906], 33).

LONGFELLOW, H. W.: *Ancient Spanish Ballads* (a chapter in *Outre-mer*, 1835).

MENÉNDEZ Y PELAYO, M.: *Tratado de los romances viejos* (in *Antología de poetas líricos castellanos*, vols. XI and XII; Madrid, 1903 and 1906).

MENÉNDEZ PIDAL, JUAN: *Leyendas del último rey godo; notas é investigaciones. Nueva edición corregida.* Madrid, 1906.

MENÉNDEZ PIDAL, RAMÓN: *Cantar de Mio Cid*, I. Madrid, 1908. [Pp. 76–103, on origin of *romance*-meter.]

—— ——: *Catálogo del romancero judío-español* (in *Cultura española*, IV [1906], 1045–1077, and V [1907], 161–199).

—— ——: *L'Épopée castillane à travers la littérature espagnole. Traduction de Henri Mérimée. Avec une préface de Ernest Mérimée.* Paris, 1910. (Chap. V, *Le "Romancero."*)

—— ——: *La leyenda de los infantes de Lara.* Madrid, 1896.

—— ——: *Notas para el romancero de Fernán González* (in *Homenaje á Menéndez y Pelayo*, Madrid, 1899, vol. I, 429–507).

MENÉNDEZ PIDAL, RAMÓN: *La penitencia del rey D. Rodrigo* (in *Revista crítica de historia y literatura*, II [1897], pp. 31–34).

——— ———: *El romancero español.* New York, 1910.

——— ———: *Los romances tradicionales en América* (in *Cultura española*, I [1906], 72–111).

——— ———: *La serranilla de la Zarzuela* (in *Studi medievali*, II [1906–7], 263–270).

——— ———: *Sobre Aluacaxi y la elegía árabe de Valencia* (in *Homenaje á Codera y Zaidín*, Zaragoza, 1904, pp. 393–409).

——— ———: *Sobre los orígenes de "El Convidado de Piedra"* (in *Cultura española*, II [1906], 449).

MÉRIMÉE, E.: Review of Saroïhandy's *Origine française*, etc. (in *Bulletin hispanique*, VII [1905], 69).

MICHAËLIS DE VASCONCELLOS, C.: *Estudos sobre o Romanceiro peninsular* (in *Revista lusitana*, II [1890], 156–179; 193–240).

——— ———: *Estudos sobre o Romanceiro peninsular* (in *Cultura española*, VII, 767–803; VIII, 1021–1057; IX, 93–132; X, 435–512; XI, 717–758; XIV, 434–483; XV, 697–732).

——— ———: *Romanzenstudien* (in *Zt. für rom. Phil.*, XVI [1892], pp. 40–89 and 397–421).

MILÁ Y FONTANALS, M.: *De la poesía heroico-popular castellana* (vol. VII of *Obras completas*, Barcelona, 1896).

——— ———: *Observaciones sobre la poesía popular, con muestras de romances catalanes inéditos* (in vol. VI of *Obras completas*, Barcelona, 1895).

MOREL-FATIO, A.: Review of RMP's *Infantes de Lara* (in *Romania*, XXVI [1897], pp. 305–320).

——— ———: Review of Michaëlis' *Romancero del Cid* (in *Romania*, I, 123–125).

OTTO, HANS: *La tradition d'Eginhard et Emma dans la poésie romancesca de la péninsule Hispanique* (in *Mod. Lang. Notes*, VII [1892], 225–243).

PARIS, GASTON: *La légende des Infants de Lara* (in *Journal des Savants*, 1898, pp. 296–309 and 321–335).

PUYMAIGRE, LE COMTE DE: *La légende des sept infants de Lara* (in *Revue des questions historiques*, 1897, pp. 246–257).

—— ——: *Notes sur un recueil de romances judéo-espagnoles* (in *Revue des études juives*, XXXIII [1896], 269–276).

—— ——: *Les vieux auteurs castillans.* Paris-Metz, 1861–2. 2 vols. [Vol. II, chaps. XIX to XXII, contains many translations.]

SALILLAS, RAFAEL: *Poesía matonesca (romances matonescos)* (in *Revue hispanique*, XV [1906], 387–452).

SAROÏHANDY, J.: *Origine française du vers des romances espagnoles* (in *Mélanges de philologie offerts à M. F. Brunot*, Paris, 1904, pp. 311–322).

TEZA, EMILIO: *Dai romanze di Castiglia.* Venezia, 1895.

TICKNOR, GEORGE: *History of Spanish Literature*, 4th American edition, Boston, 1879; 1st period, chaps. VI and VII; 2d period, chap. XXXII.

WOLF, F. J.: *Beiträge zur spanischen Volkspoesie aus den Werken Fernán Caballero's.* Wien, 1859.

—— ——: *Proben portugiesischer und catalanischer Volksromanzen, mit einer literar-historischen Einleitung über die Volkspoesie in Portugal und Catalonien.* 1856.

—— ——: *Ueber die Lais, Sequenzen, und Leiche.* Heidelberg, 1841.

—— ——: *Ueber die Romanzenpoesie der Spanier* (in *Studien zur Geschichte der spanischen und portugiesischen Nationalliteratur*, Berlin, 1859, pp. 303–554).

ROMANCES POPULARES
ROMANCES VIEJOS TRADICIONALES

I

(W. 13*a*)

[BERNALDO DEL CARPIO]

Con cartas y mensajeros — el rey al Carpio envió;
Bernaldo, como es discreto, — de traición se receló;
las cartas echó en el suelo — y al mensajero habló:
— Mensajero eres, amigo, — no mereces culpa, no;
mas al rey que acá te envía — dígasle tú esta razón: 5
que no lo estimo yo á él, — ni aun cuantos con él
   son;
mas, por ver lo que me quiere, — todavía allá iré yo. —
Y mandó juntar los suyos: — de esta suerte les habló:
— Cuatrocientos sois, los míos, — los que comedes mi
   pan:
los ciento irán al Carpio, — para el Carpio guardar;   10
los ciento por los caminos, — que á nadie dejen pasar;
doscientos iréis conmigo — para con el rey hablar;
si mala me la dijere — peor se la he de tornar. —
Por sus jornadas contadas — á la corte fué á llegar.
— Manténgavos Dios, buen rey, — y á cuantos con
   vos están.   15

1

— Mal vengades vos, Bernaldo, — traidor, hijo de mal
    padre:
dite yo el Carpio en tenencia, — tú tómaslo de heredad.
— Mentides, el rey, mentides, — que no dices la ver-
    dad;
que si yo fuese traidor, — á vos os cabría en parte.
20 Acordársevos debía — de aquella del Encinal,
cuando gentes extranjeras — allí os trataron tan mal,
que os mataron el caballo, — y aun á vos querían
    matar:
Bernaldo, como traidor, — de entre ellos os fué á
    sacar:
allí me distes el Carpio — de juro y de heredad:
25 prometístesme á mi padre, — no me guardastes verdad.
— Prendedlo, mis caballeros, — que igualado se me ha.
— Aquí, aquí, los mis doscientos, — los que comedes mi
    pan,
que hoy era venido el día — que honra habemos de
    ganar. —
El rey, de que aquesto viera, — de esta suerte fué á
    hablar:
30 — ¿Qué ha sido aquesto, Bernaldo, — que así enojado
    te has?
¿Lo que hombre dice de burla — de veras vas á tomar?
Yo te dó el Carpio, Bernaldo, — de juro y de heredad.
— Aquesas burlas, el rey, — no son burlas de burlar;
llamástesme de traidor, — traidor hijo de mal padre:
35 el Carpio yo no lo quiero, — bien lo podéis vos guar-
    dar;
que cuando yo lo quisiere, muy bien lo sabré ganar. —

II

(W. 17)

ROMANCE DEL CONDE FERNÁN GONZÁLEZ

— Buen conde Fernán González, — el rey envía por
    vos,
que vayades á las cortes — que se hacían en León;
que si vos allá vais, conde, — daros han buen galardón;
daros ha á Palenzuela — y á Palencia la mayor;
daros ha las nueve villas, — con ellas á Carrión;   5
daros ha á Torquemada, — la torre de Mormojón.
Buen conde, si allá no ides, — daros hían por traidor.
Allí respondiera el conde — y dijera esta razón:
— Mensajero eres, amigo, — no mereces culpa, no;
que yo no he miedo al rey, — ni á cuantos con él son. 10
Villas y castillos tengo, — todos á mi mandar son,
de ellos me dejó mi padre, — de ellos me ganara yo:
los que me dejó mi padre — poblélos de ricos hombres,
las que yo me hube ganado — poblélas de labradores;
quien no tenía más de un buey, — dábale otro, que
    eran dos;   15
al que casaba su hija — dóle yo muy rico don:
cada día que amanece, — por mí hacen oración;
no la hacían por el rey, — que no la merece, non;
él les puso muchos pechos, — y quitáraselos yo.

III

(W. 16)

[FERNÁN GONZÁLEZ]

Castellanos y leoneses — tienen grandes divisiones.
El conde Fernán González — y el buen rey don Sancho
    Ordóñez,
sobre el partir de las tierras, — y el poner de los mo-
    jones,
llamábanse hi-de-putas, — hijos de padres traidores;
5 echan mano á las espadas, — derriban ricos mantones:
no les pueden poner treguas — cuantos en la corte sone,
pónenselas dos hermanos, — aquesos benditos monjes.
Pónenlas por quince días, — que no pueden por más,
    non,
que se vayan á los prados — que dicen de Carrión.
10 Si mucho madruga el rey, — el conde no dormía, no;
el conde partió de Burgos, — y el rey partió de León.
Venido se han á juntar — al vado de Carrión,
y á la pasada del río — movieron una quistión:
los del rey que pasarían, — y los del conde que non.
15 El rey, como era risueño, — la su mula revolvió;
el conde con lozanía — su caballo arremetió;
con el agua y el arena — al buen rey ensalpicó.
Allí hablara el buen rey, — su gesto muy demudado:
— ¡Cómo sois soberbio, el conde! — ¡cómo sois desme
    surado!
20 si no fuera por las treguas — que los monjes nos han
    dado,

la cabeza de los hombros — ya vos la hubiera quitado;
con la sangre que os sacara — yo tiñera aqueste vado. —
El conde le respondiera, — como aquel que era osado:
— Eso que decís, buen rey, — véolo mal aliñado;
vos venís en gruesa mula, — yo en ligero caballo;   25
vos traéis sayo de seda, — yo traigo un arnés tranzado;
vos traéis alfanje de oro, — yo traigo lanza en mi mano;
vos traéis cetro de rey, — yo un venablo acerado;
vos con guantes olorosos, — yo con los de acero claro;
vos con la gorra de fiesta, — yo con un casco afinado;   30
vos traéis ciento de mula, — yo trescientos de caballo. —
Ellos en aquesto estando, — los frailes que han allegado:
— ¡Tate, tate, caballeros! — ¡tate, tate, hijosdalgo!
¡Cuán mal cumplistes las treguas — que nos habíades
    mandado! —
Allí hablara el buen rey: — Yo las cumpliré de grado. — 35
Pero respondiera el conde: — Yo de pies puesto en el
    campo. —
Cuando vido aquesto el rey, — no quiso pasar el vado;
vuélvese para sus tierras; — malamente va enojado.
Grandes bascas va haciendo, — reciamente va jurando
que había de matar al conde — y destruir su condado, 40
y mandó llamar á cortes; — por los grandes ha enviado:
todos ellos son venidos, — sólo el conde ha faltado.
Mensajero se le hace — á que cumpla su mandado:
el mensajero que fué — de esta suerte le ha hablado.

IV

(W. 20)

[LOS INFANTES DE LARA]

¡Ay Dios, qué buen caballero — fué don Rodrigo de
  Lara,
que mató cinco mil moros — con trescientos que llevaba!
Si aquéste muriera entonces, — ¡qué gran fama que
  dejara!
no matara á sus sobrinos — los siete infantes de Lara,
5 ni vendiera sus cabezas — al moro que las llevaba.
Ya se trataban sus bodas — con la linda doña Lambra:
las bodas se hacen en Burgos, — las tornabodas en
  Salas:
las bodas y tornabodas — duraron siete semanas;
las bodas fueron muy buenas, — mas las tornabodas
  malas.
10 Ya convidan por Castilla, — por Castilla y por Navarra:
tanta viene de la gente, — que no hallaban posadas,
y aun faltan por venir — los siete infantes de Lara.
Helos, helos por do vienen — por aquella vega llana;
sálelos á recebir — la su madre doña Sancha.
15 — Bien vengades, los mis hijos, — buena sea vuestra
  llegada.
— Nora buena estéis, señora, — nuestra madre doña
  Sancha. —
Ellos le besan las manos, — ella á ellos en la cara.
— Huelgo de veros á todos, — que ninguno no faltaba,

y más á vos, Gonzalvico, — porque á vos mucho amaba.
Tornad á cabalgar, hijos, — y tomedes vuestras armas, 20
y allá iréis á posar — al barrio de Cantaranas.
Por Dios os ruego, mis hijos, — no salgáis de las po-
    sadas,
porque en semejantes fiestas — se urden buenas lanza-
    das. —
Ya cabalgan los infantes — y se van á sus posadas;
hallaron las mesas puestas — y viandas aparejadas.   25
Después que hubieron comido — pidieron juego de
    tablas,
si no fuera Gonzalvico, — que su caballo demanda.
Muy bien puesto en la silla — se sale para la plaza,
y halló á don Rodrigo — que á una torre tira varas,
con una fuerza crecida — á la otra parte pasa.   30
Gonzalvico, que esto viera, — las suyas también tirara:
las suyas pesan muy mucho, — á lo alto no llegaban.
Cuando esto vió doña Lambra, — de esta manera
    hablara:
— Adamad, dueñas, amad — cada cual de buena gana,
que más vale un caballero — que cuatro de los de
    Salas. —
                                                          35
Cuando esto oyó doña Sancha, — respondió muy
    enojada:
— Calledes vos, doña Lambra, — no digáis la tal
    palabra;
si los infantes lo saben, — ante ti lo matarán.
— Callases tú, doña Sancha, — que tienes por qué
    callar,
que pariste siete hijos, — como puerca en muladar. — 40

Gonzalvico, que esto oyera, — esta respuesta le da:
— Yo te cortaré las faldas — por vergonzoso lugar,
por cima de las rodillas — un palmo y mucho más. —
Al llanto de doña Lambra — don Rodrigo fué á llegar:
45 — ¿Qué es aquesto, doña Lambra? — ¿quién te ha
        querido enojar?
Si me lo dices, yo entiendo — de te lo muy bien vengar,
porque á dueña tal cual vos — todos la deben honrar. —

V

(W. 24)

[LOS INFANTES DE LARA]

Pártese el moro Alicante — víspera de sant Cebrián;
ocho cabezas llevaba, — todas de hombres de alta
        sangre.
Sábelo el rey Almanzor, — á recibírselo sale;
aunque perdió muchos moros, — piensa en esto bien
        ganar.
5 Manda hacer un tablado — para mejor las mirar,
mandó traer un cristiano — que estaba en captividad.
Como ante sí lo trujeron — empezóle de hablar,
díjole: — Gonzalo Gustos, — mira quien conocerás;
que lidiaron mis poderes — en el campo de Almenar:
10 sacaron ocho cabezas, — todas son de gran linaje. —
Respondió Gonzalo Gustos: — Presto os diré la ver-
        dad. —
Y limpiándoles la sangre, — asaz se fuera á turbar;
dijo llorando agramente: — ¡Conózcolas por mi mal!

la una es de mi carillo; — ¡las otras me duelen más!
de los infantes de Lara — son, mis hijos naturales. — 15
Así razona con ellos, — como si vivos hablasen:
— ¡Dios os salve, el mi compadre, — el mi amigo leal!
¿Adónde son los mis hijos — que yo os quise encomendar?
Muerto sois como buen hombre, — como hombre de
fiar. —
Tomara otra cabeza — del hijo mayor de edad: 20
— Sálveos Dios, Diego González, — hombre de muy
gran bondad,
del conde Fernán González — alférez el principal:
á vos amaba yo mucho, — que me habíades de heredar. —
Alimpiándola con lágrimas — volviérala á su lugar,
y toma la del segundo, — Martín Gómez que llamaban: 25
— Dios os perdone, el mi hijo, — hijo que mucho pre-
ciaba;
jugador era de tablas — el mejor de toda España,
mesurado caballero, — muy buen hablador en plaza. —
Y dejándola llorando, — la del tercero tomaba:
— Hijo Suero Gustos, — todo el mundo os estimaba; 30
el rey os tuviera en mucho, — sólo para la su caza:
gran caballero esforzado, — muy buen bracero á ventaja.
¡Ruy Gómez vuestro tío — estas bodas ordenara! —
Y tomando la del cuarto, — lasamente la miraba:
— ¡Oh hijo Fernán González, — (nombre del mejor de
España, 35
del buen conde de Castilla, — aquel que vos baptizara)

matador de puerco espín, — amigo de gran compaña!
nunca con gente de poco — os vieran en alianza. —
Tomó la de Ruy Gómez, — de corazón la abrazaba:
40 — ¡Hijo mío, hijo mío! — ¿quién como vos se hallara?
nunca le oyeron mentira, — nunca por oro ni plata;
animoso, buen guerrero, — muy gran feridor de espada,
que á quien dábades de lleno — tullido ó muerto que-
daba. —
Tomando la del menor, — el dolor se le doblara:
45 — ¡Hijo Gonzalo González! — ¡Los ojos de doña
Sancha!
¡Qué nuevas irán á ella — que á vos más que á todos
ama!
Tan apuesto de persona, — decidor bueno entre damas,
repartidor en su haber, — aventajado en la lanza.
Mejor fuera la mi muerte — que ver tan triste jornada! —
50 Al duelo que el viejo hace, — toda Córdoba lloraba.
El rey Almanzor cuidoso — consigo se lo llevaba,
y mandó á una morica — lo sirviese muy de gana.
Ésta le torna en prisiones, — y con hambre le curaba.
Hermana era del rey, — doncella moza y lozana;
55 con ésta Gonzalo Gustos — vino á perder su saña,
que de ella le nació un hijo — que á los hermanos
vengara.

VI

(W. 26)

[LOS INFANTES DE LARA]

Á cazar va don Rodrigo, — y aun don Rodrigo de
    Lara;
con la gran siesta que hace — arrimádose ha á una
    haya,
maldiciendo á Mudarrillo, — hijo de la renegada,
que si á las manos le hubiese, — que le sacaría el alma.
El señor estando en esto — Mudarrillo que asomaba: 5
— Dios te salve, caballero, — debajo la verde haya.
— Así haga á ti, escudero, — buena sea tu llegada.
— Dígasme tú, el caballero, — ¿cómo era la tu gracia?
— Á mí dicen don Rodrigo, — y aun don Rodrigo de
    Lara,
cuñado de Gonzalo Gustos, — hermano de doña
    Sancha;   10
por sobrinos me los hube — los siete infantes de Salas.
Espero aquí á Mudarrillo, — hijo de la renegada;
si delante lo tuviese, — yo le sacaría el alma.
— Si á ti dicen don Rodrigo, — y aun don Rodrigo de
    Lara,
á mí Mudarra Gonzales, — hijo de la renegada,   15
de Gonzalo Gustos hijo, — y alnado de doña Sancha:
por hermanos me los hube — los siete infantes de
    Salas:
tú los vendiste, traidor, — en el val de Arabiana;
mas si Dios á mí me ayuda, — aquí dejarás el alma.

20 — Espéresme, don Gonzalo, — iré á tomar las mis armas.

— El espera que tú diste — á los infantes de Lara:
aquí morirás, traidor, — enemigo de doña Sancha. —

VII

(W. 42)

[RETO DE LOS DOS ZAMORANOS]

Riberas de Duero arriba — cabalgan dos Zamoranos:
las armas llevan blancas, — caballos rucios rodados,
con sus espadas ceñidas, — y sus puñales dorados,
sus adargas á los pechos, — y sus lanzas en las manos,
5 ricas capas aguaderas — por ir más disimulados,
y por un repecho arriba — arremeten los caballos:
que, según dicen las gentes, — padre é hijo son entrambos.
Palabras de gran soberbia — entre los dos van hablando:
que se matarán con tres, — lo mesmo harán con cuatro,
10 y si cinco les saliesen, — que no les huirían el campo,
con tal que no fuesen primos — ni menos fuesen hermanos,
ni de la casa del Cid, — ni de sus paniaguados,
ni de las tiendas del rey, — ni de sus leales vasallos:
de todos los otros que haya, — salgan los más esforzados.
15 Tres condes lo han oído, — todos tres eran cuñados.

— Atendednos, caballeros, — que nos estamos ar-
    mando. —
Mientras los condes se arman, — el padre al hijo ha
    hablado:
— Tú bien vees, hijo mío, — aquellos tablados altos
donde dueñas y doncellas — nos están de allí mirando;
si lo haces como bueno, — serás de ellas muy honrado; 20
si lo haces como malo, — serás de ellas ultrajado;
más vale morir con honra — que no vivir deshonrado,
que el morir es una cosa — que á cualquier nacido es
    dado. —
Estas palabras diciendo, — los condes han allegado.
Á los encuentros primeros — el viejo uno ha derrocado; 25
vuelve la cabeza el viejo, — vido al hijo mal tratado,
arremete para allá, — y otro conde ha derribado;
el otro desque esto vido — vuelve riendas al caballo;
los dos iban en su alcance; — en Zamora lo han cerrado.

VIII

(W. 45)

[TRAICIÓN DE VELLIDO DOLFOS]

— Rey don Sancho, rey don Sancho, — no digas que
    no te aviso
que de dentro de Zamora — un alevoso ha salido:
llámase Vellido Dolfos, — hijo de Dolfos Vellido,
cuatro traiciones ha hecho, — y con ésta serán cinco.
Si gran traidor fué el padre,—mayor traidor es el hijo.— 5

Gritos dan en el real: — ¡Á don Sancho han mal herido:
muerto le ha Vellido Dolfos, — gran traición ha co-
    metido! —
Desque le tuviera muerto, — metióse por un postigo, —
por las calles de Zamora — va dando voces y gritos:
10 — Tiempo era, doña Urraca, — de cumplir lo prome-
    tido.

IX
(W. 47)
[EL RETO DE LOS ZAMORANOS]

Ya cabalga Diego Ordóñez, — del real se había salido
de dobles piezas armado — y un caballo morcillo:
va á reptar los Zamoranos — por la muerte de su primo,
que mató Vellido Dolfos, — hijo de Dolfos Vellido.
5 — Yo os riepto, los Zamoranos, — por traidores fe-
    mentidos,
riepto á todos los muertos, — y con ellos á los vivos;
riepto hombres y mujeres, — los por nascer y nascidos;
riepto á todos los grandes, — á los grandes y los chicos,
á las carnes y pescados, — á las aguas de los ríos. —
10 Allí habló Arias Gonzalo, — bien oiréis lo que hubo
    dicho:
— ¿Qué culpa tienen los viejos? — ¿qué culpa tienen
    los niños?
¿qué merecen las mujeres, — y los que no son nascidos?
¿por qué rieptas á los muertos, — los ganados y los
    ríos?

Bien sabéis vos, Diego Ordóñez, — muy bien lo tenéis
    sabido,
que aquel que riepta concejo — debe de lidiar con
    cinco. —   15
Ordóñez le respondió: — Traidores heis todos sido. —

X

(W. 50)

ROMANCE DE FERNÁN D'ARIAS, FIJO DE ARIAS GONZALO

Por aquel postigo viejo — que nunca fuera cerrado,
vi venir pendón bermejo — con trescientos de caballo:
en medio de los trescientos — viene un monumento
    armado
y dentro del monumento — viene un cuerpo de un
    finado;
Fernán D'Arias ha por nombre, — fijo de Arias Gon-
    zalo.   5
Llorábanle cien doncellas, — todas ciento hijasdalgo;
todas eran sus parientas — en tercero y cuarto grado:
las unas le dicen primo, — otras le llaman hermano;
las otras decían tío, — otras lo llaman cuñado.
Sobre todas lo lloraba — aquesa Urraca Hernando: 10
¡y cuán bien que la consuela — ese viejo Arias Gonzalo!
— Calledes, hija, calledes, — no hagades tan gran
    llanto,
que si un hijo me han muerto, — ahí me quedaban
    cuatro.

No murió por las tabernas, — ni á las tablas jugando;
15 mas murió sobre Zamora — vuestra honra resguar-
dando.

XI

(W. 31)

[POR EL VAL DE LAS ESTACAS]

Por el val de las Estacas — pasó el Cid á mediodía,
en su caballo Babieca: — ¡oh qué bien que parecía!
El rey moro que lo supo — á recibirle salía,
dijo: — Bien vengas, el Cid, — buena sea tu venida,
5 que si quieres ganar sueldo, — muy bueno te lo daría,
ó si vienes por mujer, — darte he una hermana mía.
— Que no quiero vuestro sueldo — ni de nadie lo
    querría,
que ni vengo por mujer, — que viva tengo la mía:
vengo á que pagues las parias — que tú debes á Castilla.
10 — No te las daré yo, el buen Cid, — Cid, yo no te las
    daría:
si mi padre las pagó, — hizo lo que no debía.
— Si por bien no me las das, — yo por mal las tomaría.
— No lo harás así, buen Cid, — que yo buena lanza
    había.
— En cuanto á eso, rey moro, — creo nada te debía,
15 que si buena lanza tienes, — por buena tengo la mía:
mas da sus parias al rey, — á ese buen rey de Castilla.
— Por ser vos su mensajero, — de buen grado las daría.

XII

(W. 55)

ROMANCE DEL REY MORO QUE PERDIÓ Á VALENCIA

Helo, helo, por do viene — el moro por la calzada,
caballero á la gineta — encima una yegua baya;
borzeguíes marroquíes — y espuela de oro calzada;
una adarga ante los pechos, — y en su mano una
zagaya.
Mirando estaba á Valencia, — como está tan bien
cercada:
— ¡Oh Valencia, oh Valencia, — de mal fuego seas
quemada!
Primero fuiste de moros — que de cristianos ganada.
Si la lanza no me miente, — á moros serás tornada,
aquel perro de aquel Cid — prenderélo por la barba:
su mujer doña Jimena — será de mí captivada,
su hija Urraca Hernando — será mi enamorada.

. . . .

El buen Cid no está tan lejos, — que todo bien lo
escuchaba.
— Venid vos acá, mi hija, — mi hija doña Urraca;
dejad las ropas continas, — y vestid ropas de pascua.
Aquel moro hi-de-perro — detenémelo en palabras,
mientra yo ensillo á Babieca, — y me ciño la mi espada. —
La doncella muy hermosa — se paró á una ventana:
el moro desque la vido, — de esta suerte le hablara:

20 — ¡Alá te guarde, señora, — mi señora, doña Urraca!
— ¡Así haga á vos, señor, — buena sea vuestra llegada!
Siete años ha, rey, siete, — que soy vuestra enamorada.
— Otros tantos ha, señora, — que os tengo dentro en
      mi alma. —
Ellos estando en aquesto, — el buen Cid que asomaba.
25 — Adiós, adiós, mi señora, — la mi linda enamorada,
que del caballo Babieca — yo bien oigo la patada. —
Do la yegua pone el pie, — Babieca pone la pata.
Allí hablara el caballo, — bien oiréis lo que hablaba:
— ¡Reventar debía la madre — que á su hijo no
      esperaba! —
30 Siete vueltas la rodea — al derredor de una jara;
la yegua que era ligera — muy adelante pasaba,
fasta llegar cabe un río — adonde una barca estaba.
El moro desque la vido, — con ella bien se holgaba;
grandes gritos da al barquero — que le allegase la
      barca:
35 el barquero es diligente, — túvosela aparejada,
embarcó muy presto en ella, — que no se detuvo nada.
Estando el moro embarcado — el buen Cid que llegó al
      agua,
y por ver al moro en salvo, — de tristeza reventaba;
mas con la furia que tiene, — una lanza le arrojaba,
40 y dijo: — ¡Recoged, mi yerno, — arrecogedme esa lanza,
que quizá tiempo verná — que os será bien deman-
      dada!

XIII

(W. 69)

[EL REY DON PEDRO Y EL PRIOR DE SAN JUAN]

Don García de Padilla, — ese que Dios perdonase,
tomara al rey por la mano — y apartólo en puridad:
— Un castillo hay en Consuegra — que en el mundo no
    hay su par,
mejor es para vos, rey, — que lo sabréis sustentar.
No sufráis más que le tenga — ese prior de Sant Joan: 5
convidédesle, buen rey, — convidédesle á yantar.
La comida que le diéredes, — como dió en Toro á don
    Joan,
que le cortéis la cabeza — sin ninguna piedad:
desque se la hayáis cortado, — en tenencia me lo dad. —
Ellos en aquesto estando, — el prior llegado ha.   10
— Mantenga Dios á tu Alteza — y á tu corona real.
— Bien vengáis, el buen prior, — digádesme la verdad:
¿el castillo de Consuegra — sepamos por quién está?
— El castillo con la villa, — señor, á vuestro mandar.
— Pues convídoos, el prior, — para conmigo yantar.   15
— Pláceme, dijo, buen rey, — de muy buena voluntad:
déme licencia tu Alteza, — licencia me quiera dar:
monjes nuevos son venidos, — irélos á aposentar.
— Vais con Dios, Hernán Rodrigo, — luego vos queráis
    tornar. —
Vase para la cocina, — do su cocinero está,   20
así hablaba con él, — como si fuera su igual:
—Tomes estos mis vestidos,—los tuyos me quieras dar,

y á hora de media noche — salirte has á pasear. —
Vase á la caballeriza — do su macho fuera á hallar.
25 — ¡Macho rucio, macho rucio, — Dios te me quiera
guardar!
Ya de dos me has escapado, — con aquésta tres serán;
si de aquésta tú me escapas, — luego te entiendo ahorrar. —
Presto le echaba la silla, — comienza de cabalgar;
en allegando á Azoguejo, — comenzó el macho á roznar.
30 Media noche era por filo, — los gallos querían cantar,
cuando entraba por Toledo, — por Toledo, esa ciudad:
antes que el gallo cantase — á Consuegra fué á llegar.
Halló las guardas velando, — comiénzales de hablar:
— Digádesme, veladores, — digádesme la verdad:
35 ¿el castillo de Consuegra — si sabéis por quién está?
— El castillo con la villa — por el prior de Sant Joan.
— Pues abrid luego las puertas; — catalde aquí donde
está. —
La guarda desque lo oyó — abriólas de par en par.
— Tomases allá ese macho, — dél muy bien quieras
curar:
40 déjesme la vela á mí, — que yo la quiero velar.
¡Velá, velá, veladores, — así mala rabia os mate!
Que quien á buen señor sirve, — este gualardón le
dan. —
El prior estando en esto — el rey que llegado ha,
halló las guardas velando, — comenzóles de hablar:
45 — Decidme, los veladores, — que Dios os guarde de mal,
¿el castillo de Consuegra — por quién se tiene ó se
está?

— El castillo con la villa — por el prior de Sant Joan.
— Pues abrid luego las puertas, — que veislo aquí
   donde está.
— Afuera, afuera, buen rey, — que el prior llegado ha.
— ¡Macho rucio, dijo el rey, — muermo te quiera
   matar!   50
Siete caballos me has muerto, — y con éste ocho serán.
Ábreme tú, buen prior, — allá me dejes entrar:
por mi corona te juro — de no hacerte ningún mal.
— Hacerlo vos, el buen rey, — agora en mi mano
   está. —
Mandárale abrir la puerta, — dióle muy bien á cenar.   55

XIV

(W. 65)

ROMANCE DE DON FADRIQUE, MAESTRE
DE SANTIAGO, . . . ETC.

— Yo me estaba allá en Coímbra — que yo me la
   hube ganado,
cuando me vinieron cartas — del rey don Pedro mi
   hermano
que fuese á ver los torneos — que en Sevilla se han
   armado.
Yo Maestre sin ventura, — yo Maestre desdichado,
tomara trece de mula, — veinte y cinco de caballo,   5
todos con cadenas de oro — y jubones de brocado:
jornada de quince días — en ocho la había andado.

Á la pasada de un río, — pasándole por el vado,
cayó mi mula conmigo, — perdí mi puñal dorado,
10 ahogáraseme un paje — de los míos más privado,
criado era en mi sala, — y de mí muy regalado.
Con todas estas desdichas — á Sevilla hube llegado;
á la puerta Macarena — encontré con un ordenado,
ordenado de evangelio — que misa no había cantado:
15 — Manténgate Dios, Maestre, — Maestre, bien seáis
        llegado.
Hoy te ha nacido hijo, — hoy cumples veinte y un
        año.
Si te pluguiese, Maestre, — volvamos á baptizallo,
que yo sería el padrino, — tú, Maestre, el ahijado. —
Allí hablara el Maestre, — bien oiréis lo que ha hablado:
20 —No me lo mandéis, señor, — padre, no queráis man-
        dallo,
que voy á ver qué me quiere — el rey don Pedro mi
        hermano. —
Di de espuelas á mi mula, — en Sevilla me hube
        entrado;
de que no vi tela puesta — ni vi caballero armado,
fuíme para los palacios — del rey don Pedro mi her-
        mano.
25 En entrando por las puertas, — las puertas me habían
        cerrado;
quitáronme la mi espada, — la que traía á mi lado;
quitáronme mi compaña, — la que me había acom-
        pañado.
Los míos desque esto vieron — de traición me han
        avisado,

que me saliese yo fuera — que ellos me pondrían en
    salvo.
Yo, como estaba sin culpa, — de nada hube curado;   30
fuíme para el aposento — del rey don Pedro mi her-
    mano:
— Manténgaos Dios, el rey, — y á todos de cabo á
    cabo.
— Mal hora vengáis, Maestre, — Maestre, mal seáis
    llegado:
nunca nos venís á ver — sino una vez en el año,
y esta que venís, Maestre, — es por fuerza ó por
    mandado.   35
Vuestra cabeza, Maestre, — mandada está en agui-
    naldo.
— ¿Por qué es aqueso, buen rey? — nunca os hice
    desaguisado,
ni os dejé yo en la lid, — ni con moros peleando.
— Venid acá, mis porteros, — hágase lo que he man-
    dado. —
Aun no lo hubo bien dicho, — la cabeza le han cortado; 40
á doña María de Padilla — en un plato la ha enviado;
así hablaba con él — como si estuviera sano.
Las palabras que le dice, — de esta suerte está ha-
    blando:
— Aquí pagaréis, traidor, — lo de antaño y lo de ogaño,
el mal consejo que diste — al rey don Pedro tu her-
    mano. —   45
Asióla por los cabellos, — echado se la ha á un alano;
el alano es del Maestre, — púsola sobre un estrado,
á los aullidos que daba — atronó todo el palacio.

Allí demandara el rey: — ¿Quién hace mal á ese
    alano? —
50 Allí respondieron todos — á los cuales ha pesado:
— Con la cabeza lo ha, señor, — del Maestre vuestro
    hermano. —
Allí hablara una su tía — que tía era de entrambos:
— ¡Cuán mal lo mirastes, rey! — rey, ¡qué mal lo
    habéis mirado!
por una mala mujer — habéis muerto un tal her-
    mano. —
55 Aun no lo había bien dicho, — cuando ya le había
    pesado.
Fuése para doña María, — de esta suerte le ha ha-
    blado:
— Prendelda, mis caballeros, — ponédmela á buen
    recado,
que yo le daré tal castigo — que á todos sea sonado. —
En cárceles muy escuras — allí la había aprisionado;
60 él mismo le da á comer, — él mismo con la su mano:
no se fía de ninguno — sino de un paje que ha criado.

XV

(W. 78a)

[ABENÁMAR]

¡Abenámar, Abenámar, — moro de la morería,
el día que tú naciste — grandes señales había!
Estaba la mar en calma, — la luna estaba crecida:
moro que en tal signo nace, — no debe decir mentira. —
Allí respondiera el moro, — bien oiréis lo que decía: 5
— Yo te la diré, señor, — aunque me cueste la vida,
porque soy hijo de un moro — y una cristiana cautiva;
siendo yo niño y muchacho — mi madre me lo decía:
que mentira no dijese, — que era grande villanía:
por tanto, pregunta, rey, — que la verdad te diría.   10
— Yo te agradezco, Abenámar, — aquesa tu cortesía.
¿Qué castillos son aquéllos? — ¡Altos son y relucían!
— El Alhambra era, señor, — y la otra la mezquita;
los otros los Alixares, — labrados á maravilla.
El moro que los labraba — cien doblas ganaba al día,   15
y el día que no los labra — otras tantas se perdía.
El otro es Generalife, — huerta que par no tenía;
el otro Torres Bermejas, — castillo de gran valía. —
Allí habló el rey don Juan, — bien oiréis lo que decía:
— Si tú quisieses, Granada, — contigo me casaría;   20
daréte en arras y dote — á Córdoba y á Sevilla.
— Casada soy, rey don Juan, — casada soy, que no
    víuda;
el moro que á mí me tiene, — muy grande bien me
    quería.

XVI

(W. 79)

ROMANCE ANTIGUO Y VERDADERO DE ÁLORA LA BIEN CERCADA

Álora, la bien cercada, — tú que estás en par del río,
cercóte el adelantado — una mañana en domingo,
de peones y hombres de armas — el campo bien guar-
    necido;
con la gran artillería — hecho te había un portillo.
5 Viérades moros y moras — todos huir al castillo:
las moras llevaban ropa, — los moros harina y trigo,
y las moras de quince años — llevaban el oro fino,
y los moricos pequeños — llevaban la pasa y higo.
Por cima de la muralla — su pendón llevan tendido.
10 Entre almena y almena — quedado se había un morico
con una ballesta armada, — y en ella puesto un cua-
    drillo.
En altas voces decía, — que la gente lo había oído:
— ¡Treguas, treguas, adelantado, — por tuyo se da el
    castillo! —
Alza la visera arriba, — por ver el que tal le dijo:
15 asestárale á la frente, — salido le ha al colodrillo.
Sacólo Pablo de rienda, — y de mano Jacobillo,
estos dos que había criado — en su casa desde chicos.
Lleváronle á los maestros — por ver si será guarido;
Á las primeras palabras — el testamento les dijo.

XVII

(W. 83)

ROMANCE DE FAJARDO[1]

Jugando estaba el rey moro — y aun al ajedrez un día,
con aquese gran Fajardo — con amor que le tenía.
Fajardo jugaba á Lorca, — y el rey moro Almería;
jaque le dió con el roque, — el alférez le prendía.
Á grandes voces dice el moro: — La villa de Lorca es
    mía. —   5
Allí hablara Fajardo, — bien oiréis lo que decía:
— Calles, buen rey, no me enojes, — ni tengas tal
    fantasía,
aunque tú me la ganases, — Lorca no se te daría:
caballeros tengo dentro — que te la defenderían. —
Allí hablara el rey moro, — bien oiréis lo que decía: 10
— No juguemos más, Fajardo, — ni tengamos más
    porfía,
que sois tan buen caballero, — que todo el mundo os
    temía.

---

[1] This text contains some of the variants given by Argote
de Molina in the *Nobleza de Andalucía.*

XVIII

(W. 85*a*)

[LA PÉRDIDA DE ALHAMA]

Paseábase el rey moro — por la ciudad de Granada,
desde la puerta de Elvira — hasta la de Vivarambla.
　　　　«¡Ay de mi Alhama!»
Cartas le fueron venidas — que Alhama era ganada:
5 las cartas echó en el fuego, — y al mensajero matara.
　　　　«¡Ay de mi Alhama!»
Descabalga de una mula, — y en un caballo cabalga;
por el Zacatín arriba — subido se había al Alhambra.
　　　　«¡Ay de mi Alhama!»
10 Como en el Alhambra estuvo, — al mismo punto mandaba
que se toquen sus trompetas, — sus añafiles de plata.
　　　　«¡Ay de mi Alhama!»
Y que las cajas de guerra — apriesa toquen al arma,
porque lo oigan sus moros, — los de la Vega y Granada.
15　　　　«¡Ay de mi Alhama!»
Los moros que el son oyeron — que al sangriento Marte llama,
uno á uno y dos á dos — juntado se ha gran batalla.
　　　　«¡Ay de mi Alhama!»
Allí habló un moro viejo, — de esta manera hablara:
20 — ¿Para qué nos llamas, rey, — para qué es esta llamada?
　　　　«¡Ay de mi Alhama!»
— Habéis de saber, amigos, — una nueva desdichada:

que cristianos de braveza — ya nos han ganado Alhama.

«¡Ay de mi Alhama!»

Allí habló un alfaquí — de barba cruda y cana: 25
— ¡Bien se te emplea, buen rey, — buen rey, bien se te
empleara!

«¡Ay de mi Alhama!»

Mataste los Bencerrajes, — que eran la flor de Granada;
cogiste los tornadizos — de Córdoba la nombrada.

«¡Ay de mi Alhama!» 30

Por eso mereces, rey, — una pena muy doblada:
que te pierdas tú y el reino, — y aquí se pierda Granada. —

«¡Ay de mi Alhama!»

XIX

(W. 101)

ROMANCE DEL REY DE ARAGÓN

Miraba de Campo-Viejo — el rey de Aragón un día,
miraba la mar de España — como menguaba y crecía;
miraba naos y galeras, — unas van y otras venían:
unas venían de armada, — otras de mercadería;
unas van la vía de Flandes, — otras la de Lombardía. 5
Esas que vienen de guerra — ¡oh cuán bien le parecían!
Miraba la gran ciudad — que Nápoles se decía;
miraba los tres castillos — que la gran ciudad tenía:
Castel Novo y Capuana, — Santelmo, que relucía,

10 aquéste relumbra entre ellos — como el sol de mediodía.
Lloraba de los sus ojos, — de la su boca decía:
— ¡Oh ciudad, cuánto me cuestas — por la gran
    desdicha mía!
cuéstasme duques y condes, — hombres de muy gran
    valía;
cuéstasme un tal hermano, — que por hijo le tenía;
15 de esotra gente menuda — cuento ni par no tenía;
cuéstasme veinte y dos años, — los mejores de mi vida:
que en ti me nacieron barbas, — y en ti las encanecía. —

XX

(MP IX, 245)

ROMANCE DEL REY MARSÍN

Ya comienzan los franceses — con los moros pelear,
y los moros eran tantos — no los dexan resollar.
Allí habló Baldovinos, — bien oiréis lo que dirá:
— Ay compadre don Beltrán, — mal nos va en esta
    batalla;
5 más de sed que no de hambre — á Dios quiero yo dar
    el alma,
cansado traigo el caballo — más el brazo del espada;
roguemos á don Roldán — que una vez el cuerno taña,
oir lo ha el emperador — qu'está en los puertos d'Es-
    paña,
que más vale su socorro — que toda nuestra sonada.—
10 Oído lo ha don Roldán — en las batallas do estaba:

— No me lo roguéis, mis primos, — que ya rogado
    m'estaba,
mas rogaldo á don Renaldos — que á mí no me lo
    retraiga,
ni me lo retraiga en villa — ni me lo retraiga en Francia,
ni en cortes del emperador — estando comiendo á la
    tabla,
que más querría ser muerto — que sufrir tal sobar-
    bada. —   15
Oído lo ha don Renaldo — que en las batallas andaba,
comenzara á decir — estas palabras hablaba:
— Oh mal oviesen franceses — de Francia la natural,
que á tan pocos moros como éstos — el cuerno mandan
    tocar,
que si me toman los corajes — que me solían tomar,   20
por éstos y otros tantos — no me daré sólo un pan. —
Ya le toman los corajes — que le solían tomar;
así se entra por los moros — como segador por pan,
así derriba cabezas — como peras de un peral;
por Roncesvalles arriba — los moros huyendo van;   25
allí salió un perro moro — que mala hora lo parió su
    madre;
— Alcaria, moros, alcaria — si mala rabia vos mate,
que sois ciento para uno — irles fuyendo delante;
¡oh mal haya el rey Marsín — que soldada os manda
    dare;
mal haya la reina mora — que vos la manda pagare;   30
mal hayáis vosotros, moros, — que la venís á ganare! —
De que esto oyeron los moros — aun ellos volvido han,
y vueltas y revueltas — los franceses fuyendo van:

á tan bien se los esfuerza — ese arzobispo Turpín:
35 — Vuelta, vuelta, los franceses, — con corazón á la lid;
más vale morir con honra — que con deshonra vivir. —
Ya volvían los franceses — con corazón á la lid,
tantos matan de los moros — que no se puede decir;
por Ronces Valles arriba — fuyendo va el rey Marsín,
40 caballero en una cebra — no por mengua de rocín;
la sangre que dél salía — las yerbas hace teñir,
las voces que él iba dando — al cielo quieren subir:
— Reniego de ti, Mahoma, — y aun de cuanto hice en
     ti;
hícete el cuerpo de plata, — pies y manos de marfil,
45 y por más te honrar, Mahoma, — la cabeza de oro te
     hiz;
sesenta mil caballeros — ofrecílos yo á ti,
mi mujer Abrayma mora — ofrecióte treinta mil,
mi hija Mataleona — ofrecióte quince mil,
de todos éstos, Mahoma, — tan solo me veo aquí,
50 y aun mi brazo derecho, — Mahoma, no lo trayo aquí,
cortómelo el encantado — ese Roldán paladín,
que si encantado no fuera — no se me fuera él así;
mas yo me iré para Roma — que cristiano quiero morir,
ése será mi padrino — ese Roldán paladín,
55 ése me baptizará, — ese arzobispo Turpín;
mas perdóname, Mahoma, — que con cuita te lo dixe,
que ir no quiero á Roma — curar quiero yo de mí. —

XXI

(W. 185)

ROMANCE QUE DICEN: POR LA MATANZA VA EL VIEJO

Por la matanza va él viejo,—por la matanza adelante;
los brazos lleva cansados — de los muertos rodear:
vido á todos los franceses — y no vido á don Beltrán.
Siete veces echan suertes — quién le volverá á buscar;
echan las tres con malicia,—las cuatro con gran
    maldad: 5
todas siete le cupieron — al buen viejo de su padre.
Vuelve riendas al caballo, — y él se lo vuelve á buscar,
de noche por el camino, — de día por el jaral.
En la entrada de un prado, — saliendo de un arenal,
vido estar en esto un moro — que velaba en un adarve: 10
hablóle en algarabía, — como aquel que bien la sabe:
— Caballero de armas blancas,—¿si lo viste acá pasar?
si le tienes preso, moro, — á oro te le pesarán,
y si tú le tienes muerto — désmelo para enterrar,
porque el cuerpo sin el alma — muy pocos dineros vale. 15
— Ese caballero, amigo, — dime tú, ¿qué señas ha?
— Armas blancas son las suyas,—y el caballo es
    alazán,
y en el carrillo derecho — él tenía una señal,
que siendo niño pequeño — se la hizo un gavilán.
— Ese caballero, amigo,—muerto está en aquel pradal; 20
dentro del agua los pies, — y el cuerpo en un arenal:
siete lanzadas tenía, — pásanle de parte á parte.

XXII

(W. 195)

ROMANCE DEL PALMERO

De Mérida sale el palmero, — de Mérida, esa ciudad:
los pies llevaba descalzos, — las uñas corriendo sangre.
Una esclavina trae rota, — que no valía un real,
y debajo traía otra, — ¡bien valía una ciudad!
5 que ni rey ni emperador — no alcanzaba otra tal.
Camino lleva derecho — de París, esa ciudad;
ni pregunta por mesón — ni menos por hospital:
pregunta por los palacios — del rey Carlos do está.
Un portero está á la puerta, — empezóle de hablar:
10 — Dijésesme tú, el portero, — el rey Carlos ¿dónde
      está?
El portero que lo vido, — mucho maravillado se ha,
como un romero tan pobre — por el rey va á preguntar.
— Digádesmelo, señor, — de eso no tengáis pesar.
— En misa estaba, palmero, — allá en San Juan de
      Letrán,
15 que dice misa un arzobispo, — y la oficia un cardenal. —
El palmero que lo oyera — íbase para Sant Juan:
en entrando por la puerta — bien veréis lo que hará.
Humillóse á Dios del cielo — y á Santa María su Madre,
humillóse al arzobispo, — humillóse al cardenal,
20 porque decía la misa, — no porque merecía más:
humillóse al emperador — y á su corona real,
humillóse á los doce — que á una mesa comen pan.
No se humilla á Oliveros, — ni menos á don Roldán,

porque un sobrino que tienen — en poder de moros está,
y pudiéndolo hacer — no le van á rescatar.   25
Desque aquesto vió Oliveros, — desque aquesto vió
    Roldán,
sacan ambos las espadas — para el palmero se van.
El palmero con su bordón — su cuerpo va á mamparar.
Allí hablara el buen rey — bien oiréis lo que dirá:
— Tate, tate, Oliveros, — tate, tate, don Roldán,   30
ó este palmero es loco, — ó viene de sangre real. —
Tomárale por la mano, — y empiézale de hablar:
— Dígasme tú, el palmero, — no me niegues la verdad,
¿en qué año y en qué mes — pasaste aguas de la mar?
— En el mes de mayo, señor, — yo las fuera á pasar.   35
Porque yo me estaba un día — á orillas de la mar
en el huerto de mi padre — por haberme de holgar:
captiváronme los moros, — pasáronme allende el mar,
á la infanta de Sansueña — me fueron á presentar;
la infanta desque me vido — de mí se fué á enamorar.   40
La vida que yo tenía, — rey, quiero vos la contar.
En la su mesa comía, — y en su cama me iba á echar. —
Allí hablara el buen rey, — bien oiréis lo que dirá:
— Tal captividad como ésa — quien quiera la tomará.
Dígasme tú, el palmerico, — ¿si la iría yo á ganar?   45
— No vades allá, el buen rey, — buen rey, no vades allá,
porque Mérida es muy fuerte, — bien se vos defenderá.
Trescientos castillos tiene, — que es cosa de los mirar,
que el menor de todos ellos — bien se os defenderá. —
Allí hablara Oliveros, — allí habló don Roldán: 50
— Miente, señor, el palmero, — miente y no dice ver-
    dad,

que en Mérida no hay cien castillos, — ni noventa á mi
    pensar,
y éstos que Mérida tiene — no tiene quien los defensar,
que ni tenían señor, — ni menos quien los guardar. —
55 Desque aquesto oyó el palmero—movido con gran
    pesar,
alzó su mano derecha, — dió un bofetón á Roldán.
Allí hablara el rey — con furia y con gran pesar:
— Tomalde, la mi justicia, — y llevédeslo ahorcar. —
Tomádolo ha la justicia — para habello de justiciar:
60 y aun allá al pie de la horca — el palmero fuera hablar:
— ¡Oh mal hubieses, rey Carlos! — Dios te quiera hacer
    mal,
que en un hijo solo que tienes — tú le mandas ahor-
    car. —
Oídolo había la reina — que se le paró á mirar:
— Dejédeslo, la justicia, — no le queráis hacer mal,
65 que si él era mi hijo — encubrir no se podrá,
que un lado ha de tener — un extremado lunar. —
Ya le llevan á la reina, — ya se lo van á llevar:
desnúdanle una esclavina — que no valía un real;
ya le desnudaban otra — que valía una ciudad:
70 halládole han al infante, — halládole han la señal.
Alegrías se hicieron — no hay quien las pueda contar.

XXIII

(W. 150)

ROMANCE DEL INFANTE VENGADOR

Helo, helo, por do viene — el infante vengador,
caballero á la gineta — en un caballo corredor,
su manto revuelto al brazo, — demudada la color,
y en la su mano derecha — un venablo cortador.
Con la punta del venablo — sacarían un arador.   5
Siete veces fué templado — en la sangre de un dragón,
y otras tantas fué afilado — porque cortase mejor:
el hierro fué hecho en Francia, — y el asta en Aragón:
perfilándoselo iba — en las alas de su halcón.
Iba buscar á don Cuadros, — á don Cuadros el traidor, 10
allá le fuera á hallar — junto el emperador.
La vara tiene en la mano, — que era justicia mayor.
Siete veces lo pensaba, — si lo tiraría ó no,
y al cabo de las ocho — el venablo le arrojó.
Por dar al dicho don Cuadros — dado ha al emperador: 15
pasado le ha manto y sayo — que era de un tornasol:
por el suelo ladrillado — más de un palmo le metió.
Allí le habló el rey — bien oiréis lo que habló:
— ¿Por qué me tiraste, infante? — ¿por qué me tiras,
    traidor?
— Perdóneme tu Alteza, — que no tiraba á ti, no: 20
tiraba al traidor de Cuadros, — ese falso engañador,
que siete hermanos tenía, — no ha dejado, si á mí no:
por eso delante de ti, — buen rey, le desafío yo. —
Todos fían á don Cuadros, — y al infante no fían, no,

25 si no fuera una doncella, — hija es del emperador,
que los tomó por la mano, — y en el campo los metió.
Á los primeros encuentros — Cuadros en tierra cayó.
Apeárase el infante, — la cabeza le cortó,
y tomárala en su lanza, — y al buen rey la presentó.
30 De que aquesto vido el rey — con su hija le casó.

XXIV

(W. 133)

ROMANCE DE DON GARCÍA

Atal anda don García — por una sala adelante,
saetas de oro en la mano, — en la otra un arco trae,
maldiciendo á la fortuna — grandes querellas le da:
— Crióme el rey de pequeño, — hízome Dios barragán:
5 dióme armas y caballo, — por do todo hombre más vale,
diérame á doña María — por mujer y por igual,
diérame á cien doncellas — para ella acompañar,
dióme el castillo de Urueña, — para con ella casar;
diérame cien caballeros — para el castillo guardar,
10 basteciómele de vino, — basteciómele de pan,
bastecióle de agua dulce — que en el castillo no la hay.
Cercáronmelo los moros — la mañana de sant Juan:
siete años son pasados — el cerco no quieren quitar,
veo morir á los míos, — no teniendo que les dar,
15 póngolos por las almenas, — armados como se están,
porque pensasen los moros — que podrían pelear.
En el castillo de Urueña — no hay sino sólo un pan,

si le doy á los mis hijos, — la mi mujer ¿qué hará?
si lo como yo, mezquino, — los míos se quejarán. —
Hizo el pan cuatro pedazos — y arrojólos al real: 20
el un pedazo de aquéllos — á los pies del rey fué á dar.
— Alá, pese á mis moros, — Alá le quiera pesar,
de las sobras del castillo — nos bastecen el real. —
Manda tocar los clarines — y su cerco luego alzar.

XXV

(W. 113)

[LOS CRUZADOS]

— Malas mañas habéis, tío, — no las podéis olvidar:
más precias matar un puerco — que ganar una ciudad.
Vuestros hijos y mujer — en poder de moros van,
los hijos en una cebra, — y la madre en un cordal.
La mujer dice: «¡ay marido!» — los hijos dicen: «¡ay
    padre!»   5
De lástima que les hube — yo me los fuera á quitar;
heridas traigo de muerte, — de ellas no puedo escapar.
Apretádmelas, mi tío, — con tocas de caminar. —
Ya le aprieta las heridas, — comienzan de caminar.
Á vuelta de su cabeza — caído lo vido estar,   10
allá se le fué á caer — dentro del río Jordán:
como fué dentro caído, — sano le vió levantar.

XXVI

(W. 117)

[LA BUENA HIJA]

Paseábase el buen conde — todo lleno de pesar,
cuentas negras en sus manos — do suele siempre rezar;
palabras tristes diciendo, — palabras para llorar:
— Véoos, hija, crecida, — y en edad para casar;
5 el mayor dolor que siento — es no tener que os dar.
— Calledes, padre, calledes, — no debéis tener pesar,
que quien buena hija tiene — rico se debe llamar,
y el que mala la tenía, — viva la puede enterrar,
pues amengua su linaje — que no debiera amenguar,
10 y yo, si no me casare, — en religión puedo entrar.

XXVII

(W. 132)

ROMANCE QUE DICE: YO ME ERA MORA MORAYMA

Yo me era mora Morayma, — morilla de un bel catar:
cristiano vino á mi puerta, — cuitada, por me engañar.
Hablóme en algarabía — como aquel que la bien sabe:
—Ábrasme las puertas, mora,—si Alá te guarde de mal.
5 — ¿Cómo te abriré, mezquina, — que no sé quién te
serás?
— Yo soy el moro Mazote, — hermano de la tu madre,

que un cristiano dejo muerto; — tras mí venía el
   alcalde.
Si no me abres tú, mi vida, — aquí me verás matar. —
Cuando esto oí, cuitada, — comencéme á levantar,
vistiérame una almejía — no hallando mi brial,   10
fuérame para la puerta — y abríla de par en par.

XXVIII

(W. 119)

ROMANCE DE RICO FRANCO

Á caza iban, á caza, — los cazadores del rey,
ni fallaban ellos caza, — ni fallaban que traer.
Perdido habían los halcones, — ¡mal los amenaza el rey!
Arrimáranse á un castillo — que se llamaba Maynés.
Dentro estaba una doncella — muy fermosa y muy
   cortés;   5
siete condes la demandan, — y así facían tres reyes.
Robárala Rico Franco, — Rico Franco aragonés:
llorando iba la doncella — de sus ojos tan cortés.
Falágala Rico Franco, — Rico Franco aragonés:
— Si lloras tu padre ó madre, — nunca más vos los
   veréis,   10
si lloras los tus hermanos, — yo los maté todos tres.
— Ni lloro padre ni madre, — ni hermanos todos tres;
mas lloro la mi ventura — que no sé cuál ha de ser.
Prestédesme, Rico Franco, — vuestro cuchillo lugués,
cortaré fitas al manto — que no son para traer. —   15

Rico Franco de cortese — por las cachas lo fué tender;
la doncella que era artera — por los pechos se lo fué á
    meter:
así vengó padre y madre, — y aun hermanos todos tres.

XXIX

(W. 151)

ROMANCE DE LA INFANTINA

Á cazar va el caballero, — á cazar como solía;
los perros lleva cansados, — el falcón perdido había,
arrimárase á un roble, — alto es á maravilla.
En una rama más alta, — viera estar una infantina;
5 cabellos de su cabeza — todo el roble cobrían.
— No te espantes, caballero, — ni tengas tamaña grima.
Fija soy yo del buen rey — y de la reina de Castilla:
siete fadas me fadaron, — en brazos de una ama mía,
que andase los siete años — sola en esta montiña.
10 Hoy se cumplían los siete años,—ó mañana en aquel día:
por Dios te ruego, caballero,—llévesme en tu compañía,
si quisieres por mujer, — si no, sea por amiga.
— Esperéisme vos, señora, — fasta mañana, aquel día,
iré yo tomar consejo — de una madre que tenía. —
15 La niña le respondiera — y estas palabras decía:
—¡Oh mal haya el caballero — que sola deja la niña!
Él se va á tomar consejo, — y ella queda en la montiña.
Aconsejóle su madre — que la tomase por amiga.
Cuando volvió el caballero — no la hallara en la mon-
    tiña:

vídola que la llevaban — con muy gran caballería.   20
El caballero desque la vido — en el suelo se caía:
desque en sí hubo tornado — estas palabras decía:
— Caballero que tal pierde, — muy gran pena merecía:
yo mesmo seré el alcalde, — yo me seré la justicia:
que le corten pies y manos — y lo arrastren por la villa.   25

XXX

(W. 153)

ROMANCE DEL CONDE ARNALDOS

¡Quién hubiese tal ventura — sobre las aguas de mar,
como hubo el conde Arnaldos — la mañana de San Juan!
Con un falcón en la mano — la caza iba cazar,
vió venir una galera — que á tierra quiere llegar.
Las velas traía de seda, — la ejercia de un cendal,   5
marinero que la manda — diciendo viene un cantar
que la mar facía en calma, — los vientos hace amainar,
los peces que andan 'nel hondo — arriba los hace andar,
las aves que andan volando — en el mástel las face
        posar.[1]

---

[1] The *Canc. de R.* of 1550 and all succeeding editions of it
insert after this verse the following lines which do not appear in the *Canc. de R.* «sin año»:

> — Galera, la mi galera, — Dios te me guarde de mal,
> de los peligros del mundo — sobre aguas de la mar,
> de los llanos de Almería, — del estrecho de Gibraltar,
> y del golfo de Venecia, — y de los bancos de Flandes,
> y del golfo de León, — donde suelen peligrar. —

10 Allí fabló el conde Arnaldos, — bien oiréis lo que dirá:
— Por Dios te ruego, marinero, — dígasme ora ese
cantar. —
Respondióle el marinero, — tal respuesta le fué á dar:
— Yo no digo esta canción — sino á quien conmigo va.

XXXI

(W. 116)

ROMANCE DE FONTEFRIDA

Fonte-frida, fonte-frida, — fonte-frida y con amor,
do todas las avecicas — van tomar consolación,
sino es la tortolica — que está viuda y con dolor.
Por allí fuera á pasar — el traidor de ruiseñor:
5 — Si tú quisieses, señora, — yo sería tu servidor.
— Vete de ahí, enemigo, — malo, falso, engañador,
que ni poso en ramo verde, — ni en prado que tenga
flor;
que si el agua hallo clara, — turbia la bebía yo;
que no quiero haber marido, — porque hijos no haya,
no:
10 no quiero placer con ellos, — ni menos consolación.
¡Déjame, triste enemigo, — malo, falso, mal traidor,
que no quiero ser tu amiga — ni casar contigo, no!

XXXII

(MP X, 362)

[EL AMANTE DESDICHADO]

En los tiempos que me vi — más alegre y placentero,
yo me partiera de Burgos — para ir á Valladolid,
encontré con un palmero; — él me fabló y dijo así:
— ¿Dónde vas tú, desdichado? — ¿Dónde vas, triste de
   ti?
¡Oh persona desdichada! — en mal punto te conocí,   5
muerta es tu enamorada, — muerta es, que yo la vi;
las andas en que la llevan — de negro las vi cobrir,
los responsos que le dicen — yo los ayudé á decir,
siete condes la llevaban, — caballeros más de mil,
lloraban las sus doncellas — llorando dicen así: 10
— ¡Triste de aquel caballero — que tal pérdida perdí. —
De que aquesto oyera, mezquino, — en tierra muerto
   caí;
desde aquéllas, dos horas — no tornara, triste, en mí;
desque me hube retornado — á la sepultura fuí,
con lágrimas de mis ojos — llorando decía así: 15
— Acógeme, mi señora, — acógeme á par de ti. —
Al cabo de la sepultura — una triste voz oí:
— Vive, vive, enamorado, — vive, pues que yo morí;
Dios te dé ventura en armas, — y en amores así,
que el cuerpo come la tierra, — y el alma pena por ti.   20

XXXIII

(D. 1577)

[LA LAVANDERA]

Yo me levantara, madre, — mañanica de Sant Joan:
vide estar una doncella — ribericas de la mar:
sola lava y sola tuerce, — sola tiende en un rosal:
mientras los paños se enjugan, — dice la niña un
    cantar:

Cantarcillo

5 «¿Dó los mis amores, dó los? — ¿Dó los andaré á
    buscar?»

Sigue el romance

Mar abajo, mar arriba, — diciendo iba el cantar,
peine de oro en las sus manos — por sus cabellos peinar.
«Dígasme tú, el marinero, — si Dios te guarde de mal,
si los viste, mis amores, — si los viste allá pasar.»

ROMANCES JUGLARESCOS

XXXIV

(W. 4)

ROMANCE DE COMO EL CONDE DON JULIÁN, PADRE DE LA CAVA, VENDIÓ Á ESPAÑA

En Ceupta está Julián, — en Ceupta la bien nombrada:
para las partes de aliende — quiere enviar su embajada;
moro viejo la escrebía, — y el conde se la notaba:
después de haberla escripto, — al moro luego matara.
Embajada es de dolor, — dolor para toda España: 5
las cartas van al rey moro —en las cuales le juraba
que si le daba aparejo — le dará por suya España.
Madre España, ¡ay de ti! — en el mundo tan nombrada,
de las partidas la mejor, — la mejor y más ufana,
donde nace el fino oro, — y la plata no faltaba, 10
dotada de hermosura, — y en proezas extremada;
por un perverso traidor — toda eres abrasada,
todas tus ricas ciudades — con su gente tan galana
las domeñan hoy los moros — por nuestra culpa mal-
   vada,
si no fueran las Asturias, — por ser la tierra tan brava. 15
El triste rey don Rodrigo, — el que entonces te mandaba,
viendo sus reinos perdidos — sale á la campal batalla,
el cual en grave dolor — ensaña su fuerza brava;

mas tantos eran los moros, — que han vencido la
batalla.

20 No paresce el rey Rodrigo, — ni nadie sabe dó estaba.
Maldito de ti, don Orpas, — obispo de mala andanza:
en esta negra conseja — uno á otro se ayudaba.
¡Oh dolor sobre manera! — ¡oh cosa nunca cuidada!
que por sola una doncella, — la cual Cava se llamaba,
25 causen estos dos traidores — que España sea domeñada,
y perdido el rey señor, — sin nunca dél saber nada.

XXXV

(W. 5)

ROMANCE DEL REY DON RODRIGO COMO PERDIÓ Á ESPAÑA

Las huestes de don Rodrigo — desmayaban y huían
cuando en la octava batalla — sus enemigos vencían.
Rodrigo deja sus tiendas — y del real se salía:
solo va el desventurado, — que no lleva compañía.
5 El caballo de cansado — ya mudar no se podía:
camina por donde quiere, — que no le estorba la vía.
El rey va tan desmayado — que sentido no tenía:
muerto va de sed y hambre, — que de velle era mancilla;
iba tan tinto de sangre — que una brasa parecía.
10 Las armas lleva abolladas, — que eran de gran pedrería;
la espada lleva hecha sierra — de los golpes que tenía;
el almete abollado — en la cabeza se le hundía;
la cara lleva hinchada — del trabajo que sufría.

Subióse encima de un cerro — el más alto que veía:
dende allí mira su gente — como iba de vencida. 15
De allí mira sus banderas, — y estandartes que tenía,
como están todos pisados — que la tierra los cubría.
Mira por sus capitanes — que ninguno parescía;
mira el campo tinto en sangre, — la cual arroyos corría.
El triste, de ver aquesto, — gran mancilla en sí tenía: 20
llorando de los sus ojos — de esta manera decía:
— Ayer era rey de España, — hoy no lo soy de una
      villa;
ayer villas y castillos, — hoy ninguno poseía;
ayer tenía criados, — hoy ninguno me servía,
hoy no tengo una almena — que pueda decir que es
      mía. 25
¡Desdichada fué la hora, — desdichado fué aquel día
en que nací y heredé — la tan grande señoría,
pues lo había de perder — todo junto y en un día!
¡Oh muerte! ¿por qué no vienes — y llevas esta alma
      mía
de aqueste cuerpo mezquino, — pues te se agrade-
      cería? 30

XXXVI

(W. 30b)

ROMANCE DE JIMENA GÓMEZ

Día era de los Reyes, — día era señalado,
cuando dueñas y doncellas — al rey piden aguinaldo,
sino es Jimena Gómez, — hija del conde Lozano,
que puesta delante el rey, — de esta manera ha hablado:

5 — Con mancilla vivo, rey, — con ella vive mi madre;
cada día que amanece — veo quien mató á mi padre,
caballero en un caballo — y en su mano un gavilán;
otra vez con un halcón — que trae para cazar,
por me hacer más enojo — cébalo en mi palomar:
10 con sangre de mis palomas — ensangrentó mi brial.
Enviéselo á decir, — envióme á amenazar.
1 . . . .

15 Rey que no hace justicia — no debía de reinar,
ni cabalgar en caballo, — ni espuela de oro calzar,
ni comer pan á manteles, — ni con la reina holgar,
ni oir misa en sagrado, — porque no merece más. —
El rey de que aquesto oyera — comenzara de hablar:
20 — ¡Oh válame Dios del cielo! — quiérame Dios consejar:
si yo prendo ó mato al Cid, — mis Cortes se volverán;
y si no hago justicia, — mi alma lo pagará.
— Tente las tus Cortes, rey, — no te las revuelva nadie;
al Cid que mató á mi padre — dámelo tú por igual,
25 que quien tanto mal me hizo — sé que algún bien me
hará. —
Entonces dijera el rey, — bien oiréis lo que dirá:
— Siempre lo oí decir, — y agora veo que es verdad,
que el seso de las mujeres — que no era natural:
hasta aquí pidió justicia, — ya quiere con él casar.
30 Yo lo haré de buen grado, — de muy buena voluntad;

---

1 Three lines are omitted here which are an obvious interpolation from another and older *romance* (*Yo me estaba en
Barbadillo*, which forms part of W. 19).

mandarle quiero una carta, — mandarle quiero llamar:
Las palabras no son dichas, — la carta camino va,
mensajero que la lleva — dado la había á su padre.
— Malas mañas habéis, conde, — no vos las puedo
    quitar,
que cartas que el rey vos manda — no me las queréis
    mostrar.   35
— No era nada, mi hijo, — sino que vades allá,
quedávos aquí, hijo, — yo iré en vuestro lugar.
— Nunca Dios atal quisiese — ni santa María lo mande,
sino que adonde vos fuéredes — que vaya yo adelante.

XXXVII

(W. 29)

ROMANCE DEL CID RUY DÍAZ

Cabalga Diego Laínez — al buen rey besar la mano;
consigo se los llevaba — los trescientos hijosdalgo.
Entre ellos iba Rodrigo — el soberbio castellano;
todos cabalgan á mula, — sólo Rodrigo á caballo;
todos visten oro y seda, — Rodrigo va bien armado;   5
todos espadas ceñidas, — Rodrigo estoque dorado;
todos con sendas varicas, — Rodrigo lanza en la mano;
todos guantes olorosos, — Rodrigo guante mallado;
todos sombreros muy ricos, — Rodrigo casco afilado,
y encima del casco lleva — un bonete colorado.   10
Andando por su camino, — unos con otros hablando,

allegados son á Burgos; — con el rey se han encontrado.
Los que vienen con el rey — entre sí van razonando;
unos lo dicen de quedo, — otros lo van preguntando:
15 — Aquí viene entre esta gente — quien mató al conde
    Lozano.
Como lo oyera Rodrigo, — en hito los ha mirado:
con alta y soberbia voz — de esta manera ha hablado:
— Si hay alguno entre vosotros, — su pariente ó
    adeudado,
que le pese de su muerte, — salga luego á demandallo;
20 yo se lo defenderé — quiera á pie, quiera á caballo. —
Todos responden á una: — Demándelo su pecado. —
Todos se apearon juntos — para al rey besar la mano;
Rodrigo se quedó solo — encima de su caballo.
Entonces habló su padre, — bien oiréis lo que ha
    hablado:
25 — Apeáos vos, mi hijo, — besaréis al rey la mano,
porque él es vuestro señor, — vos, hijo, sois su vasallo.
Desque Rodrigo esto oyó — sintióse más agraviado:
las palabras que responde — son de hombre muy eno-
    jado.
— Si otro me lo dijera, — ya me lo hubiera pagado;
30 mas por mandarlo vos, padre, — yo lo haré de buen
    grado. —
Ya se apeaba Rodrigo — para al rey besar la mano;
al hincar de la rodilla, — el estoque se ha arrancado.
Espantóse de esto el rey, — y dijo como turbado:
— Quítate, Rodrigo, allá, — quítate me allá, diablo,
35 que tienes el gesto de hombre, — y los hechos de león
    bravo. —

Como Rodrigo esto oyó, — apriesa pide el caballo:
con una voz alterada, — contra el rey así ha hablado:
— Por besar mano de rey — no me tengo por honrado;
porque la besó mi padre — me tengo por afrentado. —
En diciendo estas palabras — salido se ha del palacio: 40
consigo se los tornaba — los trescientos hijosdalgo:
si bien vinieron vestidos, — volvieron mejor armados,
y si vinieron en mulas, — todos vuelven en caballos.

XXXVIII

(W. 52)

ROMANCE DEL JURAMENTO QUE TOMÓ EL CID AL REY DON ALONSO

En sancta Gadea de Burgos, — do juran los hijos-
    dalgo,
allí le toma la jura — el Cid al rey castellano.
Las juras eran tan fuertes, — que al buen rey ponen
    espanto;
sobre un cerrojo de hierro — y una ballesta de palo:
— Villanos te maten, Alonso, — villanos, que no hi-
    dalgos,   5
de las Asturias de Oviedo, — que no sean castellanos;
mátente con aguijadas, — no con lanzas ni con dardos;
con cuchillos cachicuernos, — no con puñales dorados;
abarcas traigan calzadas, — que no zapatos con lazo;
capas traigan aguaderas, — no de contray, ni frisado; 10
con camisones de estopa, — no de holanda, ni labrados;

caballeros vengan en burras, — que no en mulas ni en
　　caballos;
frenos traigan de cordel, — que no cueros fogueados.
Mátente por las aradas, — que no en villas ni en
　　poblado,
15 sáquente el corazón — por el siniestro costado,
si no dijeres la verdad — de lo que te fuere preguntado,
si fuiste, ni consentiste — en la muerte de tu hermano.—
Jurado había el rey, — que en tal nunca se ha hallado;
pero allí hablara el rey — malamente y enojado:
20 — Muy mal me conjuras, Cid, — Cid, muy mal me has
　　conjurado;
mas hoy me tomas la jura, — mañana me besarás la
　　mano.
— Por besar mano de rey — no me tengo por honrado;
porque la besó mi padre — me tengo por afrentado.
— Vete de mis tierras, Cid, — mal caballero probado,
25 y no vengas más á ellas — dende este día en un año. —
— Pláceme, dijo el buen Cid, — pláceme, dijo, de grado,
por ser la primera cosa — que mandas en tu reinado.
Tú me destierras por uno, — yo me destierro por
　　cuatro. —
Ya se parte el buen Cid, sin al rey besar la mano,
30 con trescientos caballeros, — todos eran hijosdalgo;
todos son hombres mancebos, — ninguno no había
　　cano.
Todos llevan lanza en puño — y el hierro acicalado,
y llevan sendas adargas, — con borlas de colorado;
mas no le faltó al buen Cid — adonde asentar su
　　campo.

XXXIX

(W. 184)

ROMANCE DE DOÑA ALDA

En París está doña Alda — la esposa de don Roldán,
trescientas damas con ella — para la acompañar:
todas visten un vestido, — todas calzan un calzar,
todas comen á una mesa, — todas comían de un pan,
sino era doña Alda, — que era la mayoral.   5
Las ciento hilaban oro, — las ciento tejen cendal,
las ciento tañen instrumentos — para doña Alda holgar.
Al son de los instrumentos — doña Alda adormido se
    ha:
ensoñado había un sueño, — un sueño de gran pesar.
Recordó despavorida — y con un pavor muy grande,   10
los gritos daba tan grandes, — que se oían en la ciudad.
Allí hablaron sus doncellas, — bien oiréis lo que dirán:
—¿Qué es aquesto, mi señora? — ¿quién es el que os
    hizo mal?
— Un sueño soñé, doncellas, — que me ha dado gran
    pesar;
que me veía en un monte — en un desierto lugar: 15
de so los montes muy altos — un azor vide volar,
tras dél viene una aguililla — que lo ahinca muy mal.
El azor con grande cuita — metióse so mi brial;
el aguililla con grande ira — de allí lo iba á sacar;
con las uñas lo despluma, — con el pico lo deshace. —   20
Allí habló su camarera, — bien oiréis lo que dirá:
— Aquese sueño, señora, — bien os lo entiendo soltar:

el azor es vuestro esposo — que viene de allén la mar;
el águila sedes vos, — con la cual ha de casar,
25 y aquel monte es la iglesia — donde os han de velar.
— Si así es, mi camarera, — bien te lo entiendo pagar. —
Otro día de mañana — cartas de fuera le traen;
tintas venían de dentro, — de fuera escritas con
    sangre,
que su Roldán era muerto — en la caza de Ronces-
    valles.

XL

(W. 171)

DOS ROMANCES DE GAIFEROS, EN LOS CUALES SE CONTIENE COMO MATARON Á DON GALVÁN

Estábase la condesa — en su estrado asentada,
tisericas de oro en mano: — su hijo afeitando estaba.
Palabras le está diciendo, — palabras de gran pesar:
las palabras eran tales — que al niño hacen llorar.
5 — Dios te dé barbas en rostro, — y te haga barragán;
déte Dios ventura en armas, — como al paladín Roldán,
porque vengases, mi hijo, — la muerte de vuestro
    padre:
matáronlo á traición — por casar con vuestra madre.
Ricas bodas me hicieron — en las cuales Dios no ha
    parte;
10 ricos paños me cortaron, — la reina no los ha tales. —
Magüera pequeño el niño — bien entendido lo ha.
Allí respondió Gaiferos, — bien oiréis lo que dirá:

— Así ruego á Dios del cielo — y á Santa María su
  Madre. —
Oídolo había el conde — en los palacios do está:
— ¡Calles, calles, la condesa, — boca mala sin verdad! 15
que yo no matara el conde, — ni lo hiciera matar;
mas tus palabras, condesa, — el niño las pagará. —
Mandó llamar escuderos, — criados son de su padre,
para que lleven al niño, — que lo lleven á matar.
La muerte que él les dijera — mancilla es de la escu-
  char: 20
— Córtenle el pie del estribo, — la mano del gavilán,
sáquenle ambos los ojos — por más seguro andar;
y el dedo, y el corazón — traédmelo por señal. —
Ya lo llevan á Gaiferos, — ya lo llevan á matar;
hablaban los escuderos — con mancilla que dél han: 25
— ¡Oh válasme Dios del cielo — y Santa María su
  Madre!
si este niño matamos — ¿qué galardón nos darán? —
Ellos en aquesto estando, — no sabiendo qué harán,
vieron venir una perrita — de la condesa su madre.
Allí habló el uno de ellos, — bien oiréis lo que dirá: 30
— Matemos esta perrita — por nuestra seguridad,
saquémosle el corazón — y llevémoslo á Galván,
cortémosle el dedo al chico — por llevar mejor señal.—
Ya tomaban á Gaiferos, — para el dedo le cortar:
— Venid acá vos, Gaiferos, — y querednos escuchar; 35
vos íos de aquesta tierra — y en ella no parezcáis más.—
Ya le daban entre señas — el camino que hará:
— Irvos heis de tierra en tierra — á do vuestro tío
  está. —

Gaiferos desconsolado — por ese mundo se va:
40 los escuderos se volvieron — para do estaba Galván.
Danle el dedo, y el corazón — y dicen que muerto lo
   han.
La condesa que esto oyera — empezara gritos dar:
lloraba de los sus ojos — que quería reventar.
Dejemos á la condesa, — que muy grande llanto hace,
45 y digamos de Gaiferos — del camino por do va,
que de día ni de noche — no hace sino caminar,
fasta que llegó á la tierra — adonde su tío está.
Dícele de esta manera, — y empezóle de hablar:
— Manténgaos Dios, el mi tío. — Mi sobrino, bien
   vengáis.
50 ¿Qué buena venida es ésta? — vos me la queráis contar.
— La venida que yo vengo — triste es y con pesar,
que Galván con grande enojo — mandado me había
   matar:
mas lo que vos ruego, mi tío, — y lo que vos vengo á
   rogar,
vamos á vengar la muerte — de vuestro hermano, mi
   padre:
55 matáronlo á traición, — por casar con la mi madre.
— Sosegaos, el mi sobrino, — vos queráis asosegar,
que la muerte de mi hermano — bien la iremos á
   vengar. —
Y ellos así estuvieron — dos años y aún más,
fasta que dijo Gaiferos — y empezara de hablar:

XLI

(W. 172)

SÍGUESE EL SEGUNDO ROMANCE

— Vámonos, dijo, mi tío, — á París esa ciudad
en figura de romeros, — no nos conozca Galván,
que si Galván nos conoce — mandar nos hía matar.
Encima ropas de seda — vistamos las de sayal,
llevemos nuestras espadas — por más seguros andar;   5
llevemos sendos bordones — por la gente asegurar. —
Ya se parten los romeros, — ya se parten, ya se van,
de noche por los caminos, — de día por los jarales.
Andando por sus jornadas — á París llegado han;
las puertas hallan cerradas, — no hallan por donde
    entrar.   10
Siete vueltas la rodean — por ver si podrán entrar,
y al cabo de las ocho — un postigo van hallar.
Ellos que se vieron dentro — empiezan á demandar:
no preguntan por mesón, — ni menos por hospital,
preguntan por los palacios — donde la condesa está;   15
á las puertas del palacio — allí van á demandar.
Vieron estar la condesa, — y empezaron de hablar:
— Dios te salve, la condesa. — Los romeros, bien
    vengáis.
— Mandedes nos dar limosna — por honor de caridad.
— Con Dios vades, los romeros, — que no os puedo
    nada dar,   20
que el conde me había mandado — á romeros no al-
    bergar.

— Dadnos limosna, señora, — que el conde no lo sabrá:
así la den á Gaiferos — en la tierra donde está. —
Así como oyó Gaiferos — comenzó de sospirar:
25 mandábales dar del vino, — mandábales dar del pan.
Ellos en aquesto estando — el conde llegado ha:
— ¿Qué es aquesto, la condesa? — aquesto ¿qué puede
    estar?
¿No os tenía yo mandado — á romeros no albergar? —
Y alzara la su mano, — puñada le fuera á dar,
30 que sus dientes menudicos — en tierra los fuera á
    echar.
Allí hablaran los romeros, — y empiezan de hablar:
—¡Por hacer bien la condesa — cierto no merece mal!
— ¡Calledes vos, los romeros, — no hayades vuestra
    parte!
Alzó Gaiferos su espada, — un golpe le fué á dar
35 que la cabeza de sus hombros — en tierra la fuera á
    echar:
allí habló la condesa — llorando con gran pesar:
— ¿Quién érades, los romeros, — que al conde fuistes
    matar?
Allí respondió el romero, — tal respuesta le fué á dar:
— Yo soy Gaiferos, señora, — vuestro hijo natural.
40 — Aquesto no puede ser, — ni era cosa de verdad,
que el dedo y el corazón — yo lo tengo por señal.
— El corazón que vos tenéis — en persona no fué á
    estar,
el dedo bien es aquéste, — que en esta mano me falta. —
La condesa que esto oyera — empezóle de abrazar:
45 la tristeza que tenía — en placer se fué á tornar.

XLII

(W. 181)

ROMANCE DE OH BELERMA

¡Oh Belerma! ¡oh Belerma! — por mi mal fuiste
    engendrada,
que siete años te serví — sin de ti alcanzar nada;
agora que me querías — muero yo en esta batalla.
No me pesa de mi muerte — aunque temprano me
    llama;
mas pésame que de verte — y de servirte dejaba.   5
¡Oh mi primo Montesinos! — lo que agora yo os ro-
    gaba,
que cuando yo fuere muerto — y mi ánima arrancada,
vos llevéis mi corazón — adonde Belerma estaba,
y servilda de mi parte, — como de vos yo esperaba,
y traelde á la memoria — dos veces cada semana;   10
y diréisle que se acuerde — cuán cara que me costaba;
y dalde todas mis tierras — las que yo señoreaba;
pues que yo á ella pierdo, — todo el bien con ella vaya.
¡Montesinos, Montesinos! — ¡mal me aqueja esta lan-
    zada!
el brazo traigo cansado, — y la mano del espada: 15
traigo grandes las heridas, — mucha sangre derramada,
los extremos tengo fríos, — y el corazón me desmaya,
los ojos que nos vieron ir — nunca nos verán en Francia.
Abracéisme, Montesinos, — que ya se me sale el alma.
De mis ojos ya no veo, — la lengua tengo turbada;   20
yo vos doy todos mis cargos, — en vos yo los traspasaba.

— El Señor en quien creéis — él oiga vuestra palabra. —
Muerto yace Durandarte — al pie de una alta montaña,
llorábalo Montesinos, — que á su muerte se hallara:
25 quitándole está el almete, — desciñéndole el espada;
hácele la sepultura — con una pequeña daga;
sacábale el corazón, — como él se lo jurara,
para llevar á Belerma, — como él se lo mandara.
Las palabras que le dice — de allá le salen del alma:
30 — ¡Oh mi primo Durandarte! — ¡primo mío de mi alma!
¡espada nunca vencida! — ¡esfuerzo do esfuerzo estaba!
¡quien á vos mató, mi primo, — no sé por qué me
dejara!

XLIII

(W. 121)

[MORIANA Y EL MORO GALVÁN]

Moriana en un castillo — juega con el moro Galván:
juegan los dos á las tablas — por mayor placer tomar.
Cada vez que el moro pierde — bien perdía una ciudad;
cuando Moriana pierde — la mano le da á besar.
5 Del placer que el moro toma — adormescido se cae.
Por aquellos altos montes — caballero vió asomar:
llorando viene y gimiendo, — las uñas corriendo sangre
de amores de Moriana — hija del rey Moriane.
Captiváronla los moros — la mañana de Sant Juane,
10 cogiendo rosas y flores — en la huerta de su padre.
Alzó los ojos Moriana, — conociérale en mirarle:
lágrimas de los sus ojos — en la faz del moro dane.

Con pavor recuerda el moro — y empezara de fablare:
— ¿Qué es esto, la mi señora? — ¿Quién vos ha fecho
    pesare?
Si os enojaron mis moros — luego los faré matare,   15
ó si las vuesas doncellas, — farélas bien castigare;
y si pesar los cristianos, — yo los iré conquistare.
Mis arreos son las armas, — mi descanso el pelear,
mi cama, las duras peñas, — mi dormir, siempre velare.
— Non me enojaron los moros, — ni los mandedes
    matare,   20
ni menos las mis doncellas — por mí reciban pesare;
ni tampoco á los cristianos — vos cumple de con-
    quistare,
pero de este sentimiento — quiero vos decir verdade:
que por los montes aquellos — caballero vi asomare,
el cual pienso que es mi esposo, — mi querido, mi amor
    grande. —   25
Alzó la su mano el moro, — un bofetón le fué á dare:
teniendo los dientes blancos — de sangre vuelto los hae,
y mandó que sus porteros — la lleven á degollare,
allí do viera á su esposo, — en aquel mismo lugare.
Al tiempo de la su muerte — estas voces fué á fablare: 30
— Yo muero como cristiana, — y también sin con-
    fesare
mis amores verdaderos — de mi esposo naturale.

XLIV

(W. 163)

ROMANCE DEL CONDE ALARCOS Y DE LA INFANTA SOLISA

Retraída está la infanta, — bien así como solía,
viviendo muy descontenta — de la vida que tenía,
viendo que ya se pasaba — toda la flor de su vida,
y que el rey no la casaba, — ni tal cuidado tenía.
5 Entre sí estaba pensando — á quien se descubriría,
y acordó llamar al rey — como otras veces solía,
por decirle su secreto — y la intención que tenía.
Vino el rey siendo llamado, — que no tardó su venida:
vídola estar apartada, — sola está sin compañía;
10 su lindo gesto mostraba — ser más triste que solía.
Conociera luego el rey — el enojo que tenía.
— ¿Qué es aquesto, la infanta? — ¿qué es aquesto, hija
    mía?
Contadme vuestros enojos, — no toméis malenconía,
que sabiendo la verdad — todo se remediaría.
15 — Menester será, buen rey, — remediar la vida mía,
que á vos quedé encomendada — de la madre que tenía.
Dédesme, buen rey, marido, — que mi edad ya lo
    pedía:
con vergüenza os lo demando, — no con gana que tenía,
que aquestos cuidados tales — á vos, rey, pertenecían.—
20 Escuchada su demanda, — el buen rey le respondía:
— Esa culpa, la infanta, — vuestra era, que no mía,
que ya fuérades casada — con el príncipe de Hungría.

No quesistes escuchar — la embajada que os venía,
pues acá en las nuestras cortes, — hija, mal recaudo
    había,
porque en todos los mis reinos — vuestro par igual no
    había,   25
sino era el conde Alarcos, — que hijos y mujer tenía.
— Convidaldo vos, el rey, — al conde Alarcos un día,
y después que hayáis comido — decilde de parte mía,
decilde que se acuerde — de la fe que dél tenía,
la cual él me prometió, — que yo no se la pedía,   30
de ser siempre mi marido, — yo que su mujer sería.
Yo fuí dello muy contenta — y que no me arrepentía.
Si casó con la condesa, — que mirase lo que hacía,
que por él no me casé — con el príncipe de Hungría:
si casó con la condesa, — dél es culpa, que no mía. —   35
Perdiera el rey en oirlo — el sentido que tenía,
mas después en sí tornado — con enojo respondía:
— ¡No son éstos los consejos, — que vuestra madre os
    decía!
¡Muy mal mirastes, infanta, — do estaba la honra
    mía!
Si verdad es todo eso — vuestra honra ya es perdida: 40
no podéis vos ser casada — siendo la condesa viva.
Si se hace el casamiento, — por razón ó por justicia
en el decir de las gentes — por mala seréis tenida.
Dadme vos, hija, consejo, — que el mío no bastaría,
que ya es muerta vuestra madre — á quien consejo
    pedía.   45
— Yo os lo daré, buen rey, — deste poco que tenía:
mate el conde á la condesa, — que nadie no lo sabría,

y eche fama que ella es muerta — de un cierto mal que
    tenía,
y tratarse ha el casamiento — como cosa no sabida.
50 Desta manera, buen rey, — mi honra se guardaría. —
De allí se salía el rey, — no con placer que tenía;
lleno va de pensamientos — con la nueva que sabía;
vido estar al conde Alarcos — entre muchos, que decía:
— ¿Qué aprovecha, caballeros, — amar y servir amiga,
55 que son servicios perdidos — donde firmeza no había?
No pueden por mí decir — aquesto que yo decía,
que en el tiempo que yo serví — una que tanto quería,
si muy bien la quise entonces, — agora más la quería;
mas por mí pueden decir — quien bien ama tarde ol-
    vida. —
60 Estas palabras diciendo — vido al buen rey que venía.
Y hablando con el rey — de entre todos se salía.
Dijo el buen rey al conde — hablando con cortesía:
— Convidaros quiero, conde, — por mañana en aquel
    día,
que queráis comer conmigo — por tenerme compañía.
65 — Que se haga de buen grado — lo que su Alteza decía:
beso sus reales manos — por la buena cortesía:
detenerme he aquí mañana — aunque estaba de par-
    tida,
que la condesa me espera — según la carta me envía. —
Otro día de mañana — el rey de misa salía;
70 asentóse luego á comer, — no por gana que tenía,
sino por hablar al conde — lo que hablarle quería.
Allí fueron bien servidos — como á rey pertenecía.
Después que hubieron comido, — toda la gente salida,

quedóse el rey con el conde — en la tabla do comía.
Empezó de hablar el rey — la embajada que traía: 75
— Unas nuevas traigo, conde, — que dellas no me
    placía,
por las cuales yo me quejo — de vuestra descortesía.
Prometistes á la infanta — lo que ella no vos pedía,
de siempre ser su marido, — y á ella que le placía.
Si otras cosas pasastes — no entro en esa porfía. 80
Otra cosa os digo, conde, — de que más os pesaría:
que matéis á la condesa — que cumple á la honra mía:
echéis fama que ella es muerta — de cierto mal que
    tenía,
y tratarse ha el casamiento — como cosa no sabida,
porque no sea deshonrada — hija que tanto quería. — 85
Oídas estas razones — el buen conde respondía:
— No puedo negar, el rey, — lo que la infanta decía,
sino que otorgo ser verdad — todo cuanto me pedía.
Por miedo de vos, el rey, — no casé con quien debía,
ni pensé que vuestra Alteza — en ello consentiría. 90
De casar con la infanta — yo, señor, bien casaría;
mas matar á la condesa, — señor rey, no lo haría,
porque no debe morir — la que mal no merecía.
— De morir tiene, el buen conde, — por salvar la
    honra mía,
pues no mirastes primero — lo que mirar se debía. 95
Si no muere la condesa — á vos costará la vida.
Por la honra de los reyes — muchos sin culpa morían,
porque muera la condesa — no es mucha maravilla.
— Yo la mataré, buen rey, — mas no será la culpa mía:
vos os avendréis con Dios — en fin de vuestra vida, 100

y prometo á vuestra alteza, — á fe de caballería,
que me tengan por traidor — si lo dicho no cumplía
de matar á la condesa, — aunque mal no merecía.
Buen rey, si me dais licencia — yo luego me partiría.
105 — Vades con Dios, el buen conde, —ordenad vuestra
    partida. —
Llorando se parte el conde, — llorando sin alegría;
llorando por la condesa, — que más que á sí la quería.
Lloraba también el conde — por tres hijos que tenía,
el uno era de teta, — que la condesa lo cría,
110 que no quería mamar — de tres amas que tenía
sino era de su madre — porque bien la conocía;
los otros eran pequeños, — poco sentido tenían.
Antes que llegase el conde — estas razones decía:
  — ¿Quién podrá mirar, condesa — vuestra cara de
    alegría,
115 que saldréis á recebirme — á la fin de vuestra vida?
Yo soy el triste culpado, — esta culpa toda es mía. —
En diciendo estas palabras — la condesa ya salía,
que un paje le había dicho — como el conde ya venía.
Vido la condesa al conde — la tristeza que tenía,
120 vióle los ojos llorosos, — que hinchados los tenía
de llorar por el camino, — mirando el bien que perdía.
Dijo la condesa al conde: — ¡Bien vengáis, bien de mi
    vida!
¿Qué habéis, el conde Alarcos? — ¿por qué lloráis, vida
    mía,
que venís tan demudado — que cierto no os conocía?
125 No parece vuestra cara — ni el gesto que ser solía;
dadme parte del enojo — como dais de la alegría.

¡Decídmelo luego, conde, — no matéis la vida mía!
— Yo vos lo diré, condesa, — cuando la hora sería.
— Si no me lo decís, conde, — cierto yo reventaría.
— No me fatiguéis, señora, — que no es la hora venida. 130
Cenemos luego, condesa, — de aqueso que en casa
    había.
— Aparejado está, conde, — como otras veces solía. —
Sentóse el conde á la mesa, — no cenaba ni podía,
con sus hijos al costado, — que muy mucho los quería.
Echóse sobre los hombros, — hizo como que dormía; 135
de lágrimas de sus ojos — toda la mesa cubría.
Mirábalo la condesa — que la causa no sabía;
no le preguntaba nada, — que no osaba ni podía.
Levantóse luego el conde, — dijo que dormir quería;
dijo también la condesa — que ella también dormiría; 140
mas entre ellos no había sueño, — si la verdad se decía.
Vanse el conde y la condesa — á dormir donde solían:
dejan los niños de fuera, — que el conde no los quería:
lleváronse el más chiquito, — el que la condesa cría.
Cierra el conde la puerta, — lo que hacer no solía. 145
Empezó de hablar el conde — con dolor y con mancilla:
— ¡Oh desdichada condesa, — grande fué la tu des-
    dicha!
— No so desdichada, el conde, — por dichosa me tenía
sólo en ser vuestra mujer: — esta fué gran dicha mía.
— ¡Si bien lo sabéis, condesa, — esa fué vuestra des-
    dicha! 150
Sabed que en tiempo pasado — yo amé á quien servía,
la cual era la infanta. — Por desdicha vuestra y mía
prometí casar con ella, — y á ella que le placía:

demándame por marido — por la fe que me tenía.
155 Puédelo muy bien hacer — de razón y de justicia:
díjomelo el rey su padre — porque de ella lo sabía.
Otra cosa manda el rey — que toca en el alma mía:
manda que muráis, condesa, — á la fin de vuestra vida,
que no puede tener honra — siendo vos, condesa,
        viva. —
160 Desque esto oyó la condesa — cayó en tierra amorte-
        cida:
mas después en sí tornada — estas palabras decía:
— ¡Pagos son de mis servicios, — conde, con que yo os
        servía!
Si no me matáis, el conde, — yo bien os consejaría:
enviédesme á mis tierras — que mi padre me ternía;
165 yo criaré vuestros hijos — mejor que la que vernía,
y os mantendré castidad — como siempre os mantenía.
— De morir habéis, condesa, — en antes que venga el
        día.
— ¡Bien parece, el conde Alarcos, — yo ser sola en esta
        vida;
porque tengo el padre viejo, — mi madre ya es fallecida,
170 y mataron á mi hermano — el buen conde don García,
que el rey lo mandó matar — por miedo que dél tenía!
No me pesa de mi muerte, — porque yo morir tenía,
mas pésame de mis hijos, — que pierden mi compañía:
hacémelos venir, conde, — y verán mi despedida.
175 — No los veréis más, condesa, — en días de vuestra
        vida:
abrazad este chiquito, — que aquéste es el que os perdía.
Pésame de vos, condesa, — cuanto pesar me podía.

No os puedo valer, señora, —que más me va que la vida;
encomendáos á Dios, — que esto hacerse tenía.
—Dejéisme decir, buen conde, —una oración que sabía. 180
— Decilda presto, condesa, —enantes que venga el día.
— Presto la habré dicho, Conde, — no estaré un Ave
    María. —
Hincó las rodillas en tierra, — esta oración decía:
«En las tus manos, Señor, — encomiendo el alma mía:
«no me juzgues mis pecados — según que yo merecía, 185
«mas según tu gran piedad — y la tu gracia infinita.»
— Acabada es ya, buen conde, —la oración que sabía;
encomiéndoos esos hijos — que entre vos y mí había,
y rogad á Dios por mí — mientra tuvierdes vida,
que á ello sois obligado — pues que sin culpa moría. 190
Dédesme acá ese hijo, — mamará por despedida.
— No lo despertéis, condesa, — dejaldo estar, que dor-
    mía,
sino que os pido perdón — porque ya se viene el día.
— Á vos yo perdono, conde, — por amor que os tenía;
mas yo no perdono al rey, — ni á la infanta su hija, 195
sino que queden citados — delante la alta justicia,
que allá vayan á juicio—dentro de los treinta días. —
Estas palabras diciendo — el conde se apercebía:
echóle por la garganta — una toca que tenía,
apretó con las dos manos — con la fuerza que podía: 200
no le aflojó la garganta — mientra que vida tenía.
Cuando ya la vido el conde — traspasada y fallecida,
desnudóle los vestidos — y las ropas que tenía:
echóla encima la cama, — cubrióla como solía;
desnudóse á su costado, — obra de un Ave María: 205

levantóse dando voces — á la gente que tenía.
— ¡Socorré, mis escuderos, — que la condesa se fina! —
Hallan la condesa muerta — los que á socorrer venían.
Así murió la condesa, — sin razón y sin justicia;
210 mas también todos murieron — dentro de los treinta
días.
Los doce días pasados — la infanta ya moría;
el rey á los veinte y cinco, — el conde al treinteno día,
allá fueron á dar cuenta — á la justicia divina.
Acá nos dé Dios su gracia, — y allá la gloria cumplida.

ROMANCES TRADICIONALES MODERNOS

XLV

(JMP, no. IX)

BERNALDO DEL CARPIO]

Íbase por un camino — el valiente don Bernaldo;
todo vestido de luto, — negro también el caballo:
por los cascos echa sangre, — y sangre por el bocado.
Con la prisa que traía — atrás deja los criados.
5 Viéralo pasar su tío, — y á un mesón fuera alcanzarlo.
— Don Bernaldo, ¿dónde vas, — que así vienes pre-
parado
con una espada en la mano — y otra en el cinto col-
gando?
— Voy libertar á mi padre, — que dicen que van á
ahorcarlo.

— Don Bernaldo, sube, sube, — tomaremos un bocado.
— Maldita la cosa quiero — hasta verlo libertado. —   10
Entre que ambos descansaban, — volvieron ya los
  criados.
Nadie les daba razón — de dónde estaba su amo,
sinon porque conocieron — el relincho del caballo.
— ¿Don Bernaldo dónde está? — Don Bernaldo está
  ocupado,
que está comiendo y bebiendo — y un momento des-
  cansando.   15
— Dígale que se dé prisa, — que á su padre van á
  ahorcarlo,
y en el medio de la plaza — hemos visto ya el tablado. —
Ciñó Bernaldo la espada — y montóse en su caballo:
por las plazas donde pasa — las piedras quedan tem-
  blando.
Sus ojos echaban fuego, — y espuma echaban sus labios: 20
por donde quiera que pasa — todos se quedan mirando.
Llegóse al medio la plaza, — y apeóse del caballo;
diera un puntapié á la horca — y en el suelo la ha tirado;
y una de las dos espadas — dióla á su tío don Basco:
— Tome esa espada, mi tío, — ríjala como hombre
  honrado;   25
que ninguno de mi sangre—habrá de morir ahorcado.

XLVI

(JMP, no. XXXI)

[LA VUELTA DEL MARIDO]

Estando yo ante mi puerta — labrando la fina seda,
vi venir un caballero — por alta Sierra Morena;
con las armas n'el caballo, — á mi marido semeja.
Atrevíme á preguntarle — si venía de la guerra.
5 — De la guerra, no, señora; — pero vengo cerca della.
¿Por qué lo entruga, señora? — ¿Por qué lo entruga,
       doncella?
— Porque tengo á mi marido — ha siete años en la
       guerra:
de los siete años que estuvo, — nunca me envió una
       letra.
— Diga, diga, la señora; — diga de qué señas era.
10 — Era alto como un pino — y galán como una estrella;
llevaba un caballo blanco — todo cubierto de seda.
— Por las señas que me dabais, — en la guerra muerto
       queda;
su cuerpo revuelto en sangre, — su boca llena de arena.
— ¡Ay, triste de mí, cuitada! — ¡Ay, de mi suerte tan
       negra!
15 ¡Siempre truje toca blanca, — ahora vestiréla prieta!
Tres hijos que me quedaron — los criaré en mi tristeza;
y, en cuanto manejen armas, — mandarélos á la guerra
para vengar á su padre — que le mataron en ella.
— Non se aflija la señora; — no se acordoje, mi dueña,
20 nin vista los negros paños, — que yo su marido era. —

XLVII

(JMP, no. XVI)

[DON BOYSO]

Camina don Boyso — mañanita fría
á tierra de Campos — á buscar la niña.
Hallóla lavando — en la fuente fría.
— ¿Qué haces ahí, mora, — hija de judía?
Deja á mi caballo — beber agua fría.   5
— Reviente el caballo — y quien lo traía;
que yo no soy mora — ni hija de judía.
Soy una cristiana, — que aquí estoy cativa,
lavando los paños — de la morería.
— Si fueras cristiana, — yo te llevaría,   10
y en paños de seda — yo te envolvería;
pero si eres mora, — yo te dejaría. —
Montóla á caballo, — por ver qué decía;
en las siete leguas — no hablara la niña.
Al pasar un campo — de verdes olivas,   15
por aquellos prados — ¡qué llantos hacía!
— ¡Ay prados! ¡Ay prados! — ¡prados de mi vida!
¡Cuando el rey mi padre — plantó aquí esta oliva,
él se la plantara, — yo se la tenía;
la reina mi madre — la seda torcía;   20
mi hermano don Boyso — los toros corría! . . .
— ¿Y cómo te llamas? — Yo soy Rosalinda;
que así me pusieron, — porque al ser nacida,
una linda rosa — n'el pecho tenía.
— ¡Pues tú, por las señas, — mi hermana serías!   25

¡Abra, la mi madre, — puertas de alegría;
por traerle nuera, — tráigole su hija!
— Para ser tu hermana, — ¡qué descolorida!
— Madre, la mi madre, — mi madre querida;
30 que hace siete años — que yo no comía,
sino amargas yerbas — de una fuente fría,
do culebras cantan, — caballos bebían. —
Metióla en un cuarto — sentóla en la silla.
— ¡Mi jubón de grana, — mi saya querida,
35 que te dejé nueva — y te hallo rompida!
— Calla, hija, calla, — hija de mi vida;
que quien te echó ésa, — otra te echaría.
— ¡Mi jubón de grana, — mi saya querida,
que te dejé nueva — y te hallo rompida!
40 — Calla, hija, calla, — hija de mi vida;
que aquí tienes madre, — que otra te echaría. —
Caminó don Boyso — que partir quería,
á tierra de moros — á buscar la niña.

XLVIII

(JMP, no. XXV)

[EL CONDE OLINOS]

¡Conde Olinos, Conde Olinos, — es niño y pasó la mar!
Levantóse Conde Olinos — mañanita de San Juan:
llevó su caballo al agua — á las orillas del mar.
Mientras el caballo bebe — él se pusiera á cantar:
5 — Bebe, bebe, mi caballo; — Dios te me libre de mal,

de los vientos rigurosos — y las arenas del mar. —
Bien lo oyó la Reina mora — de altas torres donde está:
— Escuchad, mis hijas todas, — las que dormís, recordad;
y oiredes á la sirena — como canta por la mar. —
Respondió la más chiquita, — (¡más le valiera callar!)   10
— Aquello no es la sirena, — ni tampoco su cantar;
aquél era el Conde Olinos, — que á mis montes va á
cazar.
— Mis morillos, mis morillos, — los que me coméis el
pan,
id buscar al Conde Olinos, — que á mis montes va á
cazar.
Al que me lo traiga vivo, — un reinado le he de dar;   15
el que me lo traiga muerto — con la Infanta ha de casar:
al que traiga su cabeza — á oro se la he de pesar. —
Po'l monte de los Acebos — cien mil morillos se van
en busca del Conde Olinos; — non le pueden encontrar.
Encontráronlo durmiendo — debajo de un olivar.   20
— ¿Qué haces ahí, Conde Olinos? — ¿Qué vienes aquí
á buscar?
Si á buscar vienes la muerte — te la venimos á dar;
si á buscar vienes la vida — de aquí non la has de llevar.
— ¡Oh mi espada, oh mi espada, — de buen oro y buen
metal;
que de muchas me libraste, — désta non me has de
faltar: 25
y si désta me librases — te vuelvo á sobredorar! —
Por la gracia de Dios Padre, — comenzó la espada á
hablar:

«Si tú meneas los brazos — cual los sueles menear,
yo cortaré por los moros — como cuchillo por pan.»

30 — ¡Oh caballo, oh caballo, — oh mi caballo ruan,
que de muchas me libraste, — désta non me has de
    faltar! —
Por la gracia de Dios Padre, — comenzó el caballo á
    hablar:
«Si me das la sopa en vino — y el agua por la canal,
las cuatro bandas de moros — las pasaré par y par.»

35 Cuando era medio día — no halló con quien pelear,
sinon era un perro moro — que no lo pudo matar.
Allí vino una paloma, — blanquita y de buen volar.
    — ¿Qué haces ahí, palomita; — qué vienes aquí á
    buscar?
    — Soy la Infanta, Conde Olinos, — de aquí te vengo á
    sacar.

40 Ya que non queda más qu'ése, — vivo no habrá de
    marchar. —
Por el campo los dos juntos — se pasean par y par.
La Reina mora los vió, — y ambos los mandó matar:
del uno nació una oliva, — y del otro un olivar:
cuando hacía viento fuerte, — los dos se iban á juntar.

45 La Reina también los vió, — también los mandó cortar:
del uno nació una fuente, — del otro un río caudal.
Los que tienen mal de amores — allí se van á lavar.
La Reina también los tiene — y también se iba á lavar.
    — Corre fuente, corre fuente, — que en ti me voy á
    bañar.

50 — Cuando yo era Conde Olinos, — tú me mandaste
    | matar;

cuando yo era olivar, — tú me mandaste cortar;
ahora que yo soy fuente — de ti me quiero vengar:
para todos' correré — para ti me he de secar. —
— *¡Conde Olinos, Conde Olinos,—es niño y pasó la mar!*

XLIX

(JMP, no. XXXVII)

[EL CONVITE]

— Vengo brindado, Mariana, — para una boda el
    domingo.
— Esa boda, don Alonso, — debiera de ser conmigo.
— Non es conmigo, Mariana; — es con un hermano mío.
— Siéntate aquí, don Alonso, — en este escaño florido;
que me lo dejó mi padre — para el que case conmigo. — 5
Se sentara don Alonso, — presto se quedó dormido;
Mariana, como discreta, — se fué á su jardín florido.
Tres onzas de solimán, — cuatro de acero molido,
la sangre de tres culebras, — la piel de un lagarto vivo,
y la espinilla del sapo, — todo se lo echó en el vino.   10
— Bebe vino, don Alonso, — don Alonso, bebe vino.
— Bebe primero, Mariana, — que así está puesto en
    estilo. —
Mariana, como discreta, — por el pecho lo ha vertido;
don Alonso, como joven, — todo el vino se ha bebido:
con la fuerza del veneno — los dientes se le han caído. 15
— ¿Qué es esto, Mariana, — qué es esto que tiene el
    vino?

— Tres onzas de solimán, — cuatro de acero molido,
la sangre de tres culebras, — la piel de un lagarto vivo,
y la espinilla del sapo, — para robarte el sentido.
20 — Sáname, buena Mariana, — que me casaré contigo.
— No puede ser, don Alonso, — que el corazón te ha
    partido.
— Adiós, esposa del alma, — presto quedas sin marido:
adiós, padres de mi vida, — presto quedaron sin hijo.
Cuando salí de mi casa, — salí en un caballo pío,
25 y ahora voy para la iglesia — en una caja de pino.—

L

(JMP, no. XLVI)

[DOÑA ALDA]

Á cazar va el rey don Pedro, — á cazar como solía;
le diera el mal de la muerte; — para casa se volvía.
Á la entrada de la puerta — vió un pastor que le decía:
— Albricias, señor don Pedro, — que dármelas bien
    podía;
5 que doña Alda ya parió, — y un hijo varón tenía.
— ¡Pues si parió doña Alda, — hijo sin padre sería! . . .
Con estas palabras y otras, — el rey subió para arriba.
— Haga la cama, mi madre, — haga la cama de oliva:
aprisa, aprisa con ella, — que presto me moriría.
10 No diga nada á doña Alda, — á doña Alda de mi vida,
que no sepa de mi muerte — hasta los cuarenta días.—
Don Pedro que se murió, — doña Alda nada sabía.

Viniera Pascua de Flores, — doña Alda no ha oído
   misa.
— Diga, diga, la mi suegra, — ¿qué vestido llevaría?
— Como eres alta y delgada, — lo negro bien te estaría. 15
— Yo no quiero llevar luto — que voy de linda parida. —
Á la entrada de la iglesia — toda la gente la mira.
— Diga, diga, don Melchor, — consejero de mi vida,
¿por qué me mira la gente, — por qué la gente me mira?
— Diréte una cosa, Alda, — que de saberse tenía: 20
aquí se entierran los reyes — cuantos lo son de Castilla,
y aquí se enterró don Pedro, — la prenda que más
   querías.
— Oh mal haya la mi suegra, — qué engañada me
   traía,
que en vez de venir de luto — vengo de linda parida!

ROMANCES ERUDITOS

LI

(W. 21)

[LA TRAICIÓN DE RUY VELÁZQUEZ]
by «un cauallero Cesario»

¿Quién es aquel caballero — que tan gran traición
hacía?
Ruy Velázquez es de Lara, — que á sus sobrinos vendía.
En el campo de Almenar — á los infantes decía
que fuesen á correr moros, — que él los acorrería;
5 que habrían muy gran ganancia, — muchos captivos
traerían.
Ellos en aquesto estando, — grandes gentes parecían;
más de diez mil son los moros, — las señas traen ten-
didas.
Los infantes le preguntan — qué gente es la que venía.
— No hayáis miedo, mis sobrinos, — Ruy Velázquez
respondía,
10 todos son moros astrosos, — moros de poca valía,
que viendo que vais á ellos, — á huir luego echarían;
que si ellos vos aguardan, — yo en vuestro socorro
iría:
corrílos yo muchas veces, — ninguno lo defendía.

82

Á ellos id, mis sobrinos, — no mostredes cobardía. —
¡Palabras son engañosas — y de muy grande falsía!   15
Los infantes como buenos — con moros arremetían;
caballeros son doscientos — los que su guarda seguían.
Él á furto de cristianos — á los moros se venía.
Díjoles que sus sobrinos — no escape ninguno á vida,
que les corten las cabezas, — que él no los defendería.   20
Doscientos hombres, no más, — llevaban en compañía.
Don Nuño que ir los vido, — oído había por su espía,
y cuando oyó las palabras — que á los moros les decía,
daba muy grandes las voces — que en el cielo las ponía.
— ¡Oh Ruy Velázquez traidor, — el mayor que ser po-
     dría: 25
¿Á tus sobrinos infantes — á la muerte los traías?
Mientras el mundo durare — durará tu alevosía,
Y la falsedad que has hecho — contra la tu sangre
     misma. —
Después que esto hobo dicho — á los infantes volvía,
díjoles: — Armáos, mis hijos, — que vuestro tío os
     vendía: 30
de consuno es con los moros, — ya concertado tenía
que os maten á todos juntos. — Ellos armáronse aína:
las quince huestes de moros — á todos cerco ponían;
don Nuño, que era su ayo, — gran esfuerzo les ponía:
— Esforzáos, no temades, — haced lo que yo hacía: 35
á Dios yo vos encomiendo, — mostrad vuestra va-
     lentía. —
En la delantera haz — don Nuño herido había,
mató muchos de los moros, — mas á él muerto lo
     habían.

Los infantes arremeten — con la su caballería:
40 mezcláronse con los moros, — á muchos quitan la vida.
Los cristianos eran pocos, — veinte para uno había;
mataron á los cristianos, — que á vida ninguno finca;
solos quedan los hermanos, — que ninguna ayuda
habían.
Encomendáronse á Dios, — *Santiago, valme*, decían:
45 firieron recio en los moros, — gran matanza les hacían;
no osan estar delante — que gran braveza traían.
Fernán González menor — á sus hermanos decía:
— Esforzad, los mis hermanos, — lidiemos con valentía,
mostremos gran corazón — contra aquesta morería.
50 Ya no habemos ayuda, — solo Dios darla podía;
ya murió Nuño Salido, — y nuestra caballería;
venguémoslos ó muramos, — nadie muestre cobardía.
Que desque estemos cansados — esta sierra nos val-
dría. —
Volvieron á pelear, — ¡oh qué reciamente lidian!
55 muchos matan de los moros, — á otros muchos herían;
muerto han á Fernán González, — seis solos quedado
habían.
Cansados ya de lidiar, — á la sierra se subían;
limpiáronse los sus rostros, — que sangre y polvo
teñían.

LII

(D. 742)

[EL MILAGRO DEL GAFO]
by *Lorenzo de Sepúlveda*

Ya se parte don Rodrigo, — que de Vivar se apellida,
para visitar Santiago, — adonde va en romería.
Despidióse de Fernando, — aquese rey de Castilla,
que le dió muchos haberes, — sin dones que dado había.
Veinte vasallos consigo — llevaba en su compañía;   5
mucho bien y gran limosna — hacía por donde iba:
daba á comer á los pobres, — y á los que pobreza
    habían.
Siguiendo por su camino — muy grande llanto oía,
que en medio de un tremedal — un gafo triste plañía,
dando voces que lo saquen — por Dios y Santa María. 10
Rodrigo cuando lo oye, — para el gafo se venía,
descendiera de la bestia, — en tierra se descendía:
en la silla lo subió, — delante sí lo ponía;
llegaron á la posada — do albergaron aquel día.
Sentados son á cenar, — comían á una escudilla.   15
Gran enojo habían los suyos, — de aquesto que el Cid
    hacía:
no quieren estar presentes, — á otra posada se iban.
Hicieron al Cid y al gafo — una cama en que dormían
ambos, cuando á media noche, — ya que Rodrigo
    dormía,
un soplo por las espaldas — el gafo dado le había; 20
tan recio fué, que á los pechos — á don Rodrigo salía.

Despertó muy espantado, — al gafo buscado había:
no lo hallaba en la su cama, — á voces lumbre pedía.
Traídole habían la lumbre, — el gafo no parecía;
25 tornado se había á la cama, — gran cuidado en sí tenía
de lo que le aconteciera, — mas vió un hombre que á él
venía
vestido de paños blancos, — y que aquesto le decía:
—¿Duermes ó velas, Rodrigo? — No duermo, le respondía,
pero díme: ¿quién tú eres — que tanto resplandecías?
30 — San Lázaro soy, Rodrigo, — yo, que á te hablar
venía;
yo soy el gafo á que tú — por Dios tanto bien hacías.
Rodrigo, Dios bien te quiere, — otorgado te tenía
que lo que tú comenzares — en lides, ó en otra guisa,
lo cumplirás á tu honra — y crecerá cada día.
35 De todos serás temido, — de cristianos y morisma,
y que los tus enemigos — empecerte no podrían.
Morirás tú muerte honrada, — no tu persona vencida,
tú serás el vencedor; — Dios su bendición te envía. —
En diciendo estas palabras — luego se desaparecía:
40 levantóse don Rodrigo — y de hinojos se ponía;
dió gracias á Dios del cielo, — también á Santa María;
ansí estuvo en oración — hasta que fuera de día.
Partiérase á Santiago, — su romería cumplía;
de allí se fué á Calahorra — adonde el buen rey yacía.
45 Muy bien lo había recebido, — holgóse con su venida,
lidió con Martín González, — y en el campo lo vencía.

LIII

(W. 61)

ROMANCE DE LOS CINCO MARAVEDÍS QUE EL REY DON ALONSO OCTAVO PEDÍA Á LOS HIJOSDALGO

En esa ciudad de Burgos — en Cortes se habían
    juntado
el rey que venció las Navas — con todos los hijosdalgo.
Habló con don Diego el rey, — con él se había consejado,
que era señor de Bizcaya, — de todos el más privado.
— Consejédesme, don Diego, — que estoy muy ne-   5
    cesitado,
que con las guerras que he hecho — gran dinero me
    ha faltado.
Querría llegarme á Cuenca, — no tengo lo necesario;
si os pareciese, don Diego, — por mí fuese demandado
que cinco maravedís — me peche cada hidalgo.
— Grave cosa me parece, — le respondiera el de Haro, 10
que querades vos, señor, — al libre hacer tributario;
mas por lo mucho que os quiero, — de mí seréis ayu-
    dado,
porque yo soy principal, — de mí os será pagado. —
Siendo juntos en las Cortes, — el rey se lo había hablado;
levantado está don Diego, — como ya estaba acordado. 15
— Justo es lo que el rey pide, — por nadie le sea negado;
mis cinco maravedís, — helos aquí de buen grado. —
Don Nuño, conde de Lara, — mucho mal se había
    enojado;

pospuesto todo temor, — de esta manera ha hablado:
20 — Aquéllos donde venimos — nunca tal pecho han
       pagado,
nos menos lo pagaremos, — ni al rey tal será dado;
el que quisiere pagarle — quede aquí como villano;
váyase luego tras mí — el que fuere hijodalgo. —
Todos se salen tras él; — de tres mil, tres han quedado.
25 En el campo de la Glera — todos allí se han juntado;
el pecho que el rey demanda — en las lanzas lo han
       atado,
y envíanle á decir — que el tributo está llegado,
que envíe sus cogedores, — que luego será pagado;
mas que si él va en persona — no será dél acatado;
30 pero que enviase aquellos — de quien fué aconsejado.
Cuando aquesto oyera el rey, — y que solo se ha que-
       dado,
volvióse para don Diego, — consejo le ha demandado.
Don Diego, como sagaz, — este consejo le ha dado:
— Desterrédesme, señor, — como que yo lo he causado,
35 y así cobraréis la gracia — de los vuestros hijosdalgo. —
Otorgó el rey el consejo: — á decir les ha enviado
que quien le dió tal consejo — será muy bien castigado,
que hidalgos de Castilla — no son para haber pechado.
Muy alegres fueron todos, — todo se hubo apaciguado;
40 desterraron á don Diego — por lo que no había pe-
       cado;
mas dende á pocos días, — á Castilla fué tornado.
El bien de la libertad — por ningún precio es comprado.

ROMANCES ARTÍSTICOS

LIV

(D. 699)

[JURAMENTO LLEVAN HECHO . . .]

Juramento llevan hecho, — todos juntos á una voz,
de no volver á Castilla — sin el conde, su señor.
La imagen suya de piedra — llevan en un carretón,
resueltos, si atrás no vuelve, — de no volver ellos, non,
y el que paso atrás volviere — que quedase por traidor. 5
Alzaron todos las manos, — en señal que se juró.
Acabado el homenaje, — pusiéronle su pendón,
y besáronle la mano — desde el chico hasta el mayor,
y como buenos vasallos, — caminan para Arlanzón
al paso que andan los bueyes — y á las vueltas que da
    el sol. 10
Desierta dejan á Burgos — y pueblos al rededor,
solas quedan las mujeres — y aquellos que niños son:
tratando van del concierto — del caballo y del azor,
si ha de hacer libre á Castilla — del feudo que da á á
    León;
y antes de entrar en Navarra, — toparon junto al
    mojón 15
al conde Fernán González, — en cuya demanda son,

con su esposa doña Sancha, — que con astucia y valor
le sacó de Castroviejo — con el engaño que usó.
Con sus hierros y prisiones — venían juntos los dos
20 en la mula que tomaron — á aquel preste cazador.
Al estruendo de las armas — el conde se alborotó;
mas conociendo á los suyos, — d'esta manera habló:
— ¿Dó venís, mis castellanos? — digádesmelo, por Dios:
¿Cómo dejáis mis castillos — á peligro de Almanzor? —
25 Allí habló Nuño Laínez: — Íbamos, señor, por vos,
á quedar presos ó muertos, — ó sacaros de prisión. —

LV

(W. 37)

ROMANCE DE LAS QUEJAS DE LA INFANTA CONTRA EL CID RUY DÍAZ

Afuera, afuera, Rodrigo, — el soberbio castellano,
acordársete debría — de aquel tiempo ya pasado
cuando fuiste caballero — en el altar de Santiago,
cuando el rey fué tu padrino, — tú, Rodrigo, el ahijado:
5 mi padre te dió las armas, — mi madre te dió el caballo,
yo te calcé las espuelas — porque fueses más honrado:
que pensé casar contigo, — no lo quiso mi pecado,
casaste con Jimena Gómez, — hija del conde Lozano:
con ella hubiste dineros, — conmigo hubieras estado.
10 Bien casaste tú, Rodrigo, — muy mejor fueras casado;
dejaste hija de rey — por tomar de su vasallo.

— Si os parece, mi señora, — bien podemos destigallo.
— Mi ánima penaría — si yo fuese en discrepallo.
— Afuera, afuera, los míos, — los de á pie y de á
    caballo,
pues de aquella torre mocha — una vira me han tirado. 15
No traía el asta hierro, — el corazón me ha pasado;
ya ningún remedio siento — sino vivir más penado.

LVI

(W. 114a)

[EL PRISIONERO]

Por mayo era, por mayo, — cuando hace la calor,
cuando canta la calandria — y responde el ruiseñor,
cuando los enamorados — van á servir al amor,
sino yo triste, cuitado, — que vivo en esta prisión,
que ni sé cuando es de día, — ni cuando las noches son, 5
sino por una avecilla — que me cantaba al albor;
matómela un ballestero; — ¡déle Dios mal galardón!
Cabellos de mi cabeza — lléganme al corvejón;
los cabellos de mi barba — por manteles tengo yo:
las uñas de las mis manos — por cuchillo tajador. 10
Si lo hacía el buen rey, — hácelo como señor;
si lo hace el carcelero, — hácelo como traidor.
Mas quién ahora me diese — un pájaro hablador,
siquiera fuese calandria, — ó tordico ó ruiseñor:
criado fuese entre damas — y avezado á la razón, 15
que me lleve una embajada — á mi esposa Leonor,

que me envíe una empanada, — no de trucha ni salmón,
sino de una lima sorda — y de un pico tajador:
la lima para los hierros — y el pico para la torre. —
20 Oídolo había el rey, — mandóle quitar la prisión.

LVII

(D. 56)

[ZAIDA REPRENDE Á ZAIDE]

— Mira, Zaide, que te aviso — que no pases por mi
    calle,
ni hables con mis mujeres, — ni con mis cautivos trates,
ni preguntes en qué entiendo, — ni quién viene á visi-
    tarme,
ni qué fiestas me dan gusto, — ni qué colores me placen.
5 Basta que son por tu causa — las que en el rostro me
    salen,
corrida de haber querido — moro que tan poco sabe.
Confieso que eres valiente, — que rajas, hiendes, y
    partes,
y que has muerto más cristianos — que tienes gotas de
    sangre;
que eres gallardo ginete, — y que danzas, cantas,
    tañes,
10 gentil hombre, bien criado, — cuanto puede imagi-
    narse;
blanco, rubio por extremo, — esclarecido en linaje,
el gallo de las bravatas, — la gala de los donaires;

que pierdo mucho en perderte, — que gano mucho en
    ganarte,
y que si nacieras mudo — fuera posible adorarte.
Mas por este inconveniente — determino de dejarte: 15
que eres pródigo de lengua, — y amargan tus libertades;
y habrá menester ponerte — quien quisiere sustentarte,
un alcázar en el pecho, — y en los labios un alcaide.
¡Mucho pueden con las damas — los galanes de tus
    partes!
porque los quieren briosos, — que hiendan y que des-
    garren;   20
y con esto, Zaide amigo, — si algún banquete les haces,
el plato de tus favores — quieres que coman y callen.
¡Costoso fué el que me hiciste! — ¡venturoso fueras,
    Zaide,
si conservarme supieras — como supiste obligarme!
Pero no saliste apenas — de los jardines de Tarfe,   25
cuando hiciste de tus dichas — y de mi desdicha alarde,
y á un morillo mal nacido — me dijeron que enseñaste
la trenza de mis cabellos — que te puse en el turbante.
No pido que me la vuelvas, — ni tampoco que la
    guardes,
mas quiero que entiendas, moro, — que en mi des-
    gracia la traes.   30
También me certificaron — como le desafiaste
por las verdades que dijo, — ¡que nunca fueran ver-
    dades!
De mala gana me río: — ¡qué donoso disparate!
Tú no guardas tu secreto, — ¿y quieres que otro lo
    guarde?

35 No quiero admitir disculpa, — otra vez vuelvo á avi-
　　sarte:
　　ésta será la postrera — que me veas y te hable. —
　　Dijo la discreta mora — al altivo Abencerraje,
　　y al despedirle replica: — «Quien tal hace que tal
　　pague.»

ROMANCE VULGAR

LVIII

(D. 1265)

EL VIOLÍN ENCANTADO

Todo el mundo me esté atento, — alargando las
    orejas,
de manera que los hombres — mulos manchegos parez-
    can;
dejen de mentir los sastres, — de presumir las mozue-
    las,
de hilar y arrojar gargajos — las descomunales viejas;
no escupan los fumadores, — y los borrachos con flema   5
estén con el vaso en mano — hasta caer en la tierra;
cesen de hablar los soldados — refiriendo en las tabernas
las batallas y combates — que ellos á su salvo inventan:
los jugadores de naipes — dejen las barajas quietas,
no sacando vaticinios — de las vanas apariencias;   10
los loteros cavilosos — no miren á las estrellas,
y de ambo y terno se olviden, — y las cábalas sus-
    pendan;
en fin, repito me estén — todas las almas atentas,
y de hito en hito escuchando — con sentidos y poten-
    cias.

15 Y suponiendo se preste — á mi mandato obediencia,
empiezo mi relación — diciendo como en Ginebra
servía á un amo muy chusco — un mozo bastante
    bestia;
y á los tres años cumplidos — que en su servicio
    emplea,
le pidió el criado al amo — de su salario la cuenta.
20 El amo se la ajustó, — y le dió por recompensa
de cada año un escudo, — sin que algo más se ex-
    tendiera.
El gran simplón del sirviente, — sin más despegar la
    lengua,
se contentó de la paga, — que la creyó muy completa;
y él se decía á sí mismo — con extrema complacencia:
25 — ¿Qué más puedo desear — que la presente riqueza?
Ya no quiero trabajar, — pues tres escudos, que cuenta
mi bolsillo, poseer — es una fortuna inmensa;
me voy á correr el mundo — y á divertirme sin rienda,
que un caudal de tres escudos — para todo tiene
    fuerzas. —
30 Esto dicho, tomó el cosque, — y á salga lo que saliera,
sin dirección ni destino — tomó la primera senda.
Á poco rato de andar, — atravesando una selva,
cantando como un jilguero, — de contento el alma
    llena,
hete aquí que al lado suyo — un enano se presenta,
35 de tan extraña figura — que al demonio se asemeja,
y le pregunta la causa — de aquel placer que demuestra.
El ginebrino responde: — ¿Cómo he de tener tristeza
cuando tengo un gran bolsillo — atestado de monedas?

El salario de tres años — lo tengo en mi faltriquera,
que compone tres escudos, — suma que no tiene cuenta. 40
— ¡Ah, dijo al punto el enano, — si yo tal suma
    tuviera,
un poderoso sería — y saldría de miserias!
Si esa suma darme quieres — yo te otorgaré por ella
las tres gracias que me pidas, — las que en cualquiera
    ocurrencia
te sacarán bien de todos — los lances en que te veas.   45
— Pues si eso todo es así, — respondió el patán con
    flema,
tomadla pues. — Y le dió — toda la suma completa.
El enano, agradecido — á dádiva tan ingenua,
le dijo: — Tu proceder — merece una recompensa,
y así dime las tres cosas — que en este mundo deseas,   50
y las verás concedidas — sin que falte ni una letra. —
El patán se alegró mucho, — y su contento renueva,
y restregando mil veces — su gran frente y sus melenas,
al fin dijo: — Pues, amigo, — yo solamente quisiera
un arco muy primoroso — con su bordón y ballesta,   55
que al objeto que apuntara — precisamente le diera;
también quisiera un violín — que, al tocarlo yo, hi-
    ciera
bailar á toditos cuantos — mis consonancias oyeran;
y por último deseo, — por la petición postrera,
que todo lo que yo pida — al punto se me conceda. —   60
Cuando el ganán concluyó, — el enano con franqueza
le dijo: — Pues concedido — está todo lo que ruegas.—
Y al punto le entregó el arco — armado con su ballesta;
le dió un violín, y le dijo — que la petición tercera

65 también le está concedida, — pues todo cuanto pidiera
ninguno le negaría. — Y el enano, cual centella,
desapareció á su vista — con la mayor ligereza.
Quedóse el patán contento, — no creyendo que en la
    tierra
más fortuna haber pudiese — que la que él experi-
    menta.
70 Á poco rato de marcha — un viejo judío encuentra
que atento miraba un árbol, — en cuyas ramas espesas
estaba un ufano mirlo, — que con muy dulces cadencias
cantaba con tanta gracia — que embelesaba la idea.
— ¡Qué ave tan primorosa! — decía el judío, ¿qué
    lengua
75 imitar podrá el acento — con que este animal se
    expresa?
¡Cualquiera cosa daría — por poder yo poseerla!
— ¿No es más que eso? el patán dijo, — pues ya podéis
    ir por ella. —
Y apuntando con su arco — el mirlo cayó en la tierra.
El usurero judío — se metió por la alameda
80 para recoger el mirlo — que ansiaba con tanta fuerza,
y sacando el ginebrino — su violín con ligereza,
empezó á tocar mil sones — de muy distintas maneras.
Al punto el viejo usurero, — á pesar de su torpeza,
empezó á bailar de modo — que se quebraba las piernas.
85 Tanto brincaba y saltaba — en medio de la maleza
que deshizo los espinos — y hasta hizo polvo las piedras,
se desgarró los vestidos, — y gritaba, ya sin fuerza:
— Señor músico, ya basta, — porque el demonio me
    lleva;

de ese maldito violín — callad el son de sus cuerdas,
pues que me sale el alma—haciendo tantas corvetas.— 90
El patán le respondía, — tocando con mayor priesa:
— Pues que desollaste á tantos,—justo es que tu piel
    perezca. —
Viendo el pícaro judío — que iba á perecer por fuerza
en medio de sus respingos, — vaivenes y zapatetas,
dijo con trémula voz, — que si paraba la fiesta 95
le ofrecía cien florines — porque cesara la gresca.
Enternecido el patán — aceptó la dicha oferta:
cesó el violín, y cesaron — las cabriolas violentas.
El usurero quedó — más blando que una manteca,
y entregó sus cien florines, — que era toda su riqueza. 100
Separáronse, y al punto — fué el judío con presteza
á un juez, y la queja expuso — del lance que dicho
    queda:
dió las señas del patán, — y con mayor evidencia,
del condenado violín—que á tanto dolor lo entrega.
Con tan seguros indicios — fué aprehendido con pres-
    teza 105
el patán, y presentado — al juez en comparecencia.
El usurero judío — reclama con entereza
sus cien florines, que dice—le ha robado aquel babieca.
El paleto renegaba, — diciendo que premio eran
de su música, y ajuste—que hicieron por suspenderla; 110
mas al fin el juez falló, — arreglado á las Pandectas,
y la sentencia de horca — por robo, al gañán decreta.
Humildemente escuchó — de su suerte la condena,
y estando al pie del suplicio — suplicó al juez que lo
    oyera.

115 — Señor, dijo, ya que voy — á sufrir la pena impuesta,
suplico se me permita — en esta hora postrera
tocar mi triste violín, — que huérfano al fin se queda.—
El usurero se opuso — con todo vigor y fuerza,
mas el juez lo concedió, — usando de su clemencia,
120 y porque debía cumplirse — del enano la promesa,
y de las tres peticiones — la proposición tercera,
que fué que lo que pidiese — todo se lo concediera.
Diéronle pues su violín, — y cuando á tocar empieza,
el juez con el escribano — y alguaciles con gran priesa
125 empezaron á bailar — con una furia sin rienda.
Conforme subía los puntos, — subían á las estrellas
las forzadas cabriolas — de toda la concurrencia.
El verdugo soltó al preso, — y sobre la misma cuerda
bailaba, más que mil trompos — bailar y rodar pudieran;
130 el usurero judío — cabriolaba con destreza,
y ya todos destrozados, — creyendo su hora postrera,
sudando á ríos y á mares, — sacada un palmo la
        lengua,
el juez con trémula voz — dijo al patán suspendiera
los ecos de su violín, — y anulaba la sentencia,
135 y á más que los cien florines — le adjudicaba por
        prenda.
Hízolo así, y se paró — al punto toda la gresca,
y al momento mandó el juez — que el usurero dijera
de aquel dinero el origen — y la veraz procedencia.
El usurero al instante — confesó robados eran,
140 y el juez decretó su muerte — sin que traslado se
        diera,
y en la horca del patán — al usurero lo cuelgan.

El gañán con su violín — se fué salvo y sin gabelas;
y este suceso tan raro — es verdad, y hay que creerla,
pues lo ha noticiado al pueblo, — con puntualidad
    extrema,
el correo que ha venido — de la ciudad de Ginebra.   145

NOTES

GRAMMATICAL PECULIARITIES OF THE
ROMANCES

The grammar of the *romances viejos* forms a complex subject in itself, and the present editor will make no attempt to treat it fully. Only a most thorough study of all the Old Spanish literary monuments could show what usages, if any, are peculiar to the *romances* and what are common in the fifteenth century and earlier. It is, however, absolutely necessary to indicate the most frequent deviations from modern usage, which occur in this collection. For a fuller, but by no means complete, treatment, the investigator is referred to the twenty-eight pages of *Observations grammaticales* which Ducamin has appended to his *Romances choisis*.

Students are urged to read the following section before attempting to translate. Some of the grammatical difficulties are mentioned in the notes as well, but not all. Many peculiarities of word forms are dealt with in the vocabulary, and hence are not touched upon here.

I. Contractions

De before pronouns and demonstratives: **dél** = *de él;* **dellos** = *de ellos;* **deste** = *de este;* etc. It is a learned reaction which has caused this natural method of writing to disappear.

103

II. Definite Article

1. The masculine form is used before feminine words beginning not only with an accented *a* sound, as in mod. Sp., but also with unaccented *a* and *e:* III, 17, **el arena**; VI, 21, **el espera**.

2. The definite article is used almost regularly before possessive adjectives, as in Italian: IV, 14, **la su madre doña Sancha**; XXXVI, 23, **las tus cortes**; and innumerable other examples. Cf. also XXIV, 21, **el un pedazo de aquéllos**.

3. The definite article is often used before a noun in the vocative case: XXII, 10, **Dijésesme tú, el portero**; XLIV, 12, **¿Qué es aquesto, la infanta?** Strictly speaking, the noun is in apposition with a pronoun of address expressed (as in the first example) or understood.

III. Personal Pronoun

1. The pronoun-object often precedes the verb in the imperative and infinitive moods, where it would now follow: XIII, 9, **en tenencia me lo dad**; XXXIX, 2, **para la acompañar**. The same order occurs more rarely with nouns: XXXIX, 7, **para doña Alda holgar**.

2. Third person pronouns may be appended to the past participle of a compound tense when the p. p. precedes the auxiliary: LVI, 20, **Oídolo había el rey** = *lo había oído*. This may be sometimes done in mod. Sp. when the auxiliary is understood. Cf. Ramsey, *Text-book of Mod. Sp.*, § 1382.

3. The position of the object pronoun is in general more variable than to-day: III, 12, **Venido se han á juntar**; XIII, 18, **irélos á aposentar**.

4. Metathesis of *d* and *l* often occurs in the interest of ease of pronunciation when the third person pronoun follows an imperative: XIII, 37, **catalde** = *catadle;* XXII, 58, **tomalde** = *tomadle*. Assimilation of the *r* of an infinitive with *l* to *ll*, a usage still common in poetry, is also found: as **velle** for *verle*.

5. The so-called ethical dative, or dative of advantage, is used in the *rs.* more extensively than now: XIII, 25, **Dios te me quiera guardar**; XXVII, 1, **Yo me era mora Morayma**; XXVII, 5, **no sé quién te serás.**

IV. Nouns

1. Nouns are frequently found in the plural with hardly any other force than that of a singular: XXVIII, 17, **por los pechos se lo fué á meter** (= *por el pecho*); XL, 14, **en los palacios do está** (= *en el palacio*); XLIV, 24, **pues acá en las nuestras cortes, hija, mal recaudo había** (= *en nuestra corte?*).

2. The diminutive ending –ico, which to-day properly has a disparaging and somewhat humorous force, is used as equivalent to –ito, or without any special force whatever. It is a popular use of the termination: XXXI, 2, **avecica;** *ibid.*, 3, **tortolica;** XXXIII, 1, **mañanica;** *ibid.*, 2, **riberica.**

3. Cf. section III, 1.

V. Verb Forms

1. Latin *t* is preserved as *d* in second person plural forms of all tenses except the imperative and preterit: Latin *–atis* > –ades (mod. –áis); *–ētis* >–edes (mod. –éis); *–ītis* >–ides (mod. –ís). Examples: I, 16, **vengades** = *vengáis;* I, 9, **comedes** = *coméis;* I, 18, **mentides** = *mentís;* etc.

2. The second person plural of the preterit shows –astes, –istes, for mod. –asteis, –isteis. The archaic form is the true etymological one from late Latin *–astis, –istis.* The mod. ending is derived by analogy from the other tenses which have an *i* before the *s* of this person. Examples: I, 25, **guardastes** = *guardasteis;* I, 24, **distes** = *disteis;* etc.

3. The future and conditional appear in process of formation from the infinitive of the verb+the present and imperfect, respectively, of **haber.** Examples: II, 3, **daros han** = *os darán;* II, 7, **daros hían** = *os darían.* The form **hía** never existed independently of its use as part of the conditional.

VI. Use of Tenses and Moods

The use of tenses in the *rs.* seems very loose, and the reader is almost forced to the conclusion that the exigencies of assonance and meter overcame all sense of exactitude. Cf. Ducamin, pp. 209–216.

1. Commonest of all is the imperfect for the present.

(*a*) In the indicative: II, 2, **las cortes que se hacían en León** (= *se hacen*).

(*b*) In the subjunctive: XIII, 1, **ese que Dios perdonase** (= *perdone*).

2. Conditional for future: XI, 10, **yo no te las daría** (= *daré*); XI, 12, **tomaría** (= *tomaré*).

3. Imperfect for preterit: XX, 17, **estas palabras hablaba** (= *habló*).

4. Perfect for preterit: LIII, 19, **de esta manera ha hablado** (= *habló*).

5. Pluperfect for preterit: II, 14, **las que yo me hube ganado** (= *me gané*).

6. Perfect for present: LIII, 6, **gran dinero me ha faltado** (= *me falta*).

7. –*ra* subjunctive for preterit indicative: II, 8, **allí respondiera el conde — y dijera esta razón** (= *respondió, dijo*). This tense also possesses all the modern shades of meaning, as witness the line, IV, 3, **Si aquéste muriera entonces, — ¡qué gran fama que dejara!** — The use of the –*ra* subjunctive for the preterit is not uncommon in mod. Sp.

8. Present subjunctive for imperative: XIII, 6, **convidédesle** = *convidadle;* ibid., 34, **Digádesme** = *Decidme*.

VII. Use of Auxiliaries

1. *Venir* and other intransitive verbs are often conjugated with *ser*, when *haber* would be required in mod. usage: I, 28, **hoy era venido el día** (= *es venido,* = *ha venido*).

2. *Haber* is used where the mod. language uses *tener,* and

ser and *estar* are employed at times without much distinction
of meaning: II, 10, **yo no he miedo al rey, ni á cuantos con
él son** (he = *tengo*, son = *están*); XLI, 27, **¿Qué es aquesto,
la condesa? — aquesto ¿qué puede estar?** In the last instance
the assonance is probably the governing factor.

3. *Tener*+infinitive is used for *tener que*, or *haber de*,+in-
finitive, to denote obligation: XLIV, 172, **porque yo morir
tenía;** *ibid.*, 179, **esto hacerse tenía.**

4. In addition to the usual auxiliaries, we find *haber, ir*
and *querer* employed without much special force of their
own.

(*a*) *Haber:* XXII, 37, **por haberme de holgar** = *por holgarme;*
also *ibid.*, 59.

(*b*) *Ir:* XIII, 32, **á Consuegra fué á llegar** (= *llegó*); XXII,
35, **yo las fuera á pasar** (= *pasé*).

(*c*) *Querer:* XIII, 30, **los gallos querían cantar** (= *cantaban*);
ibid., 50, **muermo te quiera matar** (= *mate*). Sometimes an
inchoative sense may be seen.

VIII. Use of Prepositions

Among the many uses of prepositions no longer regular
may be noted as most common:

1. Omission of *á* before the infinitive depending on a verb
of motion: XXII, 58, **llevédeslo ahorcar;** *ibid.*, 60, **fuera
hablar.** But in many cases, as in these two, one may suppose
the *á* to have become merged in the following *a* sound. Such
is not the case in XXXI, 2, **van tomar.**

2. *De* instead of *á* after *comenzar* and *empezar:* XIII, 28,
comienza de cabalgar; V, 7, **empezóle de hablar.**

3. *Para* instead of *á:* XIII, 20, **vase para la cocina.** This
use is common in popular speech to-day.

BERNARDO DEL CARPIO

(MF, 130–172; MP, XI, 176–216)

Bernardo (or **Bernaldo**) **del Carpio**, the famous champion of Spain and slayer of Roland at Roncesvaux (Sp. *Roncesvalles*), is probably an entirely fictitious character, the only purely imaginary hero of the Old Spanish epic. His legend was developed with many variants in epics now lost; it is reported in the Latin chronicles of Lucas of Tuy and the Archbishop Rodrigo, and in the Castilian *Crónica general* of Alfonso X. The best-known version runs as follows: the Count of Saldaña was secretly married to Ximena, sister of Alfonso II (el Casto) of Asturias. Bernardo was born of the union. Alfonso discovered the secret, imprisoned the Count, put the princess in a convent and took the child to be educated at court, where he early became noted for his courage. When Alfonso entered into an alliance with Charlemagne, the Spanish nobles rebelled and compelled their king to repudiate all connection with the foreigner. Bernardo took a prominent part in this and led the Spanish forces against Charlemagne, who crossed the Pyrenees to punish his faithless ally. The French were defeated at Roncesvaux, with the loss of Roland and other leaders. Soon after Bernardo learned of his father's imprisonment and asked Alfonso to free him, but met with refusal. He lived out of Spain until the reign of Alfonso III (el Magno), whom he aided in many battles. The king promised many times to release the Count of Saldaña, but never kept his word. At last, while attending the Cortes at León, Bernardo openly charged him with perjury, and was exiled. He built the castle of El Carpio and made war upon Alfonso, finally extorting a serious promise of his father's liberty, in exchange for El Carpio. But the Count had died three days before the messengers had arrived at his prison; his body was set on horseback and led out to meet Bernardo, whose greeting was directed to a corpse. After this great disappointment, Bernardo left León, and died in upper Aragon. — The story that Bernardo vanquished Roland in single combat at Roncesvaux does not appear before the sixteenth century.

The battle of Roncesvaux occurred in 778. (For details concerning it, see note on XX.) Alfonso II reigned 791–842, and Alfonso III from 866 to 874. These dates alone show the impossibility of the legendary account. The name Bernardo is itself French, not Spanish. It is thought that the origin of the hero may be found in a real Bernardo of Ribagorza (Upper Aragon), said to be a relative of Charlemagne; but the epic Bernardo is a pure invention, a sort of epitome of Spanish valor to correspond to the French Roland. The poems about him certainly did not appear till after 1100.

No. I is the only *r. viejo* on Bernardo. (Cf. XLV.) It represents the scene between Alfonso III and the hero just before his exile, but varies widely from the account given in the *1ª Crónica general*. Here Bernardo's father is barely mentioned and the dispute turns on the possession of El Carpio, which in the version of the Chronicle did not yet exist. (Cf. *Cr. gen.*, pp. 371–374.) The *r.* probably derives from a late epic of the fourteenth century.

It is unfortunate that there is no good ballad on the dramatic meeting of Bernardo with his dead father. (*Cr. gen.*, p. 375.) There are several of the erudite and artistic periods, but none so complete as the poem by Mrs. Hemans, «Bernardo del Carpio.»

I. 1. **al Carpio.** Seven Carpios are known. Tradition connects Bernardo with one near Alba de Tormes, not far from Salamanca. Cf. MF, 147, n. 4.

4. A proverbial line, appearing in many ballads, as II, 9. Cervantes makes Sancho quote it, *D. Quijote*, II, 10.

9. **comedes**, mod. *coméis*. (See *Gram. pec.*, V, 1.) **Los que coméis mi pan** is also a common phrase in the *rs.*

10, 11. **los ciento.** The article was used regularly before a noun expressing part of a whole previously given; in mod. Sp. it would be suppressed. In l. 12 the meter did not allow it.

13. **la.** An indefinite feminine often found. *Razón* may have been understood at first.

18. **el rey.** The use of the definite article before a noun in the vocative will be found repeatedly. See *Gram. pec.*, II, 3.

20. **aquella** (supply *batalla*) **del Encinal.** No battle of El Encinal is mentioned in the *Cr. gen.* in this passage. W. 13, a slightly modernized version of the same poem, calls it *El Romeral.* Nothing is known of either place or battle.

28. **era venido,** for *ha venido.* Cf. *Gram. pec.*, VII, 1. **habemos,** mod. *hemos.*

FERNÁN GONZÁLEZ

(MF, 173–193; MP, XI, 217–241; RMP, *Notas para el romancero de Fernán González*)

Count Fernán González is preeminently the Castilian hero, as Bernardo and the Cid are representatives of the national feeling of Spain against other countries. The Count is cred-ited with having, after many struggles, freed Castile from allegiance to the king of León, and having thus paved the way for the establishment of the separate kingdom of Castile. Not much is known of his real history. He was one of the counts appointed by the kings of León to govern Castile as a dependency. He helped Ramiro II of León defeat the Moors near Osma in 933. Later he quarreled with Ramiro and was imprisoned by him at León, but he was soon released, and his daughter married the king's son Ordoño. This prince succeeded his father in 950 or 951, but the alliance did not prevent Fernán González from fighting him and his successor Sancho el Gordo (r. 955–967). In the course of a war with García of Navarre, whose sister Sancha he had married, the Castilian count was imprisoned in Pamplona (960), but was soon set free. United with the other Christian rulers he fought the common enemy, the Caliph of Cordova, Alhakim II, and was defeated at San Esteban de Gormaz. He died at an advanced age in 970. Castile was practically freed from dependence on León during his rule, but the title of king of Castile was not adopted by his successors till 1037.

Tradition has liberally added romantic details, and represents the bickering count as an unconquered hero and patriot. An early epic undoubtedly existed, but has been lost. It was superseded by a long poem in 4-line monorime stanzas (*cuaderna vía*) written about 1250 by a monk of San Pedro de Arlanza, *El Poema de Fernán González,* and based in part on the epic. (See the edition of C. Carroll Marden, Baltimore, 1904.) A later epic, with romantic details developed at greater length, has left traces in the *Crónica de 1344,* which used it as a source.

In brief, the legend states that the count warred with constant success against the Moors, and slew king Sancho of Navarre. He was summoned to the Cortes by Sancho I (el Gordo) of León, and attended against his will. While there he sold the king a horse and hawk, which were to be paid for on a certain date. For every day which passed without payment beyond the time set, the price was to be doubled.[1] Fernán González was then invited into Navarre to marry Sancha, daughter of the Sancho whom he had slain; but her brother García threw him into prison to avenge his father's death. Sancha, however, rose to the occasion, released the Count and escaped with him to Castile, where his subjects were found about to march in force upon Navarre, drawing a stone image of the Count as their leader (LIV). After this he fought García several times, on one occasion taking him prisoner and releasing him at the request of Sancha.

Meanwhile three years had passed and the Count had not attended the Cortes at León. King Sancho sent him a per-

---

[1] On this curious transaction and the phrase "al gallarín," used in the *Crónica rimada* to describe it, see C. Pitollet, *Notes au poema de Fernán González, Venta del caballo y del azor,* in *Bulletin hispanique,* IV, 157–160; and RMP, *Ép. cast.,* p. 54.

emptory summons which Fernán González obeyed; he appeared at court and demanded payment for his horse and
hawk. Sancho imprisoned him, but he was again rescued by
his wife; this time she obtained permission to visit him and
he departed dressed in her clothes. He ravaged Leonese
territory until he obtained an interview with Sancho at the
ford of Carrión (III). The king had postponed payment for
the horse and hawk so long that all Spain would not equal
the sum due, and he was persuaded to free Castile from vas-
salage in lieu of coin. The Count, after more wars with the
Moors, died peacefully at Burgos.

II. The origin of this poem is not precisely known; it is
certainly late in spirit, and may represent an episode of the
late epic on the Count. We must suppose that a lost ending
existed, in which Fernán González decides to obey the summons in spite of his bold words. The Cortes referred to may
be either of the two which he attended, probably the second.

2. The Cortes at this time embraced only the nobles and
clergy, and would more properly be called *Concilio*. The
real Cortes with the third estate did not appear in León till
1188. León was the capital of the kingdom of that name, and
at times also of Galicia, Asturias and Castile, when all four
chanced to be united.

3. **daros han** = *os darán*. See *Gram. pec.*, V, 3.

4-6. The towns mentioned all lie in the province of Palencia, Old Castile. **Palencia** itself, capital of the province, with
16,000 inhabitants, is the only one of any present-day importance. The **nueve villas**, of which four no longer exist, lay
to the north of Palencia, and were allied among themselves.
Carrión (*de los Condes*), two miles north of Palencia on the
river Carrión, was the ancestral home of the family of Carrión, so prominent in the Cid legend. On these place-names,
see RMP, *Notas*, p. 461, n. 2.

Palencia la mayor. Ducamin suggests that **mayor** may
contrast with **Palenzuela**, "little Palencia." But more likely

it is a mere epic epithet; as *Poema del Cid*, v. 3151, «Valencia la mayor.» Cf. MF, p. 298, n. 2.

8. **Respondiera, dijera.** See *Gram. pec.*, VI, 7.

10. **no he miedo al rey, ni á cuantos con él son;** cf. *Gram. pec.*, VII, 2.

12. **de ellos ... de ellos** = *los unos ... los otros.*

III. This poem is undoubtedly derived from the fourteenth century epic which was used for the *Crónica de 1344*. The last four lines are to be regarded as a spurious addition made by the editors of the first *Cancionero de rs.* to join it with no. II, which was supposed to be its continuation.

2. **Sancho Ordóñez** is an error for Sancho I (el Gordo). He was the half-brother, not the son, of Ordoño III, whom he succeeded.

6. **sone;** on the adventitious *e*, see *Introduction*, § VII.

9. **que se vayan,** 'to allow them to go.'

14. **los del rey,** supply *dijeron.*

15. **la su mula;** the definite article will be found constantly used with the possessive pronoun, as in Italian. See *Gram. pec.*, II, 2.

17. **el arena;** mod. Sp. would use *la* in this case, but not before **agua.** See *Gram. pec.*, II, 1.

24. **buen rey.** The epithet, here inappropriate, is used as a formula. Cf. RMP, *Cantar de Mio Cid* (Madrid, 1908), p. 329.

32. **los frailes que han allegado;** a common elliptical construction; a word "behold" may originally have been supplied before the noun.

THE INFANTES DE LARA

(MF, 202–218; MP, XI, 265–289; RMP, *Leyenda de los Infantes de Lara*)

The story of the **Infantes de Lara** (or **Salas,** the earlier term) in its simplest form is this: During the rule in Castile of Garci Fernández, son of Fernán González, the seven Infantes came to Burgos to attend the wedding of their uncle Ruy Velázquez with doña Lambra (IV). The youngest, Gonzalvo, became involved in an unfortunate quarrel over a *tablado* (see IV, 29, note) with Alvar Sánchez, cousin to the bride. Sánchez was killed, and a general mêlée ensued. The incipient feud was finally hushed, and the Infantes even accompanied the newly married pair to their home at Barbadillo, near Lara. But doña Lambra, following her revengeful instinct, orders a servant to strike Gonzalvo's breast with a cucumber wet in blood, an act considered a deadly insult. The man, pursued, takes refuge under her cloak (an asylum as sacred as a church), but the Infantes kill him none the less. Doña Lambra calls upon her husband for vengeance. Ruy Velázquez carries through a deep-laid plot: still feigning friendship with the family of Salas, he sends Gonzalo Gústioz, father of the Infantes, on an embassy to the Moor Almanzor at Cordova, but with secret instructions to the latter to slay the messenger. The Infantes are betrayed into the hands of the Moors (LI) and slain, on the plain of Almenar; their heads are sent to Almanzor (V). But Gonzalo Gústioz escaped the treachery which was intended to end his whole race; spared through the pity of the Moorish ruler he lived to lament the death of his children and to return home. His bastard son Mudarra, child of his captivity, later avenged the murder of his half-brothers by slaying Ruy Velázquez (VI) and the revengeful doña Lambra.

This theme was treated in at least two Old Spanish epics, of which only scanty fragments are preserved in the *Crónicas*. The *rs. viejos* here given represent the tradition of the second of them. It is probable that there was a basis of fact for the first part of the story, but all we know certainly is that a **Gonzalo Gústioz** actually lived at the court of Castile in the latter part of the tenth century, and that **Almanzor** (died 1002), the famous general and prime minister of the Cordovan Caliph Hishâm II, was his contemporary. A *Roderico Velazquiz* is mentioned in a Castilian document of 988. **Lambra**

(Latin *Flamula*) was common as a name of women in the tenth century, and **Mudarra** (Arabic in origin) was frequently borne by Spaniards of the period. True or false, the legend gives a just idea of the family vendettas, the obligatory vengeances common to all primitive peoples. In Spain they continued up to the firm rule of Ferdinand and Isabella.

The chronological order of the *rs.* dealing with the Infantes de Lara is IV, LI, V, VI.

IV. The beginning of the feud is here presented in a form considerably at variance with the original story. Alvar Sánchez and the squire with the bloody cucumber have disappeared, and a petty squabble between the ladies of the rival families is given as the cause of all the subsequent bloodshed.

The immediate source of this ballad is not certainly known, but it is far distant from any known version of a chronicle or epic. Another *r. viejo* almost parallel to this exists, beginning *Á Calatrava la vieja* (W. 19), which is a little nearer the original story, but more obscure and disconnected.

1. **Lara**, a town, and the district named from it, about thirty miles southeast of Burgos. **Salas** is a smaller town within the district (*alfoz*) of Lara. Salas was the home of the Infantes, and Lara of Rodrigo Velázquez; but in the later versions the Infantes also were called by the more comprehensive title.

2. It is not certain what battle is referred to here; possibly there is a reminiscence of the Vado de Cascajares (cf. LII, l. 8, note), where Garci Fernández defeated the Moors. See RMP, *Leyenda*, p. 27, n. 1; p. 88; p. 345.

3. **dejara** = *hubiera dejado*. (Cf. below, **matara, vendiera**.) The use is modern also. **que** is a peculiarly Spanish expletive.

7. **Salas**, an obvious error for *Lara*.

8. **duraron siete semanas.** This expression is either a poetic exaggeration or proves the antiquity of the material. The expense and duration of wedding celebrations became so

unbridled that in 1258 Alfonso X and the Castilian Cortes passed a law limiting the number of persons who could be invited to a wedding, and prohibiting a celebration of more than two days in length. Similar restrictions were continued by later kings. Cf. Wolf, *Ueber eine Sammlung*, p. 28, n. 1.

11. **tanta viene de la gente**, mod. *tanta gente viene.*

13. Cf. XII, l. 1.

14. **Doña Sancha** was also the sister of Ruy Velázquez.

21. **Cantaranas.** A street of that name existed till recently in Burgos, but the scene of this poem seems to be laid in Lara. The appellation is common for streets in Spanish towns. (*Leyenda*, p. 177, and n. 3.)

29. **torre**, in other versions called *tablado*, a mock castle loosely built of boards, set up for the knights to knock down, if they had skill and strength enough, with javelins (*bohordos*, **varas**). It was a favorite pastime of the nobles up to the fourteenth century. (*Leyenda*, p. 5, n. 1.)

30. Durán reads: *á la otra parte pasaban*, in which case **varas** is clearly the subject of the verb. Wolf's reading is probably an error for *pasan*.

35. **un caballero**; Durán suggests *mi caballero*, which makes better sense.

37. **la tal**, mod. *tal.*

39. **Callases** = *calles* = *calla*. See *Gram. pec.*, VI, 1*b* and 8.

40. A tradition, common in the Middle Ages and later, attributed disgrace to the woman who had more than one child at a birth. The insult here is purely gratuitous; although in late legend the seven Infantes were vaguely associated with such a stigma, it had no place in the original story, and the difference in age of the Infantes is clearly indicated in no. V.

42–43. On this punishment which was inflicted by law on prostitutes in the thirteenth century, see RMP, *Leyenda*, p. 87, and n. 1.

46. **entiendo de te lo muy bien vengar**, mod. *pienso vengártelo muy bien.*

V. This ballad, which depicts the most dramatic scene of the whole story, is derived with some modification from the second epic on the Infantes, preserved in the *Crónica de 1344.* In the enumeration of the heads one name, Gustios González (the sixth son), has been omitted. The patronymic, which varies in the text, should be in every case González. The qualities assigned to Gonzalo's sons form, taken all together, a pretty complete picture of the ideal medieval knight. Cf. *Leyenda*, p. 26, n. 2.

An interesting traditional ballad on this subject has recently been found among the Spanish Jews of the Orient. (Cf. note to LVIII, l. 70.) It was published in the *Revue hispanique*, X, 605. A semi-artistic version from a MS. collection in Barcelona is printed in MP, IX, 183. Cf. also *ibid.*, p. 265.

1. There are several Saints Cyprian, but the most famous was once Bishop of Carthage. His day in the Roman calendar is Sept. 16.

9. **Almenar,** a village sixty miles southeast of Salas.

14. **carillo.** Nuño Salido is meant, the tutor of the Infantes, who accompanied them and died with them. Cf. no. LI.

22. **Fernán González** should be *Garci Fernández,* as is shown by the corresponding passage in the *Crón. de 1344.* (*Leyenda,* 281.)

31. The idea seems to be: 'Your aid in hunting was alone enough to make the king esteem you,' or 'You were the only one whom the king cared to have with him on his hunt.'

33. **Gómez,** an error for *Velázquez,* which gives the correct length to the half-line.

53. **hambre,** obviously an error, perhaps for *amor.*

VI. One of the most widely known *rs.* Lockhart translated it, and Victor Hugo expanded it into one of his *Orientales* (no. XXX, *Romance mauresque*), which begins:

«Don Rodrigue est à la chasse,
Sans épée et sans cuirasse.»

The ballad is remotely derived from the second *cantar de gesta*. There, however, the two enemies are each backed by an armed force; Mudarra by agreement fights Ruy Velázquez in single combat, overcomes him, and takes him home to be put to death by torture. There is a later redaction of the *r.* printed by R. Fouché-Delbosc, *Revue hispanique*, V, 251–254.

1. **y aun;** a formula of emphatic repetition with the addition of a new element. Cf. XVII, l. 1.

3. **renegada.** Here a mere term of insult, as Mudarra's mother had never been a Christian.

5. See note on III, 32.

18. **Arabiana**, a name which does not appear in the early chronicles, but was later substituted for Almenar as the scene of the tragedy. The Arabiana is a stream near Almenar, and the present-day «campos de Arabiana» a narrow valley some twelve miles northeast of that village.

21. **El espera.** Cf. III, 17, note.

22. A line given immortality by Sancho Panza, who quoted it in triumph to his master, on one of the rare occasions when he rebelled against him (*D. Quijote*, II, 60). The last hemistich may be made good meter by reading *nemigo*. Cf. *Leyenda*, p. 104, n. 2; and p. 423, n. 5.

THE CID

(MF, 219–300; MP, XI, 290–371)

Ruy Díaz (= Rodrigo, son of Diego), called El Campeador (*The Champion*, one who fought in single combat before an army) and El Cid (Arabic *sîdî*, "my lord"), is the most famous and most sung of Spanish national heroes. His historical figure began soon after his death to be obscured by a great variety of poetic legends, which from the first epic down to the play of Corneille drew further and further away from the facts. Modern investigation has succeeded in recovering a firm outline of the Cid's deeds and character.

Fernando I (died 1065) had succeeded in uniting under his rule the kingdoms of Castile, León and Galicia, but at his death he divided his dominions among his children, leaving Castile to Sancho, León to Alfonso, Galicia to García, and two fortified cities to his daughters, Toro to Elvira and Zamora to Urraca. War was sure to result. Sancho II soon set out to gain the whole for himself. He defeated Alfonso and García, and took Toro from Elvira, but while besieging Urraca was slain before the walls of Zamora (1072, cf. no. VIII). Alfonso (the VI) then became ruler of the three kingdoms, and reigned long and successfully, warring against the Moors.

Ruy Díaz was born of noble lineage either at Burgos or the near-by village of Bivar in the first half of the eleventh century. He fought under Sancho against his brothers and at the siege of Zamora, and in a short time was promoted to high rank. Alfonso had just cause of grievance against the Cid, but he received him, and gave him a princess of the royal blood in marriage (1074 or a little earlier), Ximena Díaz, daughter of the Count of Oviedo. He employed him on a mission to the Moors of Seville; but soon after (1081) exiled him on the pretext that he had made war without permission.

Rodrigo then began an independent existence as captain of mercenaries in the pay of the Moorish king of Saragossa. He fought Christians and rival Moors indiscriminately, by force and by intrigue, but always with success. Soldiers of both races served under him; he himself adopted Moorish costume, and received his famous appellation from the Arabs. He had a share in maintaining the then king of Valencia upon his throne, and when this king was dethroned, the Cid besieged and captured the city for himself (1094), in spite of the opposition of Alfonso, of the Count of Barcelona and of various Moorish rulers. He ruled in Valencia with an iron hand, maintaining himself there against all comers till his death in 1099. His wife and followers were obliged to abandon the place in 1102. One of his daughters married a Count of Barcelona, and another a Prince of Navarre. The Cid was evidently a man of extraordinary force and ability, and his character, which has been harshly criticized for cruelty and irreligion, was well within the bounds prescribed by his age.

The epic muse began very soon after his death to idealize his figure. The *Poema del Cid*, c. 1140?, (edition by RMP, Madrid, 1900) one of the greatest monuments of medieval literature, is built about an imaginary event, the marriage of the hero's daughters to the Infantes de Carrión, who proved to be cowards and bullies, and were divorced. It describes the adult career of the Cid as that of a great warrior, pious Christian and obedient vassal of Alfonso. Other poems of the same period existed without doubt. Later epics followed a process of development which was the natural result of the people's curiosity for more details in the life of their favorite hero, and filled in his youthful years with romantic adventures. Only one of the latest and most degenerate poems is preserved, the *Crónica rimada* (fourteenth century; printed in *Bibl. de Aut. Esp.*, XVI, 651–662).

The first epic period (twelfth century) added to history various poetic details of the Siege of Zamora (nos. VII, VIII, IX, X); the story of the oath exacted by the Cid from Alfonso VI at Santa Gadea in Burgos (XXXVIII); the marriage of the Cid's daughters to the Infantes de Carrión; and the battle won against king Búcar by the Cid's dead body strapped on horseback.

The second epic expansion (thirteenth and fourteenth centuries), devoted to the Cid's youth or *Mocedades*, contains the marriage of the Cid to Ximena, daughter of Count Gómez de Gormaz whom he had slain (XXXVI, XXXVII); the vision of St. Lazarus in the form of a leper (LII); the duel with the Aragonese champion Martín González; the fantastic expedition of the Cid and king Fernando into France, with discomfiture of all opponents; and the prominent part played by the Cid in the distribution of kingdoms at Fernando's death. The romantic love of the hero for Ximena, with the resultant conflict between duty and passion, the trial which Diego

Laínez makes of his son's courage (W. 28), have been given wide currency by Guillén de Castro and Corneille, but they are artistic inventions not earlier than the late sixteenth century.

Special collections of the Cid ballads have often been made. The first *Romancero del Cid*, compiled by Juan de Escobar (1612), was often reprinted, and most of the editions contained 102 poems; Keller's *Romancero del Cid* (1840) has 154, and that of C. Michaëlis de Vasconcellos (1871) includes 205. For Herder's translation of the Cid ballads, see *Bibliography* under Herder.

Chronologically the *rs.* concerning the Cid in the present collection may be placed in this order: XXXVI, XXXVII, LII, LV, VII, VIII, IX, X, XXXVIII, XII. XI contains nothing to indicate its proper place in the sequence.

SIEGE OF ZAMORA

Nos. VII, VIII, IX and X deal with the Siege of Zamora, as described in the stirring epic which was summarized in the *Primera crónica general*.[1] According to this story, Sancho encamped with his army before the strong city and sent the Cid to demand its surrender. (Cf. no. LV.) Urraca refused, and Sancho, accusing the Cid of complicity with her, exiled him, but immediately repented and recalled him. The king then attacked the place in vain, but after seven years put the inhabitants in straits for food. The Zamorans were about to yield when Vellido Dolfos, with the tacit consent of Urraca, escaped from the city, pretending to be a deserter, and treacherously killed the king, who would not heed the loyal warning

---

[1] It is supposed with reason that beside two versions of the *Poema del Cid* and two of the *Rodrigo* (cf. note to XXXVI and XXXVII) there existed two other epics, the *Cantar del rey don Fernando* or *de la partición de los reinos* and the *Cantar del cerco de Zamora*. The latter was utilized in the *Primera crónica general;* the former was not, but appears *prosified* in the *Crón. de 1344.* See MP, XI, 322–335; and RMP, *Ép. cast.*, 57–79.

sent him from Zamora (VIII). The traitor returned to the
town, closely pursued by the Cid. Then Diego Ordóñez, one
of the besieging knights, formally accused the city of treachery,
and challenged it (IX). According to the laws of the time,
he was compelled to fight in the lists with five Zamorans
one after another. The champions were the five sons of Arias
Gonzalo, the aged friend and adviser of Urraca. Ordóñez
slew three of them, but the third forced him out of the lists,
and the contest was left undecided: «et assi finco este pleyto
por judgar» (*Cr. gen.*, pp. 505–518).

The Cid does not figure actively in this series of *rs.*, and
yet his presence as an important character in the events is
constantly felt.

VII. The episode related in this fine ballad is quite independent of anything in the *Primera crónica general.* There
are other versions (W. 41, 42*a*).

20. **si lo haces,** ' if you behave.'

22. **que no vivir;** the expletive *no* after a comparative is
seen to be of old use, though to-day sometimes considered a
Gallicism.

VIII. Apparently a condensed relic of the original *cantar.*
The account in the *1ª crónica* is much more circumstantial.
It relates that Dolfos obtained the king's confidence and then
stabbed him in the back. A contemporary historian, however, the monk of Silós, says that the Zamorans sent out a
bold knight who made a dash, slew Sancho face to face, and
escaped in safety. Thus it appears that Vellido Dolfos, who
shares the traitors' corner in Spanish popular history with
the bishop don Orpas, may owe his obloquy to a poet who
needed a villain for his tale.

IX. This widely known ballad is closely allied to the *1ª
crónica,* and may be a descendant of the original epic. The
words of challenge seem to have been a consecrated formula,

and are repeated with little variation in a number of *rs.* on this subject (W. 47*a*, 47*b*). D. Quijote in his speech to the town with the braying alcaldes (II, 27) cites this case as a classic example of a challenge to a whole town. Again, in the *entremés* of Cervantes entitled *Los dos habladores*, Roldán says: «con cinco estaba obligado á reñir antiguamente el que desafiaba de común; como se vió en don Diego Ordóñez y los hijos de Arias Gonzalo, cuando el rey don Sancho . . .» According to the *Siete Partidas* of Alfonso el Sabio the *riepto* (as distinguished from the *desafío*) was made only to one accused of treachery, and the challenged party, if defeated, was dishonored for the rest of his life.

X. Here is presented a scene not known to the *1ª crónica;* neither is Fernando there given as the name of one of Arias Gonzalo's sons. The same theme is treated in another *r.* (W. 50*a*), not quite equal to this.

Title. **Fernán D'Arias.** Although the name appears written in this way, the **D** is really part of *Fernand(o)*.

1. **que nunca fuera cerrado.** Damas Hinard translates: «qui n'avait jamais dû être fermée.» The words seem to mean, however, 'which never was closed.' The *Primera crón. gen.* (p. 511*a*) puts these words into the mouth of Vellido Dolfos, as he promises King Sancho to teach him the way to capture Zamora: «et yo mostraruos e el postigo que los çambranos llaman dArena, por o entraremos la villa, *ca nunqua aquel postigo se cierra.*»

2. **trescientos de caballo,** moď. *de á caballo.*

14. **ni á las tablas jugando,** i.e. in a quarrel arising over the game, which proved fatal to several knights of legend. Cf. W. 173, beginning.

XI. An episode not connected with any other known poem or chronicle. There is a revised version (W. 32), but neither one indicates which of the Cid's three sovereigns is the king mentioned.

In this connection one may quote an interesting poem of the *Romancero general* (D. 244). The author protests against the extent to which the Castilian muse is busied with Moorish subjects (cf. note to no. LVII) to the neglect of the national heroes. He asks:

«Los Ordoños, los Bermudos,
Los Rasuras y Mudarras,
Los Alfonsos, los Enricos,
Los Sanchos, y los de Lara,
¿Qué es de ellos? ¿y qué es del Cid?
¡Tanto olvido á gloria tanta!»

And farther on:

«Buen Conde Fernán-González,
Por el val de las Estacas,
Nuñovero, Nuñovero,
Viejos son, pero no cansan.»

This patriotic poet had a keen literary sense which selected three of the oldest *rs.* as his examples. *Nuñovero* is W. 168.

1. **val de las Estacas.** There is a *Valdestacas* in the province of Toledo. Cervantes jestingly refers to this line in the Quijote (I, 17).

2. **Babieca,** the Cid's famous charger, is said to have survived him two years, and to have been buried in front of the door of S. Pedro de Cardeña, within which was its master's tomb.

7. (*Digo*) **que no quiero.**

12. **por bien, por mal;** ' willingly, by force.'

17. **Por ser vos,** ' because you are.'

XII. On this " incomparable cantarcillo," see C. Michaëlis de Vasconcellos, *Romanzenstudien*, I (in *Zeitschrift für rom. Phil.*, XVI, 40–89). The poem seems to be a sporadic product of the fifteenth century, not connected with any known epic, except that the last part (l. 25 to end) is a version of the flight of Búcar, king of Morocco, whose defeat by the Cid is related both in the *Poema del Cid* (l. 2408 and following) and the Chronicles (*Cr. gen.*, pp. 605–607). This ballad was a great favorite, and traditional versions have been found in Catalonia (W. 129), in Portuguese territory (three or more in number, *Rom. geral*, II, 317–327, and cf. C. M. de Vasconcellos, *Estudos* in *Cult. esp.*, XI, 717, ff.) and among the Jews of Tangier (RMP, *Catál.*, no. 6).

1. Cf. IV, 13, and XXIII, 1. These are all old ballads, and it is not certain that any one borrowed from another.

6–7. These lines may represent part of an old "Elegy on Valencia" written by a Moor at the time of the loss of the city. See Michaëlis, *op. cit.*, pp. 49–57; *Cr. gen.*, pp. 576–578; and RMP, *Sobre Aluacaxí y la elegía árabe de Valencia*.

11. **Urraca Hernando** was the name, not of a daughter of the Cid, but of the strong-minded princess who held Zamora against Sancho. (Cf. LV, VIII.) Mme. Michaëlis suggests that this part of the poem may be a remnant of some legend about her.

13. **que,** ' for.'

29. This line is explained by the Portuguese versions from the Azores and Madeira. In them it appears that Búcar's mare was the mother of Babieca, which the Cid had captured in a battle some time before. It is curious that this traditional account, of unknown origin, should be so much more plausible than the version of the *Crón. de 1344.* The author or poet whose invention is there set down, desiring to account for the horse in some way, could think of nothing better than to make him a present to the Cid in his boyhood. And Babieca outlived him two years!

XIII. (MF, 307; MP, XII, 112–115)

Doubtless direct oral tradition supplied the details of this lively anecdote of the reign of Pedro I, called *el cruel* or *el justiciero* (reigned 1350–69). That it has a basis in fact is shown by these words of the so-called *Cuarta crónica general* (quoted by MP, XII, 114): «Después desto fecho, por volturas de un pariente de doña María de Padilla, que se decía Juan García de Padilla, el rey don Pedro corrió desde Sevilla fasta Consuegra al Prior de Sant Juan, e en dos noches e dos días le corrió fasta el Castillo de Consuegra, e non le alcanzó e tornóse á Sevilla.» There is another version of the *r*. (W. 69*a*).

The Order of St. John of Jerusalem, called also of the Hospitallers and of the Knights of Malta, was a foreign order, created during the crusades and later introduced into Spain.

1. **D. García de Padilla**, a relative of María de Padilla, the king's mistress during a long period of years.

3. **Consuegra**, a town thirty-five miles southeast of Toledo. Alfonso IX granted it to the military order of St. John in 1183.

6. **convidédesle** = *convidéisle* = *convidadle*.

7. This is the reading of MP (XII, 113). W. reads *dió el Toro;* D., *dió Toro.* The reference is to D. Juan el tuerto (*the deformed*), a prince of royal blood, but rebellious, whom Alfonso XI, Pedro's father, invited to dine at Toro and caused to be slain as he was entering the palace (1326). **Toro** is a town on the extreme eastern edge of the kingdom of León, between Zamora and Valladolid. It has lost its former importance.

The laconic brevity of the reference in this line, which does not even take the trouble to name the author of the deed, is an example of something that must always be borne in mind in reading the *rs.*: that the audience which listened to them was supposed to be, and was, entirely familiar with the events related and their circumstances. Hence the abrupt beginnings, sudden transitions and obscure references.

9. **me lo dad;** *dádmelo* is required to-day.

13. **por quién está?** ' to whom it owes allegiance.'

19. **Vais,** mod. *id.*

23. **salirte has,** *te saldrás.*

25. **te me quiera guardar.** (See *Gram. pec.*, III, 5.) Standard modern Castilian would omit the **me** rather than allow

the conjunctive forms of the first and second person pronouns to stand together.

26. **de dos;** no particular noun is necessarily understood with this indefinite feminine.

29. **Azoguejo,** 'the little market-place' (see *Vocabulary*); a name preserved in squares at Segovia and Valladolid, but not now known as a town.

30. This line is the same as that beginning the well-known *r.* of *Conde Claros* (W. 190), and was certainly borrowed thence. There is difference of opinion as to the source of the expression in the first hemistich. Ticknor (I, 121, n. 3) says " the counting of time by the dripping of water is a proof of antiquity in the ballad [*Conde Claros*] itself." MF (p. 369) states that the figure is not taken from a time-keeping device which would be a proof of age, but from a balance. — Cervantes quotes «Media noche era por filo» (*D. Quijote*, II, 9). — **querían;** an example of the use of *querer* without additional force: **querían cantar**=*cantaban.* (See *Gram. pec.*, VII, 4.) But one may interpret, 'were about to crow.'

31. Toledo does not lie in the route from Seville to Consuegra, but Seville is nowhere mentioned in the ballad.

32. **antes que el gallo cantase;** the Spanish cock is said to crow twice, once at midnight, and once at dawn. This explains the apparent contradiction in ll. 30 and 32.

37. **catalde** = *catadle.* See *Gram. pec.*, III, 4.

39. **tomases** = *toma.* Cf. IV, 39.

41–42. These lines are a splenetic monologue of the Prior, as he reflects on his adventure. — **así mala rabia os mate,** 'pest take you.'

54. **Hacerlo vos,** *hacerlo á vos.*

XIV. (MF, 305; MP, XII, 115–125)

The Grand Master of the Order of Santiago was murdered at the command of his half-brother Pedro I in 1358, and the deed is one of the blackest in a black reign. The facts of the

invitation to the palace, the dismissal of all Fadrique's at-
tendants, and the murder before Pedro's eyes are as here
stated; the other details are traditional and might or might
not be true.   Doña María, however, is exonerated by history
from the odious responsibility she received in the poem; she
was a kind-hearted person who did her best to mitigate the
effects of Pedro's temper.   Fadrique had been concerned in
numerous rebellions against the king, but at this time was
supposed to be loyal and in his service.   The military order
of Santiago de la Espada was one of the three most powerful
in Spain, and was founded about 1170.

No. XIV is a dramatic and genuinely popular ballad, which
has been translated by Lockhart.   The device of putting the
first part of the narration in the first person and the rest in the
third is not uncommon in popular poetry.   A fine traditional
version exists in Asturias (JMP, no. XII) and one has been
found in Tangier (RMP, *Catál.*, no. 7).

1. **Coímbra** should be *Jumilla*, a town in Murcia which
the Grand Master had just captured.   The name of the Portuguese city must be a late substitution in analogy with the
original form of the first line of W. 104.

5. **de mula, de caballo,** 'on mules, on horse.'   *De á caballo*
would be used to-day, and some other turn be substituted for
the first phrase.

7. A formula occurring practically unchanged in two *rs.*
of the Carolingian cycle (W. 173 and 191).

13. **Puerta Macarena,** the north gate of Seville.

14. **ordenado de evangelio.**   There were three degrees of
clerics ordained for different parts of the Roman Catholic
service: 1, ordained to chant the epistles, the *ordenado de
epístola* (*epistolero, subdiácono*); 2, ordained for the Gospels,
the **ordenado de evangelio** (*evangelistero, diácono*); 3, ordained for the mass, the *ordenado de misa* (*misacantano, sa-
cerdote*).   The cleric of the lowest rank was not allowed to
perform the service of either of the other two, nor he of the
second to usurp the office of the third.

16. **año**, mod. *años*.

18. Cf. LV, 4. In the present case **ahijado** is loosely used and means simply 'the one sponsored.' It should properly be applied to the Maestre's son.

22. **hube curado.** See *Gram. pec.*, VI, 5.

24. **palacios**, the Alcázar of Seville, a famous example of mudéjar architecture, begun by Pedro I himself. Antiquarians have not been able to identify the exact room in which the murder took place.

29. Supply *dijeron* before the first **que.**

51. **Con la cabeza lo ha; lo** perhaps refers back to **mal;** or **haberlo con** may equal the commoner phrase *habérselas con,* 'to be working at.'

52. **una su tía.** mod. *una tía suya.* In the following year Don Pedro caused the death of his aunt, doña Leonor, queen of Aragon, sister of Alfonso XI; and some reminiscence of her may be at the bottom of this passage.

56. Damas Hinard, alone among commentators, ignores the reference to **doña María**, and makes the subsequent punishment refer to the rash aunt. In that case **le** in l. 55 has for its antecedent **tía** and not **rey.** Such an interpretation is more plausible than the hasty and unnatural repentance of Don Pedro; and one may easily suppose that **doña María** is a late interpolation for *la su tía.* Observe that at present the hemistich is one syllable too long, and that the proposed reading would correct the meter.

FRONTIER BALLADS

XV. (MF, 314; MP, XII, 186–192; RMP, *Ép. cast.*, 173–176)

This and the three following poems are examples of the *romances fronterizos*, or frontier ballads (cf. the Scotch "border ballads"). They relate episodes in the never-ending struggle of Christians against Moors, which was the chief business of the Christian kingdoms from the invasion of Spain by Tárik and Músá in 711 till the capture of Granada by Ferdinand and Isabella in 1492, and even afterward in the rebellion of the moriscos (1568–71). It is not surprising that the Moors play a prominent part in all four of the great medieval epic cycles, or that in later times lively skirmishes or unusual events should be celebrated in verse. Nearly all of the *rs. fronterizos* are of the fifteenth century (one is of the fourteenth and several of the sixteenth), and it is safe to suppose in nearly all cases that each poem was composed very soon after the event it celebrates, and that it has undergone comparatively little change since then.

«Joya incomparable de la poesía castellana,» says Milá, «son los romances fronterizos. Hijos de una sociedad todavía heroica y ya no bárbara, inspirados por el más vivo espíritu nacional, reflejan al mismo tiempo algo de las costumbres, de los trajes y edificios, y aun, si bien en pocos casos, de la poesía del pueblo moro.»

Abenámar is one of the few which are supposed to have their root in Moorish popular poetry. (Cf. XVIII and XXVII.) The comparison of a besieged city to a maiden wooed (l. 20 ff.) is common in Arabic verse but not known in western Europe at this time outside Spain.

Chateaubriand twice imitates this poem in his novel *Les Aventures du dernier Abencérage*. The first part of the *r.* furnishes the substance of the conversation between Aben-Hamet and his guide, near the beginning of the story; and the last four lines become the song of Aben-Hamet, toward the close.

The king referred to must be Juan II, who in 1431 won the battle of La Higueruela, near Granada. According to Lafuente Alcántara (*Historia de Granada*, 1843–46, III, 232), on the morning of the battle he did question one of his Moorish allies, Yúsuf Ibn Alahmar, concerning the conspicuous landmarks of Granada, visible in the distance. But even in that case the poem is purely fanciful in detail, as it is also very effective. There is another less poetic version (W. 78) adapted to the Christian view-point, in which the king attacks and captures the city.

6. **Yo te la diré; la** must refer to *verdad*, which is implied, though not expressed in the previous lines.

13. **El Alhambra** (mod. *La Alhambra*, see *Gram. pec.*, II, 1), the famous palace of the Moorish kings of Granada, situated on an eminence above the city. It was built chiefly in the thirteenth and fourteenth centuries. — **la mezquita**, probably the main mosque, located in the center of the city on the spot now occupied by the Sagrario, next the Cathedral.

14. **los Alixares**, a summer-palace no longer in existence, which stood on the south slope of the Cerro del Sol, east of the Alhambra, near the present cemetery. — The agreement of **la otra, los otros** with the predicate noun instead of *castillo* is an example of attraction.

17. **Generalife**, a summer-house and garden still further up the hill than the Alhambra.

18. **Torres Bermejas**, towers so named from the reddish hue of their stonework. They stand apart from the Alhambra and nearer the city, and are now used as a military prison.

22. **víuda** stands in an *i–a* assonance, which shows that it must have been accented on the *i*, in accordance with its derivation from Latin *vĭdŭam*. Later the diphthong *iu* passed over into the commoner *iú*.

XVI. (MF, 314–315, 418; MP, XII, 193–194)

Álora la bien cercada, a rigorously historical ballad with a first line of strangely haunting quality, was probably composed soon after the event which it narrates. Its early date and popularity are testified to in the *Laberinto* of Juan de Mena (1444), which contains these lines:

«Aquel que tu vees con la saetada
. . . .
Deja su sangre tan bien derramada
Sobre la villa no poco cantada,
El Adelantado Diego de Ribera, . . .»

(Copla CXC.)

A commentator of the end of the same century, Fernán Núñez (1499), gives this note to the third line quoted: «Álora, conviene á saber; y esto dice por un cantar que se hizo sobre la muerte del dicho Adelantado, que comienza, *Álora, la bien cercada, tú que estás á par del río.*»

The Adelantado of Andalusia, Diego Gómez de Rivera, was killed in May, 1434, before the walls of Álora, a town twenty miles northwest of Malaga, on the river Guadalhorce.

5. **Viérades** = *vierais*, 'you might have seen.'
12. **que** = *de modo que.*

XVII. (MF, 316; MP, XII, 201–204)

A popular anecdote, the hero of which is probably Alonso Yáñez Fajardo, a prominent noble of the middle of the fifteenth century, Adelantado of Murcia and Alcaide of Lorca. He ruled the district of Murcia, Cartagena and Lorca with great independence, fighting now against the Moors, now against the Castilian monarch, Enrique IV. He was on friendly terms with the king of Granada, Ibn Isma'il II, who is the «rey moro» mentioned.

1. **y aun.** Cf. note on VI, 1.
4. **el alférez le prendía.** Juan de Timoneda (*Rosa española*, 1573), who usually attempted to correct errors in preceding editions, reads «el orfil que le prendía.» The word intended in both cases is undoubtedly *alfil*, the 'bishop' in the game of chess.

XVIII. (MF, 317; MP, XII, 209–211)

This *r.* was translated by Byron (*A very mournful ballad on the siege and conquest of Alhama*), and is perhaps even better known than its intrinsic qualities deserve. Ginés Pérez de Hita first published it (*Historia de los bandos de los Zegríes*, etc., 1595), and he declares that it was taken from an Arabic poem which was so much repeated in Granada after the loss of Alhama that the authorities, fearing its depressing effect, prohibited the singing of it. Hita's statement as to the Moorish source is borne out by the consistently Moorish point of view and by the accuracy of some details. Elegies on the loss of cities were common in Arabic poetry. (Cf. note to XII, 6–7.) There are two other versions of the *r*. (W. 85 and 85*b*). The present one alone has a refrain, and perhaps on that account is the best known; it was translated also by "Monk" Lewis. See *Introduction*, § VI, note 1.

The «rey moro» here is Muley Abu-l Hasan (died 1485), the father of Muhammed Abu 'Abdallah ("Boabdil"), the last Moorish king of Granada. Alhama, "the key to Granada," is a city, once a strong fortress, twenty miles southwest of that capital. It was captured by the Castilian forces in 1482, and its loss presaged the downfall of the Moorish kingdom.

2. **puerta de Elvira, la de Vivarambla;** gates respectively at the north end of the city and near the center. The latter no longer exists, but the Plaza de Bibarrambla, near the Cathedral, commemorates its site.

3. This refrain was wrongly translated by Byron "Woe is me, Alhama!"

8. **el Zacatín,** a narrow street leading east from the Plaza de Bibarrambla toward the Alhambrá hill. It doubtless was a favorite station of second-hand clothes-dealers, hence the name. (Cf. *Vocabulary*.) **Alhambra.** See note on XV, 13.

14. **la Vega,** the rich plain extending west from the city down the valley of the Genil.

28. **los Bencerrajes.** Abu-l Hasan put to death some of the renowned family of the Abencerrages, who sided with his wife 'Aisha, mother of Boabdil, against his favorite Zorayah (Isabel de Solís), a captive Spanish girl.

29. **los tornadizos;** Pedro Venegas, a child of the Cordovan family of Egas, lords of Luque, was captured by Moors at the age of eight. He adopted Islâm, and married the sister of the Yûsuf Ibn Alahmar mentioned in the note to no. XV.

He was known among the Moors as The Turncoat (Sp. *el tornadizo*). His son, Abu'l Kasim Venegas, became the favorite and vizir of king Muley Abu'l Hasan; hence the reference. See Lafuente Alcántara, *Hist. de Granada*, III, 223–240 and 391.

XIX. (MF, 324; MP, XII, 278)

Alfonso V (el Magnánimo, born 1385) reigned over Aragon, Catalonia, Valencia and Sicily from 1416 to 1458, but passed most of his life outside Spain. The years from 1420 to 1442 were spent in the conquest of the kingdom of Naples, which Louis and René of Anjou disputed with him. The ballad, possibly written by some soldier in his army, is a striking depiction of what might have been his thoughts just before his final sterile victory.

Lockhart translated a slightly different form of the poem (W. 101*a*).

1. **Campo-Viejo**, Italian *Campo Vecchio*, called also *Campus Neapolis* and *campo dei nostri*, a plain northeast of Naples outside the Porta Capuana. See B. Croce, *Leggende napoletane*, Napoli, 1905, p. 33, n. 1.

9. **Castel Novo** (*Nuovo*); **Capuana** (= *Castel Capuano*); **Santelmo**; three fortresses in Naples, respectively on the water-front, at the east end and on the hill to the west. All are still in existence.

14. **hermano**; don Pedro de Aragón, famed for his valor, who was killed by a cannon-shot in 1438. A poem by Mrs. Hemans, " The King of Arragon's Lament for his Brother," is merely an expansion of this line.

CAROLINGIAN CYCLE
(MF, 327–379; MP, XII, 320–445)

The *rs.* of the Carolingian cycle differ completely from those based on Spanish history in that they all have their ultimate source in the French epic tradition which first appeared in the *Chanson de Roland* (eleventh century) and was then developed in innumerable poems having the Emperor Charlemagne as their central figure and the Twelve Peers as their chief heroes. As these knights directed their energies mainly against the Saracens of Spain, it was natural that Spain should often be the seat of the Carolingian epics. It was natural, too, that when the French poems became known across the Pyrenees, the Spanish *juglares* should seize upon them as matter likely to interest their hearers and adapt them to the new environment.

The *rs.* of this cycle (there are thirty-seven in the *Primavera*) are all such adaptations. But they vary greatly in originality, from those which can easily be traced to definite French sources (no. XX) to those whose story appears to be due entirely to native invention (no. XXII), although the interest still centers about the court of Charlemagne. Sometimes the stories have passed through the intermediate stage of a romance of chivalry (*libro de caballería*), and sometimes the immediate source is quite unknown.

The Carolingian *rs.* tend to prolixity and most of them are of the juglaresque type (nos. XXXIX to XLIII).

XX

According to Menéndez y Pelayo the *Romance del rey Marsín* is the chief exception to the rule that the Spanish ballads are original in form even when derived from a foreign source. It evidently comes from the *Chanson de Roland* (cf. ll. 1049–92, 2570–91, ed. Gröber), but has been greatly altered, not for the better. There exists a fragmentary variant of this poem, which begins *Domingo era de ramos* (W. 183).

The famous battle of Roncesvaux (Sp. *Roncesvalles*) took place in 778 in a pass of the Pyrenees. Charlemagne had been invited into Spain by the Arab emir of Saragossa, but the city shut its gates against him and he retired to France.

While the army was defiling through the mountains its rearguard was attacked and annihilated, by Basque mountaineers, according to the French chroniclers; by Arabs, according to the Arabian historians. Among many others were killed "Eggihardus" and "Hrodlandus," prefect of the Marches of Brittany. Charlemagne was never able to avenge this defeat, and it quickly passed into popular tradition, and later into epic poetry.

In the *Chanson de Roland*, Charlemagne conquered all of Spain except Saragossa. The king of that city feared a battle and offered to become his vassal, sending him presents and hostages. The Emperor retreated through the mountains, but the Moorish king treacherously fell upon his rearguard, which included Roland and the other Peers, and slew them every one. But Charlemagne returned, utterly defeated the pagans, and captured Saragossa, the king of which had already died from a wound given him by Roland. The dramatic interest of the poem is furnished by the death of the hero Roland and the treachery of his stepfather, Ganelon.

Title. **Marsín**, in the *Chanson de Roland*, *Marsilie*, king of Saragossa.

3, 4. **Baldovinos, Beltrán**; no such warriors are known to the *Chanson*, though the young son of Ganelon is called *Baldewins*.

6. **del espada**, mod. *de la espada*.

12. **Renaldos** (Fr. *Renaud*, Ital. *Rinaldo*) is not a character of the *Chanson de Roland*, but became the real hero of the late artistic epics concerning the Peers.

18. **oviesen** = *hubiesen* = *tuviesen* = *tengan*. 'Ill betide the Frenchmen from their native France.'

21. **me**; ethical dative, not to be translated.

38. **tantos de los moros**, mod. *tantos moros*.

40. **cebra**. Whether or not the zebra was ever really ridden by the Arabs, it seems to have been considered by the Spaniards a fine steed. (Cf. XXV, 4.) Sancho remarks of the supposed Dulcinea: «sin espuelas hace correr la hacanea

como una cebra» (*D. Quijote*, II, 10). — **rocín** means here simply 'horse.'

45. **hiz** = *hice*, which would fit the assonance equally well. Of course, no image of Muhammed was ever made by a devout Mussulman, as his religion expressly forbids the worship of images.

47. **Abrayma**, in the *Chanson*, *Bramimunde*. Marsín's daughter is not mentioned there.

51. **encantado.** The tradition that Roland was invulnerable does not appear in French before the thirteenth century.

XXI

No **Beltrán** (*Bertrand*) is known to the *Chanson de Roland*, though several appear in later French poems. This r. has been compared to a passage of the *Chanson* (ll. 2184–90, ed. Gröber) where Roland goes over the battle-field seeking out the dead Peers, but the analogy is of the slightest.

There is another later and longer Castilian version (W. 185a), and two traditional ones have been found in Portuguese (*Rom. geral*, I, 207–211). A most irreverent parody beginning «Por la dolencia va el viejo» (D. 1669) appeared as early as the *Cancionero de rs.*, and proves the popularity of the old ballad.

8. Cf. XLI, 8. There are many such formulæ, borrowed from one poem into another, especially among the Carolingian rs. This one indicates the care taken by travelers in a hostile land to avoid notice.

12. **si lo viste;** i.e. *te pregunto si lo viste.*

XXII

The ballad of the Palmer has no connection with any other known tradition, French or Spanish. The special prominence given Mérida, a city not important under Spanish rule, seems to point to an origin in that district.

1. **Mérida** was famous and prosperous under Roman, Visigothic and Moorish sway, but is now utterly decadent. It contains the most extensive Roman ruins on the Peninsula, — two bridges, an arch, two acqueducts, theater, amphitheater, etc.

10. **dijésesme tú**, *dime tú*.

14. **San Juan de Letrán**, Italian *San Giovanni in Laterano*, 'St. John Lateran,' a famous church in Rome, — not Paris. A fantastic geography is to be expected in the Carolingian *rs.*; W. 176 places Paris on the banks of the Duero.

22. **los doce**, ' the twelve Peers,' — Oliver and Roland being of the number.

39. **Sansueña**, which in material taken from the French epics refers to Saxony, was transferred by Spanish writers to a more familiar spot, and interpreted to mean Saragossa, as it probably does here. Cf. *D. Quijote*, II, 26, «la ciudad de Sansueña, que así se llamaba entonces la que hoy se llama Zaragoza.»

46. **vades**, mod. *vayáis*.

58–60. Cf. *Gram. pec.*, VIII, 1.

XXIII. (MF, 358 and 389; MP, XII, 407–408)

A spirited ballad, which from its mention of the "Emperor" seems to belong with the cycle of Charlemagne. Otherwise the subject is quite isolated. The ending appears forced and late. The special insistence on the mystic number seven (not uncommon in the *rs.*, cf. XXIX, 8, 9; XLI, 11) and the reference to dragon's blood have been thought to point to a northern origin. The number seven, however, was commonly thought by Spaniards to possess special virtues; for this reason Alfonso X divided his code of laws into *siete partidas*. Cf. J. Menéndez Pidal, *Colección*, p. 81, note. Lockhart translated this poem (*The Avenging Childe*).

1. Cf. XII, 1, note.

5. **sacarían un arador;** a realistic expression, but none the

less genuine Castilian, as is shown by the proverb: «No se saca arador con pala de azadón.» In some of the ballads of king Roderick (W. 3*a*, 3*b*) the king employs a curious attention in his love-making:

«sacándole está aradores — de su odorífera mano.»

9. **perfilar** seems to be used for *afilar*. Damas Hinard and Puymaigre both translate: «Il allait l'aiguisant dans (sur) les ailes de son faucon.»

10. Cf. *Gram. pec.*, VIII, 1.

22. 'I had seven brothers, and he has left none but me.'

XXIV. (MF, 390; MP, XII, 494–496)

The two stratagems of war related here are well known to medieval literature (see O. M. Johnston, *Sources of the Spanish Ballad on D. García*, in *Revue hispanique*, XII (1905), 281–298), but no other story comes close enough to this to prove any borrowing. It is quite within the range of possibility that the episode occurred as related, but in that case the hero still awaits identification.

7. **para ella acompañar.** Cf. XXXIX, 2 and 7, and *Gram. pec.*, III, 1.

8. **Urueña,** a city in the province of Valladolid on the slope of the Monte de Torozos. It has well preserved ancient walls. — **para con ella casar,** 'that I might live there with her.'

12. The day of St. John the Baptist has been an occasion of festivities and love-making all over Europe. On that day young men and maidens among both Spaniards and Moors go out early to gather flowers and celebrate the definitive advent of summer. In the *rs.* the expression **mañana de San Juan** became almost stereotyped as a phrase to fix the time of any event, whether appropriate to the day or not. (Cf. XXX, 2; XXXIII, 1; XLIII, 9.) In the present case there is possibly an implied reproach that the Moors broke the un-

written truce of the holiday. Remarks on the peculiar cus-
toms of the day and of the night before, like those of our
Hallowe'en, may be found in the foreword to Lockhart's
"Song for the Morning of the Day of St. John the Baptist";
in Durán, no. 112, note; and in Damas Hinard, *Rom. esp.*,
II, 285, n. 49.

22. **Alá le quiera pesar;** one might read *les* or, with Durán,
á Alá.

XXV. (MF, 391; MP, XII, 497)

A fragment of unknown origin, but evidently dealing with
two crusaders.

4. **cebra;** see note to XX, 40.

8. **tocas de caminar;** Covarrubias (*Tesoro de la lengua,*
1611) says: «En algunas partes de Espana no traen los hombres caperuças ni sombreros, y usan de unas tocas revueltas
en la cabeça, como son los Vizcaynos y Montañeses.»

10. **Á vuelta de su cabeza,** 'when he (the uncle) turned
his head.'

12. **levantar,** *levantarse.*

XXVI

Translated by Bowring (p. 276).

Traditional versions of Tangier (RMP, *Catál.*, no. 119)
add that the king overheard the conversation between father
and daughter, and married the girl.

3. **palabras para llorar,** 'words to cause tears.'

XXVII. (MF, 388; MP, XII, 498)

Like **Abenámar** and **Paseábase el rey moro,** this *r.* may be
a translation or imitation of a Moorish song. It is also an
excellent example of the fact, often to be observed, that
many of these short poems receive a mysterious charm from
their fragmentary character; in a complete state they might

prove to be commonplace. There are translations by Bowring (p. 40) and Ticknor (I, 110).

1. **de un bel catar,** 'fair to see.' The mod. phrase would be *de buen ver.*

XXVIII. (MP, XII, 507–508)

The theme of **Rico Franco,** "Honor avenged," occurs in popular poems all over Europe, as well as nearer to our purpose in Asturias, Castile, Portugal and among the Spanish Jews (RMP, *Catál.*, no. 85; MP, X, 322; Alonso Cortés, p. 24). Some of the Portuguese versions (*Rom. geral*, I, 148–155) are closely connected with the Castilian one; others (*ibid.*, I, 409–414) much resemble the Asturian (MP, X, 100–105). For comparative references it may suffice here to point to the notes of Child on "Lady Isabel and the Elf-Knight " (*Eng. and Scottish Pop. Ballads*, no. 4, I, 22) and of G. Doncieux on «Renaud le tueur de femmes» (*Rom. populaire de la France*, no. XXX, p. 351). The theme is traced back to a Dutch song, «Heer Halewijn,» which Doncieux accepts in turn as merely a popular rendering of the Biblical story of Judith and Holofernes. In any case, **Rico Franco** is so far removed in story from «Heer Halewijn,» and is in itself so vigorous, spontaneous and effective, that it has all the appearance of entire originality.

8. **de sus ojos tan cortés;** one might expect *corteses*, which would fit the assonance equally well (cf. **reyes,** two lines above); but **cortés** can be construed to agree with **doncella.**

14. **cuchillo lugués.** This phrase, carefully avoided by most translators and commentators (e.g. Puymaigre), is explained by Damas Hinard and St. Prato (*Romania*, XII, 615) to mean 'Luccan knife.' The *coltello lucchese*, according to Prato, became typical, just as Pistoia gave its name to the pistol. **lugués** also means 'of Lugo' (a Spanish city), but there seems to be no special appropriateness in that reference. In the two Portuguese versions from Madeira the weapon

is called a *punhal ingrez* ('English dagger'). One Azores version gives *punhal frances*, and two others make the adjective *joanez*, explained by Th. Braga (*Hist. da poesia pop. port.*, II, 272) as "genovez" ('Genoese'). «Cuchillico de ciprés» sing the Jews of Andrinopolis.

15. «Je couperai de mon manteau des ornements qui ne sont plus à porter» (Puymaigre).

XXIX. (MF, 391; MP, XII, 520)

The supernatural note struck here is very rare in Spanish poetry. The strange apparition from a tree-top, the enchantment, the mysterious departure of the maiden, are traits of a kind one would expect to find in Celtic poetry; but no source of this *r.* has been discovered there. A very similar Portuguese traditional ballad was printed by Almeida-Garrett (*O caçador, Rom. geral*, I, 238). Many other Portuguese versions (*ibid.*, I, 230–263) have traits of resemblance with *La Infantina*, but are contaminated with the *hija del rey de Francia* theme (W. 154). For modern versions in Castilian see Olmeda, p. 74, RMP, *Catál.*, no. 114, and *Rom. esp.*, pp. 122–124.

Bowring (p. 118) and Lockhart both translated this *r.*

3. **roble.** The oak calls to mind the druids, and seems to have been a tree especially associated with enchantments. Cf. Th. Braga, *Hist. da poesia pop. port.*, I, 93–94.

25. '(The sentence shall be) that . . .'

XXX. (MF, 392; MP, XII, 531–533)

The Italian Berchet began his collection of translated *rs.* with this poem, and remarked to the reader: "If you do not enjoy this *romance*, if you do not penetrate its hidden meaning, stop here, follow me no farther; you would be bored and I should be sorry for it." Longfellow underwent the nameless charm of *El Conde Arnaldos:*

> "Most of all, the Spanish ballad
> Haunts me oft, and tarries long,
> Of the noble Count Arnaldos
> And the sailor's mystic song."

He incorporated a free rendering into his poem, and added

> "In each sail that skims the horizon,
> In each landward-blowing breeze,
> I behold that stately galley,
> Hear those mournful melodies;
>
> Till my soul is full of longing
> For the secret of the sea,
> And the heart of the great ocean
> Sends a thrilling pulse through me."

("The Secret of the Sea," in "The Seaside and the Fireside.")

Merely the power of music may be exemplified here, but many, like Berchet and Lockhart, who also made a translation, have seen a mystical and religious meaning, quite in accord with one side of Spanish character. The words of the song itself, given in the note, hardly bear out the second interpretation. The wonderful effects of song upon all creatures have been a popular theme from Orpheus down. The example nearest at hand is the Catalan ballad, «El poder del canto» (Milá, *Romancerillo*, no. 207). The only modern traditional version of *Conde Arnaldos* comes from the Tangier Jews (RMP, *Catál.*, no. 143), and it completes the story by adding that the Count was enticed from home by the mysterious mariner:

> «Tiró la barca el navío — y el infante fué á embarcar.
> Con el ruido del agua — el sueño le fué á llevar;
> con el golpe del martillo — el infante fué á acordar:
> — ¿Quién es ése, cuál es ése — que á mí quiere cautivar,
> siendo yo el conde Fernando, — muchacho y para casar? —
> Otro día de mañana — su resgate fué á llegar, —
> llegar vió siete navíos, — todos en su busquedad.»

It is possible that the old form, truncated and vague as it is, may be more attractive without this newly found addendum.

There is also a metrical rendering of *Conde Arnaldos* by Bowring (p. 78).

1. ¡Quién . . . ventura! 'Would I might be so fortunate!' In mod. Sp. the optative construction with *¡quien!* and the past subjunctive expresses a wish in which the speaker is subject, and it may be so construed in this case. It was not always so, however, as is shown in LVI, 13.

5. de un cendal, mod. *de cendal*.

12. fué á dar = *dió*. Cf. *Gram. pec.*, VII, 4, *b*.

XXXI. (MP, XII, 530-531)

"*Fontefrida*," says Baist, "is a motif from the natural history of the Physiologus, made popular by preaching." The *Physiologus*, or *Bestiary*, was a medieval collection of zoological stories taken from the fabulous Greek naturalists and provided with morals by Christian writers. It was extremely popular, and gave rise to many fables, and, in the Church, to sermon-apologues. In them it is stated that the turtle-dove takes only one consort in its life; that after his death the dove, "mourning for its lost mate, seeks the solitary places of the earth for its habitation, rests upon no green branch, and drinks from no clear spring, but chooses the dead limb for its home and muddies with beak or feet the water which is to satisfy its thirst" (Philip S. Allen, *Turtel-taube*, in *Mod. Lang. Notes*, XIX, 175–177). See the same article for references to the theme in German, Danish, Greek, Old French and Italian folk-songs, and a German translation of *Fontefrida* by Eichendorff. The nightingale in the rôle of villain does not appear outside of the *romance*, if we except a fugitive allusion in a Portuguese popular song noted by J. Leite de Vasconcellos (*A rola viuva na poesia popular portuguesa*, in *Mod. Lang. Notes*, XXI, 33).

The gentle melancholy of the Spanish ballad has often been admired.

1. This line is not easy to render in a way to convey the charm of the original. Bowring's version (p. 387) cannot readily be bettered.

> "Fount of freshness, fount of freshness,
> Fount of freshness and of love."

There is also a translation in Ticknor, I, 111.

2. **van tomar,** mod. *van á tomar.*

XXXII. (MP, X, 133)

Translated by Bowring (p. 80) and by Lockhart under the title "Valladolid." The *r.* has steadily kept its hold upon the people. It was well known in the sixteenth century. (Cf. MP, IX, 220, 278.) Much altered traditional versions have recéntly been collected (MP, X, 132, 192; RMP, *Rs. trads.*, no. 17, and *Catál.*, no. 56; Alonso Cortés, pp. 32–34; Ledesma, p. 164; Milá, *Romancerillo*, no. 227); and its vitality is shown by the adaptation that was sung at the time of the death of Queen Mercedes, first wife of Alfonso XII (died 1878), beginning:

> «¿Dónde vas, rey Alfonsito? — ¿Dónde vas, triste de ti?
> — Voy en busca de Mercedes, — que ayer tarde no la vi.»
>
> (MP, X, 134)

11. **perdí;** to make sense should be *perdió,* which does not fit the assonance. Durán (no. 292) reads «que tal pérdida pierde aquí,» which contains one syllable too many.

13. **desde aquéllas, dos horas,** 'for two hours from that time.' Durán reads «y por más de doce horas.»

20. **cuerpo** is the object, and **tierra** the subject, of **come.**

XXXIII

This dainty little *r. villanesco* was erroneously ascribed by Durán to Alfonso de Alcaudete, who wrote a gloss upon it, not the poem itself. Neither Wolf nor Menéndez y Pelayo seem to have regarded it as popular, and it has somewhat the air of a *r. trovadoresco*, but Ducamin and RMP (*Notas al rom. de F. G.*, p. 486) place it in the popular class. It was translated by Bowring (p. 145).

1. **mañanica, riberica**, are popular diminutives without much additional force.

2. **ribericas de la mar.** The locative use of a noun without a preposition is common in certain phrases, especially «orillas del mar.»

3. A bush, whether of rose or cactus, is still the only clothes-line of Spanish country districts.

XXXIV–XXXV. (MF, 107–129; MP, XI, 133–175)

According to the legend of Roderick, the last Gothic king in Spain, there was in Toledo a mysterious house, never opened, to which each king in succession added a padlock. Roderick, curious and eager for treasure, broke into the house, and found within only a chest containing a painting of men dressed with the costume and arms of Arabs, and an inscription saying: "When this chest is opened, such men as these shall invade and conquer Spain." The prophecy was soon fulfilled. Count Julian, governor for the king in northern Africa, had at court a daughter called La Cava or Florinda, who fell a victim to Roderick's desires. Julian, to avenge his daughter, betrayed his post to the Arabs, and assisted them to invade Spain. Roderick was defeated in an eight-day battle on the Guadalete and fled alone to Portugal, near Viseo. There he met a hermit who received special command from heaven to hear his confession. The weary king was assigned the penance of being shut in a tomb with a serpent which gnawed him till he died.

The legend has been used by Southey for an English epic, "Roderick the Last of the Goths," but its contents are almost wholly original with the poet. Walter Scott's "Vision of Don Roderick" utilizes the fated king only as a peg on which to hang a glowing account of the Peninsular War.

Sober history knows very little of this poetic tale of punished presumption. The woman in the case is altogether lacking. Roderick (reigned 710–711) gained the throne by force of arms, defeating the sons of Witiza, his predecessor. Witiza's sons invoked aid from Africa, and readily obtained it. The Visigothic traitor Julian becomes in history Olban, a Christian Berber, who had been on friendly terms with Witiza and had long defended the stronghold of Ceuta against the invading Arabs. He took advantage of the appeal of the deposed princes to make peace with the Arabs, and accompanied Tárik in his conquest of Spain. Roderick was defeated in the battle of Lake Janda, where he was probably killed; the Arab chroniclers report that his riderless horse and one of his golden boots were found in a quagmire near the battle-field. The Arabs who had begun the invasion as allies of the sons of Witiza, soon dropped the rôle and made themselves masters of all Spain, with the exception of the corner in Asturias where Pelayo and his followers held out among the mountains and began the reconquest. The movement, as far as the Arabs were concerned, was merely part of the rapid conquest of northwestern Africa which took place 707–709 under the leadership of the general Músá ibn Noseyr and his lieutenant Tárik. The invading army was led by Arabs but was composed mostly of Berbers.

The legendary version does not appear in Christian chronicles till four centuries after the events. There existed probably poems based on traditions of the fall of Roderick, but they are lost, and only a few mangled fragments preserved

in the *Crón. de 1344.* Pedro de Corral's *Coronica sarrazyna*
(c. 1443) added a mass of pure fiction to previous tradition
and first gave wide currency to the story of the king's penance.
This book was the source of the *rs.* here given, which are
rather late, and are classed by something of a stretch among
the *juglarescos.*

The authority on the subject is Juan Menéndez Pidal's
Leyendas del último rey godo (Madrid, 1906).

XXXIV. 2. **partes de aliende,** 'distant parts.'

8–15. A reminiscence of two chapters of the *Crón. gen.*
which follow the story of Roderick: the *Loor de España* and
Duelo de España (pp. 310–314).

15. **Asturias,** the mountainous northern province of Spain
where Pelayo with a small band of followers held out against
the invaders and furnished a foothold for the reconquest.

21. **don Orpas** or *Oppas,* a bishop who, with the sons of
Witiza, began the battle on the side of Roderick and deserted
him at the critical moment. Orpas is called sometimes a son
of Witiza and sometimes a brother; and Julian's wife is
spoken of as his sister.

26. **sin . . . nada,** 'without anything ever being known
of him.'

XXXV. Translated by Lockhart and distantly imitated by
Victor Hugo, in *La Bataille perdue,* no. XVI of *Les Orientales.*
Hugo describes the emotions of a Turkish vizir, Reschid,
after he has been defeated by the Greeks.

2. According to the *Crón. gen.,* the battle on the Guadalete
lasted eight days.

8. **velle,** mod. *verle.*

22–25. Maese Pedro, after D. Quijote has smashed his
marionettes (II, 26), remarks:

«puedo decir con el rey Don Rodrigo,

> Ayer fuí señor de España,
> Y hoy no tengo una almena
> Que pueda decir que es mía.»

This is also the only passage which Hugo followed closely (stanza 12):

> «Hier j'avais des châteaux; j'avais de belles villes,
> Des grecques par milliers à vendre aux juifs serviles;
> J'avais de grands harems et de grands arsenaux.
> Aujourd'hui, depouillé, vaincu, proscrit, funeste,
> Je fuis . . . De mon empire, hélas! rien ne me reste.
> Allah! je n'ai plus même une tour à créneaux.»

XXXVI and XXXVII. (MF, 270–278; MP, XI, 348–349)

These two ballads are closely connected in matter and origin. They are included among the *juglarescos* for want of more certain knowledge, although two good judges, Dozy and Menéndez y Pelayo, considered them a product of the early sixteenth century, and in the second of the two the latter critic professes to detect the hand of a «poeta culto.» Both are derived with some change from a form of the *Rodrigo* or *Mocedades del Cid*. There is of course no historical foundation for the events described.

There are two versions accessible to us of the poem relating the youthful adventures of the Cid. The first is known only through the prose chronicle written in 1344 and not yet printed. (Cf. MP, XI, 322–324; RMP, *Ép. cast.*, 122–137.) The object of its author was to inform the eager public of the early life of a hero whose adult career was already sufficiently familiar. The Cid is depicted as a respectful vassal of noble lineage and signal courage. His remarkable feats are inventions of the poet. As regards his marriage, it is stated that Rodrigo killed Count Gómez de Gormaz in a quarrel; Ximena, a daughter of the latter, then presented herself to the king and asked for Rodrigo as her husband, because she believed he would become the most powerful noble in the realm. The king granted her request and wrote to Rodrigo, offering him pardon and a wife. The young hero accepted both with gratitude, and the marriage was celebrated with pomp.

The second version of the Rodrigo is preserved in verse (*Crónica rimada, Bibl. de Aut. Esp.*, XVI, 651–662). It is undoubtedly later, and changes the Cid's character to that of a rebellious, overbearing noble, who keeps his king in constant fear and subjection. That this portrait made an effective appeal to the populace of the day when it was written is shown by its acceptance in the *rs*. The *Crónica rimada* specifies the cause of the quarrel which led to the death of Count Gómez; it was because he had made a foray into the lands of Diego Laínez and stolen his cattle. Ximena asks for Rodrigo's hand more to preserve peace in the kingdom than for personal reasons. The Cid, instead of responding gladly to the king's invitation, fears treachery, comes defiantly, is married against his will and departs in a huff. In this changed attitude it is not hard to see the spirit of the turbulent reigns and violent deeds of Alfonso XI and Pedro el Cruel. (Cf. notes on XIII, 7, and XIV.)

The *romanceristas* of the latter sixteenth century could not accept, if they knew it, the story of the raid on a neighbor's estate, for the nation had outgrown the condition of misgovernment which permitted such anarchy; they therefore invented a hunting-quarrel as the cause of the duel (W. 28). The love of Ximena for the Cid is indicated in the later *rs*. (cf. no. LV), but it remained for Guillén de Castro, in the drama *Las mocedades del Cid* (1599?), to develop the powerful conflict between love and duty which Corneille made famous all over Europe.

XXXVI. Cf. *Crónica rimada*, ll. 341–382. As a poem no. XXXVI is inferior to the following ballad. It contains lines borrowed from other *rs*. of greater age and unity. One passage omitted in this text is taken from *Á Calatrava la vieja*

(W. 19); line 17 seems to be a reminiscence of the juglaresque
ballads on the Marquis of Mantua and Count Dirlos (W. 165
and 164); line 34 recalls at once no. XXV, l. 1, where the expression is more in place than here. But the poem contains
much good epic matter; the student should compare it with
Corneille's *Cid*, IV, 4, and V, 6 and 7. There exist two other
versions (W. 30 and 30*a*), shorter and, according to some,
earlier. Traditional versions have been collected in Tangier
and Orán (RMP, *Catál.*, no. 3).

3. **Lozano**, originally an adjective applied to Count
Gómez, was misunderstood by later generations to be a proper
name in itself.

20 ff. The impotent king, a puppet in the hands of his
powerful vàssals, is a characteristic figure in the decadent
period of the epic, in France and Italy as well as Spain.

24. **igual.** As Puymaigre points out, the Old French word
per had a similar meaning:

> «O est Rollanz le catanie
> Ki me jurat cume *sa per* a prendre?»
> (*Chanson de Roland*, ed. Gröber, ll. 3709-10.)

28-29. **que no era natural,** 'is most extraordinary.' The
modern-sounding comment of the king probably would not
have occurred to a contemporary of the Cid. As presented
in this ballad, Jimena's sudden veering seems queer enough;
the *Crónica rimada* makes it clear that she sacrificed herself
from a patriotic desire to stifle an incipient feud by the most
effectual means. The sacrifice did not appear great in an
age when matches depended very little on the inclination of
either party. In the older poem Jimena makes complaint
to the king in these terms:

> «Rey, dueña so lasrada, e aveme piedat.
> . . . .
> Ffijo de Diego Laynes fissome mucho mal;
> prissome mis hermanos, e matome a mi padre.
> A vos que sodes rey vengome a querellar.
> Señor, por merced, derecho me mandat dar.»

The king fears that in the troubled state of his kingdom Castile may be added to the rebels if he grants her request. She kisses his hand and says:

«Mostrarvos he assosegar a Castilla e a los reynos otro tal.
Datme a Rodrigo por marido, aquel que mato a mi padre.»

36. **vades** = *vayades* = *vayáis*.

XXXVII. *Crónica rimada*, ll. 387–429; cf. RMP, *Ép. cast.*, pp. 141–147. The *r.* follows the earlier epic quite closely in spots, but omits Rodrigo's marriage with Jimena, which is there represented as taking place immediately and is the cause of the hero's angry departure. The series of antitheses in lines 4–10 is very likely imitated from *Castellanos y leoneses* (no. III, 25–31).

9. **afilado,** 'pointed,' if this be the correct reading. Another reading is *afinado* (cf. III, 30).

14. **preguntando;** D. reads *publicando.* In all probability the original form was *pregonando.*

21. **Demándelo su pecado; su** may refer either to Rodrigo or to the dead count.

31–39. Cf. *Crónica rimada*, ll. 405–410.

«Rodrigo finco los ynojos por le bessar la mano.
El espada traya luenga; el rey fue mal espantado.
A grandes voses dixo: Tiratme alla esse pecado.
Dixo estonce don Rodrigo: Querria mas un clavo,
que vos seades mi señor, nin yo vuestro vassallo.
Porque vos la besso mi padre, soy yo mal amansellado.»

XXXVIII. (MF, 221, 290–292; MP, XI, 302, 354–355)

The *1ª crónica general* (p. 519) relates the story of the famous oath exacted by the Cid in Sta. Gadea from Alfonso VI, to the effect that he had no hand in the death of his brother Sancho. The Cid there expresses the wish that the king, in case his oath prove false, may be slain treacherously. The *Crónica particular del Cid*, an extract from one of the later chronicles (printed 1512), adds the detail that his slayer should not be a native of León or Castile. No. XXXVIII is probably related to a degenerate form of the *Cantar del Cerco de Zamora* (cf. p. 121, note); but the exaggerated details of the king's threatened punishment seem to be an invention of this *romancerista*, as also the strange symbols of the **cerrojo** and **ballesta**. In the *1ª crónica* Alfonso swears upon a Bible.

Modern historians find that the oath was exacted of Alfonso by twelve *compurgatores*, of whom the Cid was one, but he is given no special prominence. Cf. RMP, *Ép. cast.*, 71–74.

1. **Sancta Gadea** or *Águeda* ('St. Agatha'), a small Gothic church still existing in Burgos.

4. **cerrojo, ballesta.** Damas Hinard (II, 135, n. 14) suggests that these may symbolize respectively the prison and the death penalty, and Ducamin notes that each has somewhat the form of a cross. The 'bolt' is still exhibited to visitors in the church of St. Agatha at Burgos.

13. **cueros fogueados.** Puymaigre and Damas Hinard translate «cuir passé au feu,» Dozy, «cuir bien tanné.» Ducamin in his glossary says: «*Cueros fogueados* doit signifier cuir bouilli, dont on paraît avoir fait grand cas au moyen âge.» He then cites passages from Littré (s. v. *cuir*) showing that *cuir bouilli* was much used for articles of value. Hatzfeld and Darmesteter define *cuir bouilli* as «cuir de vache qu'on a fait bouillir avec de la cire et de la résine pour le rendre à la fois solide et flexible.»

22–23. Two lines borrowed from XXXVII, 38–39.

24. **mal caballero probado**, a set phrase like *buen caballero probado*, 'known for a faithless knight.'

XXXIX. (MF, 351–352; MP, XII, 368–371)

"One of the most admired of all Spanish ballads," says Lockhart in the note at the head of his translation. It is a representation by indirection and suggestion of the scene told in the *Chanson de Roland* with the utmost possible simplicity and directness (ll. 3705–3722, ed. Gröber). Prcphetic dreams of precisely similar nature to this are, however, attributed to Charlemagne in the *Chanson* (as ll. 2525–54, 2555–69). The reader should not fail to compare this poem with the corresponding passage of the French epic, although the result is rather to the disadvantage of the Spanish. «Nuestro romance es bello,» says Milá, «pero el trozo del *Rollans* es más que bello.»

A better translation than Lockhart's is that of Sir Edmund Head (in Ticknor, I, 121). There are traditional versions among the Spanish Jews (RMP, *Catál.*, no. 21).

7. **para doña Alda holgar.** See *Gram. pec.*, III, 1.

21. **bien oiréis lo que dirá.** The frequent repetition of this and other rime-formulæ is characteristic of the more artificial *rs. juglarescos.* This phrase reminds us too that these poems were meant to be sung or recited by the minstrel to an assembled throng.

XL and XLI. (MF, 344–346; MP, XII, 378–384)

Gaiferos, who appears as *Gaifiers* in the *Chanson de Roland* (ed. Gröber, l. 798) and other French epics, has been identified with an historical personage (Latin *Waifarius*), a duke of Aquitania, who, from his strongholds in southwestern France, made war against Pépin le bref until he was assassinated in 769. But the adventures related in the three well-known Spanish ballads on Gaiferos have nothing to do with his real deeds. The first two, given here, are quite native in matter, and have endured in the oral tradition of Asturias to the present day (JMP, no. XXI). The third (W. 173) is much longer and was given fame by Cervantes (*D. Quijote*, II, 26) in the adventure of the marionettes. Milá and RMP (*Ép. cast.*, 18–21) point out the remarkable similarity of detail between the adventures of Gaiferos in this *r.* and those of Waltarius Aquitanus (a contemporary of Attila, fifth century) as described in a tenth-century Latin poem by the monk Ekkehard.

No. XL was translated by Lockhart.

XL

21–22. A formula which is copied without much change in a later *r.* concerning the siege of Troy (W. 109, ll. 66–67). The 'hawk-hand' is the left (cf. Ducamin, p. 81, n. 2), and so also is the 'stirrup-foot.'

31 ff. The stratagem here related is a commonplace of folk-lore and the medieval epic.

32. The name **Galván** is taken from the cycle of Arthur and the Round Table: 'Gawain.'

42. Durán reads *empezara á.*

XLI

8. Cf. XXI, 8.

27. **estar** instead of *ser,* can be due only to the exigencies of the assonance.

37. **Quien**, as relative pronoun, may refer to a plural antecedent in mod. Sp.

XLII. (MF, 350; MP, XII, 423–425)

An episode of the battle of Roncesvaux is depicted in this well-known and often parodied ballad. The heroes, both Frenchmen, are both creations of the Spanish muse. **Durandarte** is simply a name made from Roland's sword *Durendal* (which even in one French epic, that of the *Quatre Fils Aymon,* is applied to a man). His love-affairs and melancholy end are dealt with in other *rs.* (W. 180, 182; other versions are given, MP, IX, 248 (2), and 323). **Montesinos** is the hero of a whole set of poems of his own (W. 175, 176, 177, 177*a*, 178, 179), mostly long and manifestly juglaresque. The lover who recommends that his heart be conveyed to his mistress is found in some of the books of chivalry; thus Amadís de Gaula to Oriana.

Durandarte and Montesinos were given their great fame by
Cervantes, who based an important scene of the *Quijote*,
that of the Cave of Montesinos (II, 22, 23) upon this poem.
(Cf. *Introduction*, § V.) Lines 6, 7 and 8 are quoted by
Cervantes with little change from this version, but after l. 8
he adds:

«sacándomele del pecho, — ya con puñal, ya con daga.»

D. 1425 is a parody of no. XLII, and D. 436 and 437 contain some sharp satirical comments upon it.

29. **de allá le salen del alma,** 'issue from his very soul.'

XLIII. (MF, 389–390; MP, XII, 387–388)

This *r.* is followed by four others (W. 122, 123, 124, 125),
more or less related to it, from which it appears that Moriana
was rescued from death by her husband; the love-lorn Galván pursued her, and met his end by a lance-thrust. The
name of the villain is the same as that of Gaiferos' stepfather in nos. XL and XLI, and some of the lines are similar
(26–27, and XLI, 29, 30). It seems likely that the story of
Moriana and the Moor Galván is a curious perversion of the
Gaiferos matter, including the rescue of Melisenda by the
hero (W. 173). There is a traditional version from Tangier
(RMP, *Catál.*, no. 61).

In this poem the paragogic *e*'s, removed by Wolf, are given
according to the text of the *Silva de Varios Romances*, 1602.
No reason is apparent for the addition of an *e* to some lines
and not to others. See *Introduction*, § VII.

18. This and the following line are quoted by D. Quijote
in interesting fashion (I, 2). The knight errant addresses the
inn-keeper: «Para mí, señor castellano, cualquiera cosa basta,
porque mis arreos son las armas, mi descanso el pelear, etc.»
The landlord replies: «Según eso, las camas de vuestra merced
serán duras peñas, y su dormir siempre velar.» There is another reference to the same words (*D. Quijote*, II, 64).

The same two lines begin another short *r.* (W. 125), thought to be older than *Moriana*.

It runs thus:

> Mis arreos son las armas, — mi descanso es pelear,
> mi cama las duras peñas, — mi dormir siempre velar.
> Las manidas son escuras, — los caminos por usar,
> el cielo con sus mudanzas — ha por bien de me dañar,
> andando de sierra en sierra — por orillas de la mar,
> por probar si mi ventura — hay lugar donde avadar.
> Pero por vos, mi señora, — todo se ha de comportar.

As RMP points out (*Inf. de Lara*, 418, n. 3), it is without any doubt a fragment of a lost ballad beginning «Á las armas, moriscote.» This line is quoted in the famous *Ensalada* of Prague[1] and in various Portuguese authors of the sixteenth century (see C. Michaëlis de Vasconcellos, *Estudos*, in *Cult. esp.*, IX, 96). Two more lines have been rescued from a music book of 1564 (MP, IX, 211), but the whole of this often quoted old ballad has never been recovered. An artistic parody on it (D. 1670) commences «Á las armas, el buen Conde,» and contains the lines

> «Mis arreos son muchos cuentos,
> Mi descanso es el burlar,» etc.

A religious parody or *r. vuelto á lo divino* (MP, IX, 211) begins «Á las armas, rey del cielo,» and the passage corresponding to W. 125 runs:

> «las armas son mis arreos,
> mi descanso es pelear,
> mi cama el duro pesebre,
> mi dormir siempre es velar,» etc.

---

[1] In the rare collection of *pliegos sueltos* which F. J. Wolf unearthed in the University Library at Prague is a curious *Ensalada de muchos romances viejos y cantarcillos* (*Ueber eine Sammlung spanischer Romanzen*, p. 17). This 'salad' or hodge-podge consists of well-known lines from *rs.* and songs worked together with some adventitious matter into meaningless verse. Its great interest lies in the preservation of fragments of old poems that are not printed elsewhere. A list, not quite complete, of the lines otherwise unknown may be found in MP, IX, 258.

The lost poem, as nearly as one can judge from the paro-
dies, related to an invasion of Spain by the French; the Moorish hero, Moriscote, is called upon to defend his country, and
replies, in part, with the words of the text.

Bowring translated W. 125 (p. 73), and Lockhart made a
free version ("The Wandering Knight's Song") which is
deemed by Saintsbury "a nearly perfect bit of verse."

31. **sin confesare** appears to make no sense. Ducamin
suggests reading *por* for **sin**, a substitution already made by
Timoneda. If the last line were omitted entirely the original
reading would do very well.

XLIV. (MF, 394; MP, XII, 535–540)

No *romance* is more widely known than this. It was much
admired by the German romanticists of the late eighteenth
century, and Friedrich Schlegel wrote a drama upon the same
theme. Bowring and Lockhart translated it, and Ticknor
calls it "one of the most tender and beautiful ballads in any
language." Taking for granted the "fundamental error" of
the exaggerated sacrifice to loyalty, which later became a
commonplace of the Spanish drama, the scenes are drawn in
a lifelike and affecting manner.

The **Conde Alarcos** is a unified poem, written by one who
had an artistic end in view. The author may be Pedro de
Riaño, who is named as such in the broadside that gives the
first printed text (prior to 1517, see RMP, *Leyenda de los Inf.
de Lara*, 121, n. 2). Following a course which in the last
analysis was that of all the so-called popular ballads, the
poem carefully designed by one man passed over to the people,
and gave the many traditional versions that are still found
in Asturias, Tangier, Portugal, Catalonia, etc. (MP, X, 116–
118; 204, 260; RMP, *Rs. trads.*, no. 8; *Catál.*, no. 64; Milá,
Romancerillo, no. 237; *Rom. geral*, I, 488–556).

No historical basis of this story is known. The author may
have invented it, or taken it from tradition.

23. quesistes, mod. *quisisteis.*

24. mal recaudo había. A vague expression, which may be rendered 'there is little opportunity.'

25. par igual; a colloquial phrase, 'equal in rank.'

42. por razón ó por justicia. There is no real opposition between these phrases. Cf. l. 155 and l. 209.

54–59. «Ce passage, qui semble indiquer qu'Alarcos aimait encore l'infante, est une maladresse du poëte.» (Puymaigre.)

79. á ella que le placía; *ella dijo que le placía.*

105. Vades; see note on XXXVI, 36. Here *id* would be the final equivalent.

114–115. The sentence is elliptical. It may be translated 'Who could believe, countess, at seeing your happy face, that as you come to meet me you are near the end of your life?' or 'Who could endure the sight of your joyful face, when,' etc.

119. al conde, 'by the count's appearance'; or perhaps an accusative correlative with tristeza.

135. Echóse sobre los hombros; a dubious phrase, probably 'he leaned back in his chair.' Puymaigre renders «il abaissa sa tête sur sa poitrine»; Damas Hinard, «il pencha sa tête sur son épouse,» which is wholly inadmissible.

141. si . . . decía, 'to tell the truth.'

154. la fe que me tenía, 'the troth which she received from me.'

158. á la fin de vuestra vida; another reading is *y que se os quite la vida.* Either is a mere rime-tag.

163. si . . . matáis. As above in l. 150, the clause introduced by si is in effect an imperative.

189. tuvierdes, *tuviereis.*

196–197. This is an instance of the *emplazamiento.* The innocent person condemned to death summons his judge to meet him before the divine tribunal within a certain time (*plazo*). The classic example is Fernando IV of Castile and León (called thence *el emplazado*) who, legend says, executed on a false charge the two brothers Carvajal. They summoned him to meet them within thirty days, and at the end of that time the king was found dead in bed (1312).

198. The subject of **diciendo** is *la condesa* understood.

199. The subject of **tenía** is *ella*.

205. **obra . . . María**, 'it took but a moment.'

207. **socorré** = *socorred*. Cf. l. 174, **hacémelos** for *hacéd-melos*.

XLV. (MP, X, 51)

On the *rs. tradicionales modernos* see *Introduction*, p. xx. Those given here were all collected in Astúrias and were first published by Juan Menéndez Pidal in his *Colección de los viejos romances que se cantan por los asturianos*, Madrid, 1885. Asturian dialect peculiarities will be noted occasionally both in vocabulary and grammar, but they are not so great as to offer much difficulty.

Concerning Bernardo del Carpio, see note to no. I. Three other versions of no. XLV have been collected in Asturias (MP, X, 49–50; Munthe, no. IV), and Portuguese ballads exist which offer a certain analogy (*Rom. geral*, II, 119–126). Historical subjects are rare in traditional ballads to-day, and still rarer is the preservation of a proper name in its correct form. Here Bernardo liberates his father in a way wholly at variance with the old story.

22. **al medio la plaza.** Cf. French *à mi-chemin*. Possibly *de* once followed **medio**, and was absorbed by its final syllable.

XLVI. (MP, X, 85–86)

A theme familiar to all countries from the time of the Odyssey on (cf. Child, *Eng. and Scot. Ballads*, II, 426–427; MP, X, 85–86). In Spain one version was printed in a broadside of 1605 (W. 156; cf. also 155), and many others have lately been collected from oral tradition in Asturias (MP, X, 84, 138), Castile (Alonso Cortés, pp. 59–60; Ledesma, p. 170),

Catalonia (e.g. Milá, *Romancerillo*, nos. 202, 203), Portugal (*Rom. geral*, I, 33–69), and South America (RMP, *Rs. trads.*, nos. 1 and 2). Cf. also M. Goyri, *Rs. que deben buscarse*, no. 50, and RMP, *Catál.*, nos. 58 and 59.

XLVII. (MP, X, 58–61)

D. Bueso is a name which appears in the *1ª crónica general* as that of a Frenchman who was slain by Bernardo del Carpio. In later times it was borne by real persons. But the hero of the present ballad may have nothing to do with them.

No *r.* de don Bueso appears in any of the old collections, but Juan Álvarez Gato, a fifteenth-century poet, bears witness that such existed, and were considered old and stale in his day. He complains that one night an ugly old woman was substituted for his mistress at her window, and he was given

> «Por palacios tristes cuevas,
> Por lindas canciones nuevas
> Los romances de don Bueso.»

Don Bueso was a burlesque character for the poets of the *siglo de oro* (cf. D. 1710, 1719 and 1646, last line); he seems to have been represented as an old Basque still susceptible to love. The *Ensalada* of Prague (see p. 157, note) cites the first line of a lost *r.* which may have been a parody on no. XXIX:

> «Á caza va el rey don Bueso — por los montes á correr.»

The modern story of Don Bueso has been found in four other Asturian versions (JMP, no. XV; Munthe, no. V; Amador, *Romanzen Asturiens*, pp. 282–283; D. I, lxv), in four from Castile (Alonso Cortés, pp. 51–56), in many from Catalonia (e.g. Milá, *Romancerillo*, no. 250) and among the Spanish Jews (MP, X, 327; RMP, *Catál.*, no. 49). There are Portuguese *rs.* about *Dom Bezo*, but the theme is wholly different. The recognition of a lost brother or sister is a common element of European folk-lore.

Nearly all the *rs.* concerning don Bueso are, like this version, cast in the rare 6+6 form, instead of the usual 8+8. JMP (pp. 296–297) and Th. Braga (*Hist. da poesia pop. port.*, II, 206–217) contend that the short meter is the older, but it is highly improbable, so far as assonating verse is concerned. Poets of the *siglo de oro* often used the 6+6 *romance*, then called *endechas*, for elegiac and amatory themes (D. II, 607–639).

23. **pusieron**, supply *nombre*.

26. **abra puertas de alegría**, 'open the gates of joy.'

32. **do culebras cantan**. «Preciosa metáfora en que se representa la seducción en forma de culebra que, como la sirena de la fábula, tiene mágica voz que atrae á quien la escucha. Muchas veces se repite esta imagen en los romances de Asturias. Siempre en siniestras ocasiones, ó para anunciar males y desgracias, canta la culebra: el genio del mal adoptó la forma de este reptil para engañar al hombre en el Paraíso» (J. M. Pidal, *Colección*, p. 149, note).

XLVIII. (MP, X, 75–76)

A poem whose dreamy nature seems rather Celtic than Spanish, and which may be remotely related to the Tristan and Isolde story. It is found in another Asturian version (JMP, XXVI), in two from Castile (Alonso Cortés, p. 8; Ledesma, p. 159), in several collected among the Spanish Jews (RMP, *Catál.*, no. 55), in South America (Ciro Bayo, *Cantos pops. amers.*, no. II), and in many Portuguese forms (*Rom. geral*, I, 263–276). There is some connection in idea with the French song «La Pernette» (Doncieux, *Romancéro pop.*, no. I).

5. **te me libre**; te is the direct object, **me** the indirect, **or** ethical dative. Cf. XIII, 25, note.

8. **las que dormís, recordad.**

> «Si dormís, las mis doncellas, — si dormides, recordad.»
>
> (*La linda Melisenda* [W. 198], l. 8.)

13. Cf. I, 9; also W. 71 and 71*a*, l. 1:

«Moricos, los mis moricos, — los que ganáis mi soldada.»

Such comparisons show how intimate is the connection between the *rs*. recited to-day and those collected from oral tradition three hundred and more years ago.

25. de muchas. Cf. XIII, 26, note.

43 ff. The legend of the two trees which spring from lovers' tombs is one of the commonest elements of folk-lore. For full comparative references, see Child, I, 96–99. — olivar, used for the assonance, means here no more than oliva. The masculine gender of the former is also to be taken into account.

XLIX. (MP, X, 99)

In the third stanza of the *Ensalada* of Prague (see p. 157, note) occurs the line:

«¿Qué me distes, Moriana, — qué me distes en el vino?»

No other trace than this, in a broadside of the middle of the sixteenth century, was preserved in the old collections, of a *r*. that was evidently popular in its day. Hence it is of exceptional interest that searchers have recovered it from the lips of peasants after a lapse of three centuries.

The solitary Asturian version may be compared with those from Tangier and León (RMP, *Catál.*, no. 86; *Romancero esp.*, pp. 125–128), from Catalonia (Milá, *Romancerillo*, no. 256; and others) and from Portugal (*Rom. geral*, I, 89–94). In English there is a slight analogy with "Lord Randal" (Child, no. 12).

Th. Braga (*Hist. da poesia pop. port.*, I, 233) sees here a relic of the Scandinavian legend of Sigurd, who forgot Brunhilde, his betrothed, on account of a potion given him by the mother of Gudrun, whom he later married. The theory is supported by the name *Gudriana*, which appears in the Catalan versions instead of **Mariana,** but the circumstances are quite different.

8–10. On the composition of witches' poisons, cf. Child, I, 156.

12. J. M. Pidal recalls in this connection the tragic story of Sancho García, son of Garci Fernández of Castile (*Crón. gen.*, p. 454). His mother desired to usurp the rule, and tried to poison him. Sancho was warned by servants of what was prepared for him, and forced his mother to drink the potion first. It is said that since then women always drink before men in Castile (cf. D. 714).

L. (MP, X, 112–115)

A form of the most famous of French popular songs, «Le roi Renaud,» which ramified all over the territory speaking Romanic languages. It in turn has been traced back to Scandinavia, and thence to Germany. See the comprehensive study of G. Doncieux: *La Chanson du Roi Renaud*, etc., in *Romania*, XXIX, 219–256. Many Spanish and Catalan versions are found, and one Portuguese. See MP, X, 110–115; 177; 259; Alonso Cortés, p. 80; RMP, *Catál.*, no. 75; Milá, *Romancerillo*, nos. 204 and 210; and *Romania*, XI, 585.

The importance of «Le roi Renaud» makes it the most desirable poem to set before the student as an example of the transmission of folk-songs. Doncieux's *Texte critique* follows:

LE ROI RENAUD

Le roi Renaud de guerre vint,
Portant ses tripes en sa main.
Sa mére étoit sur le créneau,
Qui vit venir son fils Renaud.

«Renaud, Renaud, réjouis-toi!
Ta femme est accouché' d'un roi.»
— «Ni de la femme, ni du fils
Je ne saurois me réjouir.

«Allez, ma mére, allez devant;
Faites-moi faire un beau lit blanc:
Guère de tems n'y demorrai,
A la minuit trépasserai.

«Mais faites-l'moi faire ici bas,
Que l'accouché' n'entende pas.»
Et quand ce vint sur la minuit,
Le roi Renaud rendit l'esprit.

Il ne fut pas le matin jour,
Que les valets ploroient tretous;
Il ne fut tems de déjeûner,
Que les servantes ont ploré.

«Dites-moi, ma mére m'ami',
Que plourent nos valets ici?»
— «Ma fille, en baignant nos chevaus,
Ont laissé noyer le plus beau.»

— «Et pourquoi, ma mére m'ami',
Pour un cheval plorer ainsi?
Quand le roi Renaud reviendra,
Plus beaus chevaus amènera.»

«Dites-moi, ma mére m'ami',
Que plourent nos servantes ci?»
— «Ma fille, en lavant nos linceuls,
Ont laissé aller le plus neuf.»

— «Et pourquoi, ma mére m'ami',
Pour un linceul plorer ainsi?
Quand le roi Renaud reviendra,
Plus beaus linceuls achètera.»

— «Dites-moi, ma mére m'ami',
Pourquoi j'entens cogner ici?»
— «Ma fill', ce sont les charpentiers
Qui raccommodent le planchier.»

— «Dites-moi, ma mére m'ami',
Pourquoi les seins sonnent ici?»
— «Ma fill', c'est la procession
Que sort pour les Rogations.»

— «Dites-moi, ma mére m'ami',
Que chantent les prêtres ici?» —
— «Ma fill', c'est la procession
Qui fait le tour de la maison.»

Or, quand ce fut pour relever,
A la messe el voulut aller;
Or, quand ce fut passé huit jours,
El voulut faire ses atours:

«Dites-moi, ma mére m'ami',
Quel habit prendrai-je aujourd'hui?»
— «Prenez le vert, prenez le gris,
Prenez le noir, pour mieus choisir.»

— «Dites-moi, ma mére m'ami',
Ce que ce noir-là signifi'?»
— «Femme qui relève d'enfant,
Le noir lui est bien plus séant.»

Mais quand el fut emmi les chans,
Trois pâtoureaus alloient disant:
«Voilà la femme du seignour
Que l'on enterra l'autre jour.»

«Dites-moi, ma mére m'ami',
Que dient ces pâtoureaus ici?»
— «Ils nous dient d'avancer le pas,
Ou que la messe n'aurons pas.»

Quand el fut dans l'église entré',
Le cierge on lui a présenté;
Aperçut, en s'agenouillant,
La terre fraîche sous son banc:

«Dites-moi, ma mére m'ami',
Pourquoi la terre est rafraîchi'?»
— «Ma fill', ne l'vous puis plus celer,
Renaud est mort et enterré.»

— «Puisque le roi Renaud est mort,
Voici les clés de mon trésor.
Prenez mes bagues et joyaus,
Nourrissez bien le fils Renaud.»

«Terre, ouvre-toi, terre, fens-toi,
Que j'aille avec Renaud mon roi!»
Terre s'ouvrit, terre fendit,
Et si fut la belle englouti'.

LI

On the *rs. eruditos*, see *Introduction*, p. xxii. On the story of the *Infantes de Lara*, see note to nos. IV–VI.

The first edition of Lorenzo de Sepúlveda's *Romances nuevamente sacados de historias antiguas de la crónica de España* appeared in 1551. The second edition (1566) contained in addition to Sepúlveda's own compositions some by a «cauallero Cesario, cuyo nombre se guarda para mayores cosas.» The *rs.* of the unknown gentleman are superior to the others in freedom and spirit. No. LI is one of his. He merely versified a chapter of the *Crónica general* published by Ocampo in 1541. Ticknor translated part of this ballad (I, 127).

22. **Nuño.** See note on V, 14.

47. **menor** =*el menor*. **Fernán González** was not the youngest, but the fourth in age, of Gonzalo Gústioz's sons.

LII

Sepúlveda made this piece of verse from the *Crónica general* of 1541. The legend does not belong to the early Cid tradition and does not appear in the *1ª crónica general* (cf. p. 120).

It is related in the *Crón. rimada*, ll. 557–579. A very similar story was told of Edward the Confessor of England (*r.* 1042–66), and it was known in Spain, since it found a place in chap. VII of the *Castigos e documentos del rey don Sancho* (end of the thirteenth century); see *Bibl. de Aut. Esp.*, vol. 51, pp. 98b, 99a.

2. The cathedral at Santiago de Compostela is supposed to contain the grave of St. James the Greater, and is one of the most famous pilgrimage resorts in Europe.

8. According to the *Crónica rimada*, this adventure took place at the Vado de Cascajar, on the Duero. The precise location of the ford is not known, but it was near San Esteban de Gormaz, southwest of Soria. Cf. RMP, *Inf. de Lara*, p. 199.

46. **Martín González;** according to tradition a champion appointed by the king of Aragon to fight with the Cid in order to decide whether the city of Calahorra should belong to Aragon or Castile (*Crón. rimada*, ll. 499–545; 580–615).

LIII. (MF, 301–302; MP, XII, 86–92)

This *r.* is taken directly from Rodríguez de Almela's *Valerio de las Historias* (1487), a compilation of historical traditions. The event is not vouched for by any valid authority, but represents in a fairly truthful way the relations between king and nobles at the time. Exemption from taxes had always been a privilege of the latter. Alfonso VIII reigned 1158–1214.

2. **las Navas;** the decisive battle of Las Navas de Tolosa (in the Sierra Morena, near the pass of Despeñaperros) was won by Alfonso in 1212 over the Almohades (Moors).

3. **don Diego;** Diego de Haro, died 1238, one of the great nobles of the time.

7. **Cuenca** was captured by Alfonso in 1177.

18. **Don Nuño de Lara**, one of the leaders of the party of Laras, who during Alfonso's minority supported him against

the Castros, who attempted to place Fernando II of León on the Castilian throne.

25. **la Glera**, the *Glera del Arlanzón*, formed by the pebbly bed of that river outside Burgos.

29. **no será dél acatado;** an awkward and obscure reading of the *Canc. de rs. sin año*, which Durán corrected to *no será desacatado*. Ducamin attempts to interpret the original, thus: «Je comprends, 'no será acatado del tributo,' c'est-à-dire il ne sera pas considéré par le tribut comme collecteur et le tribut refusera de se livrer à lui.» This seems strained. The reading of the *Silva de varios romances* (1550), *de ellos no será acatado*, is certainly wrong. The corresponding passage in Almela shows clearly that Durán's correction conveys the right meaning, and probably was the correct form, distorted by a mere misprint. Almela reads: «que embie ahi aquel cogedor que los ha de coger, y que nos le daremos este pecho como siempre dieron aquellos donde venimos, y *quanto es al su cuerpo non venga acá, ca donde él viniesse facerle hemos conoscimiento como á nuestro Señor natural, y guardaremos toda su honra:* mas aquellos que le esto consejaron y quisieren ser cogedores vengan acá, y hallarán tal recaudo qual á nos cumple de les dar, assi como siempre ficieron aquellos donde venimos.» The passage covering the whole *r.* is quoted by MP, XII, 88–91.

40. **por lo que no había pecado,** 'for an offense which he did not commit.'

42. Almela: «La libertad y franqueza no es comprada por oro.» It is a classical quotation, coming from the Æsopian fable of *The Dog and the Wolf:* «Non bene pro toto libertas venditur auro.» The phrase has a long history in Spanish literature, beginning with the *1ª crónica general* (p. 73b, l. 47) and including the *Libro de los Enxemplos* (no. CLXXVI), Juan Ruiz's *Libro de buen amor* (copla 206, ed. Ducamin), Fernán Pérez de Guzmán (MP, I, 234) and the *Corbacho* of Martínez de Toledo (ed. Pérez Pastor, p. 18). See K. Pietsch, in *Mod. Lang. Notes*, 1909, pp. 55–56. Pietsch, however, fol-

lows the curious blunder of Clemencín (edition of *D. Quijote*, I, Prólogo, note 14), already exposed by MP (XII, 91), and considers the present *r.* as *by* Diego López de Haro, a poet of the *Cancionero general* of 1511, instead of *about* D. Diego de Haro.

LIV. (MP, XI, 239–240; RMP, *Notas para el rom. de Fernán González,* 477–479)

Some have considered this poem popular, but it is clearly artificial in most respects. RMP classes it as "semi-erudite," i.e. a *r.* the material for which was taken from an early chronicle, worked over and filled out by a late poet. Menéndez y Pelayo thinks Lope de Vega might be the author. For the story, see p. 111 and cf. *1ª crón. gen.,* pp. 414*b*–415*b*.

10. **á las vueltas que da el sol,** 'se guidant sur le soleil' (Damas Hinard).

17–20. When the princess released Fernán González from prison she was unable to remove his fetters. An archpriest who was out hunting met the pair and took advantage of the count's helplessness to offer violence to doña Sancha. He was however slain with his own dagger, and his mule aided the fugitives materially.

24. **Almanzor,** the "ever-victorious" general and prime minister of Hishâm II, caliph of Cordova. He ravaged the Christian states toward the end of the tenth century and died in 1002.

LV. (MF, 283–285; MP, XI, 350–351; *Crón. gen.,* 506–508)

A very well-known ballad which was once thought to be older than it is. The last three lines are contrary to the spirit of the true *r. viejo,* and in fact the last six sound like the invention of a would-be archaic poet, appended to an older fragment.

The scene is in Zamora, when the Cid was sent to Urraca

as ambassador. The notion that Urraca loved the Cid first
appears here; it was amplified in the dramas of Guillén de
Castro and Corneille. It is a sentimental perversion of a
statement in the Chronicles that the two were educated together in the house of Arias Gonzalo. There is a translation
of the first eleven lines in Ticknor, I, 130.

2. **debría,** *debería.*

3. The *1ª crónica general* states (p. 487a and 506b) that the
Cid was knighted by Fernando I during the siege of Coimbra.
That Portuguese city was captured by Fernando in 1064.
The ceremony of knighting always took place at an altar of
St. James.

12. **destigallo,** an unknown word which the earliest editions bear. Later editions of the *Canc. de rs.* read *castigallo.*
Durán corrected to *desviallo.* Ducamin suggests *desligallo,*
which seems natural and makes good sense. We need not
suppose, with Ducamin, that the Cid intends to follow the
example of Count Alarcos; by the royal influence a divorce
might have been procured.

13. **discrepallo;** this verb is ordinarily used only as intransitive. «Discrepallo doit se traduire: aller contre le fait
accompli, contre le mariage sanctionné par l'église» (Ducamin).

LVI

Six lines of this poem were printed as early as 1511 *(Canc.
general,* compiled by Hernando del Castillo). The nearly
perfect rime and lyric tone indicate that it is the work of a
cultured poet of the end of the fifteenth century. It is therefore strictly to be classed as a *r. trovadoresco.* It has been
translated by Lockhart and Bowring.

Modern traditional versions have been found in Catalonia
(Milá, *Romancerillo,* no. 239), Castile, Andalusia and Portugal
(C. Michaëlis de Vasconcellos, *Estudos,* in *Cultura esp.,* XI,
p. 724 ff.; Alonso Cortés, pp. 20, 22).

1–3. This little spring-song could be paralleled many times in the works of Provençal and Galician poets. As an example take a passage from the historical *Poema de Alfonso Onceno* (fourteenth century; stanzas 411–413):

«Allí quando vienen las flores
E los árboles dan fruto,
Los leales amadores
Este tienpo preçian mucho,

Asy commo el mes de mayo
Cuando el ruy-sennor canta,
Rresponde el papagayo
De la muy fermosa planta.

La calandra del otra parte,
Del muy fermoso rrosal,
El tordo que departe
El amor que mucho ual.»

13. **quién . . . diese**, 'would that some one would give me.' Cf. note on XXX, 1.

15. **criado fuese**, *con tal que fuese criado.*

18. **lima sorda.**

«El diablo trae una sorda lyma
Con que las vidas nos viene tajando,»

says an anonymous writer of the *Cancionero de Baena* (c. 1445; MP, I, 170). Juan del Encina includes among the goods of a poor student (*La Almoneda;* in MP, VII, xlix)

«una buena lima sorda
para excusar alcabalas.»

Judging by the poets' familiarity with this special implement, jail-breaking must have been a highly developed profession in the turbulent fifteenth century.

LVII

A *r. morisco*, with all the gallantries and refinements of its class. A great number of such poems were written about 1600, of all degrees of merit. It is needless now to dwell on the fact, once stoutly denied, that the substance of these poems is purely imaginary, that the characters are fictitious and that the customs described have nothing to do with real Moorish habits of life.[1] (Cf. Wolf, *Studien*, pp. 518–533.) If the *rs. moriscos* are faithful pictures of manners in any time and place, it is not of Granada under the rule of the Moors, but of court life at Valladolid and Madrid in the latter half of the sixteenth century. Probably not even so much can be said for them. In historical value they are to be compared exactly to G. Pérez de Hita's *Historia de los bandos de los Zegríes*, etc. (1595); that is to say, they relate romantic adventures of love and war, with a sprinkling of Moorish names, costumes and a few real customs. But there are in these essentially artificial verses many ingenious conceits and many brilliant descriptions. For a time they crowded out the old national subjects (see note on no. XI).

Of no. LVII Durán says: «Es composición tan bella y popular que se inserta en todas las colecciones de su género desde fines del siglo XVI en que se compuso, hasta el día. De él se han hecho muchas imitaciones y algunas parodias.» Proof of its contemporary popularity is found in another *r.* (D. 257) which declares that «Mira, Zaide, que te aviso» was repeated by sailors, tailors, apothecaries, kitchen-maids, men, women and children, until poor Zaide had no street left to pass through. It is only one of nineteen in Durán's collection which relate the loves and jealousies of Zaida and Zaide the talkative. Long series dealing with one hero were the rule

[1] Durán, who lived in the controversial period, still believed that the *rs. moriscos* reflected Moorish manners. There is, however, little excuse for Epiphanius Wilson, who persists in that notion (preface to his translations, *Moorish Ballads*, in *The World's Great Classics*).

in the *rs. moriscos*, and every author felt at liberty to add a new adventure.

37. **Abencerraje.** See note on XVIII, 28.

38. **«Quien tal hace, que tal pague,»** 'As a man sows, so let him reap.'

LVIII

On the *rs. vulgares*, see *Introduction*, p. xix; Durán, I, xxviii–xxxiii; Wolf, *Studien*, 542–551.

No. LVIII may date from the seventeenth century, although the broadside from which it is taken was printed in the nineteenth. It is an example of one class of "blind-beggar ballads," that dealing with romances and folk-lore, — the novelesque class. The *rs. vulgares* embrace many other subjects, such as Spanish history, lives of saints, captivity in Africa, etc., and particularly the life stories of thieves and rogues. *El violín encantado* is a bit of folk-lore; it appears in almost identical form in Grimm's *Kinder- und Hausmärchen* («Der Jude im Dorn»); in the English translation, "The Magic Fiddle").

The exordium to the reciter's audience is a characteristic feature of the vulgar ballad and is especially well developed in this specimen. It is unnecessary to point out in detail the rime-tags, careless language and unnatural psychology that distinguish this kind of *r*. The style is marked by prosiness and loose diction; in the grammar the reader will note frequent omissions of the conjunction *que* after a verb of saying, a colloquial construction.

The transition from the noble old ballads to this fitly represents the reduction of a high-spirited people to a state of intellectual impotence under the civil and religious despotism that began with the Emperor Charles V.

11–12. The sort of lottery here referred to is that in which five numbers are drawn by lot from among ninety, and ticket-holders are rewarded according to the lucky numbers or combinations of them which they have picked. It is no longer in use in Spain, but the Italian state lottery of to-day and the "policy" of the United States are of similar type. The classic example of a 'tern' is the "nigger-gig," 4–11–44.

70 ff. The attitude displayed in this poem toward the Jews may be taken as typical of the Spanish and even European point of view in the sixteenth, seventeenth and eighteenth centuries. The Jews had enjoyed perfect freedom and even special privileges in Castile prior to 1200; after that time the lower classes became more and more hostile to them, partly on account of the preachings of certain Roman Catholics, and partly from envy of their wealth and prosperity and rancor at their alleged extortions. The Castilian and other monarchs of the Peninsula received great services from the money and ability of the Jews, and stood by them long after popular persecution of them had begun; but the time came when the rulers followed the main current, and a series of laws imposing restrictions and disabilities upon the Jews culminated in the decree for their expulsion from all Spanish territory (March 31, 1492), which has been called the one grave error of Ferdinand and Isabella. The exiles scattered all over the Mediterranean region, and it is in their colonies, especially in Tangier, Salonika and Constantinople, that have been recently collected the interesting *rs.* referred to in many notes. See RMP, *Catálogo del romancero judío-español.*

VOCABULARY

ABBREVIATIONS

EMPLOYED IN THE VOCABULARY

adj.	adjective	*intr.*	intransitive
adv.	adverb	*m.*	masculine
arch.	archaic	*mod.*	modern
conj.	conjunction	*pl.*	plural
dim.	diminutive	*p. p.*	past participle
f.	feminine	*prep.*	preposition
fig.	figuratively	*pr. n.*	proper noun
impers.	impersonal	*pron.*	pronoun
interj.	interjection	*refl.*	reflexive
interr.	interrogative	*tr.*	transitive

The articles, pronouns and demonstrative adjectives are omitted, unless there is some special reason for their presence.

Adjectives having a masculine termination in –o and feminine in –a are given in the masculine form only.

VOCABULARY

A

á, to, at, in, by, with; of, from;
uno — uno, one by one; —
que, to the end that.

abajo, down; río —, down
stream.

abarca, *f.*, coarse leather san-
dal.

Abenámar, *pr. n. m.*

Abencerraje, *pr. n. m.*

abollar, to dent.

abrasar, to burn, set on fire.

Abrayma, *pr. n. f.*

abrazar, to embrace.

abrir, to open (*tr. and intr.*).

acá, hither, here.

acabar, to finish, end.

acatar, to respect.

acebo, *m.*, holly-tree.

acento, *m.*, accent.

aceptar, to accept.

acerado, of steel, steel-tipped.

acero, *m.*, steel.

acicalar, to polish.

acompañar, to accompany.

aconsejar, to advise, give
counsel; *refl.*, to take counsel.

acontecer, to happen, befall.

acordar, to resolve, determine, agree upon; *refl. with*
de, to remember; se me
acuerda, I remember.

acordojarse (*Asturian word,
cf. arch.* cordojo, *anguish*),
to grieve, sorrow.

acorrer, to help, succor.

adamar, to love passionately.

adarga, *f.*, shield (*of leather,
oval or heart-shaped*).

adarve, *m.*, flat top of a
wall.

adelantado, *m.*, the former
title of the military and
civil governor of a frontier
province.

adelante, ahead, forward.

adeudado, *m.*, one under ob-
ligations to another, re-
tainer.

adiós, farewell, good-by.

adjudicar, to adjudge, award.

admitir, to admit, accept.

adonde, whither; (*arch. for*
donde *or* en donde) where;
adónde, *same interr.*

adorar, to adore.

adormescido (*arch. for* ador-mecido), drowsy, sleepy.

adormirse (*arch.*), to fall asleep.

afeitar, to trim, cut the hair of.

afilar, to whet, grind; to sharpen, point.

afinado, fine, of fine material.

afligirse, to be afflicted, repine.

aflojar, to loosen, let go.

afrentar, to insult.

afuera, away.

agora (*arch. for* ahora), now.

agradecer, to be grateful (*to one for something*).

agradecido, grateful.

agramente (*arch. for* agria-mente), bitterly.

agraviar, to offend, injure.

agua, *f.*, water.

aguadero, *adj.*, waterproof.

aguardar, to await.

aguijada, *f.*, goad.

águila, *f.*, eagle.

aguililla, *f.*, eaglet.

aguinaldo, *m.*, Christmas *or* New Year's present.

ahí, there.

ahijado, *m.*, godchild. *See note to* XIV, 18.

ahincar (*arch.*), to press.

ahogarse, to be drowned.

ahora, now.

ahorcar, to hang (*on a gallows*).

ahorrar, to spare.

aína, quickly.

ajedrez, *m.*, chess.

ajustar, to make out, draw up.

ajuste, *m.*, agreement, settlement.

ala, *f.*, wing.

Alá, *pr. n. m.*, Allah.

alameda, *f.*, poplar grove.

alano, *m.*, mastiff.

Alarcos, *pr. n. m.*

alarde, *m.*, boasting; hacer —, to boast.

alargar, to lengthen, stretch out.

alazán,–na, *adj.*, sorrel (*color*).

albergar, *tr.*, to harbor, shelter; *intr.*, to lodge.

albor, *m.*, dawn.

alborotar, to excite, alarm.

albricias, *f. pl.*, reward for bringing good tidings.

alcaide, *m.*, jailer, warden.

alcalde, *m.*, mayor; justice of the peace.

alcance, *m.*; en su —, in pursuit of him.

alcanzar, to reach, obtain; to overtake.

alcaria, ? (XX, 27).

alcázar, *m.*, fortress.

Alda, *pr. n. f.* (*French* Alde, Aude).

alegrarse, to rejoice.

alegre, merry, glad, light-hearted.

alegría, f., joy, pleasure; festivity.

alevosía, f., perfidy.

alevoso, treacherous, false.

alfanje, m., simitar (a short, curved, one-edged sword).

alfaquí, m., wise man, doctor.

alférez, m., standard-bearer. See note to XVII, 4.

algarabía, f., Arabic language.

algo, pron., anything, something; adv., any, somewhat.

alguacil, m., constable.

Alhama, pr. n.

Alhambra, pr. n. f.

alianza, f., alliance, league.

Alicante, pr. n. m.

aliende, arch. for allende.

alimpiar (arch. for limpiar), to clean, wash.

aliñado, p. p., prepared, arranged; véolo mal —, I think it can ill be done.

Alixares, pr. n. m. pl., Alijares.

alma, f., soul; esposa del —, dear wife.

Almanzor, pr. n. m.

almejía, f., small cheap cloak worn by poor Moors.

almena, f., merlon (of a battlement; the raised part between two embrasures).

Almenar, pr. n.

Almería, pr. n. (important seaport southeast of Granada; 47,000 inhabitants).

almete, m., helmet.

alnado, m., husband's son by another woman, stepson.

Alonso, pr. n. m., Alfonso.

Álora, pr. n.

altar, m., altar.

alterar, to change, perturb.

alteza, f., highness.

altivo, proud.

alto, high, lofty, tall; loud.

alzar, to raise.

allá, there, thither.

allegar, tr., to bring near; intr. (arch. for llegar), to arrive.

allén, arch. for allende.

allende, adv. and prep., beyond.

allí, there, then; por —, that way.

ama, f., nurse.

amainar, to die down, soften (of wind).

amanecer, to dawn.

amar, to love.

amargar, to embitter; to offend.

amargo, bitter.

ambo, m., "saddle" (combination of two numbers in the lottery).

ambos, -as, adj. and pron., both.

amenazar, to threaten.

amenguar, to disgrace, dishonor.

amigo, -a, *m. and f.*, friend, lover.

amo, *m.*, master.

amor, *m.*, love; object of love; *pl.*, loved one; amours, love-affairs; tener mal de —, to be love-sick.

amortecido, fainting, swooning.

andanza; de mala —, ill-starred, unlucky.

andar, to go, move, walk; (XXIX, 9) to pass.

andas, *f. pl.*, litter, bier.

ánima, *f.*, soul.

animal, *m.*, animal.

animoso, gallant, brave.

ansí, *arch. for* así.

ansiar, to long for.

antaño, *adv.*, last year, long ago.

ante, before.

antes, before; — que, before.

anular, to annul.

añafil, *m.*, straight Moorish trumpet.

año, *m.*, year.

apaciguar, to calm, pacify.

aparejar, to prepare, make ready.

aparejo, *m.*, means, equipment.

apariencia, *f.*, appearance; conjecture.

apartado, retired, apart.

apartar, to lead aside; to separate.

apearse, to alight, dismount.

apellidarse, to be surnamed.

apenas, barely, scarcely; no . . . —, no sooner.

apercebir (*arch. for* apercibir), to prepare, make ready.

aposentar, to lodge, assign lodgings.

aposento, *m.*, room.

aprehender, to seize, take into custody.

apretar, to compress, bind tight, draw tight.

apriesa, quickly, at once.

aprisa = apriesa.

aprisionar, to imprison, confine.

aprovechar, to profit, avail.

apuesto, attractive, neat.

apuntar, to aim at.

aquejar, to pain.

aquel, -lla, -llo, *adj.*, that; *pron.*, that one, he who.

aquese, *arch. for* ese.

aqueste, *arch. for* este.

aquí, here.

Arabiana, *pr. n.*

arada, *f.*, plowed ground.

arador, *m.*, mite (*insect which burrows under the skin*).

Aragón, *pr. n.*, Aragon.

aragonés, –sa, *adj.*, Aragonese.

árbol, *m.*, tree.

arco, *m.*, bow.

arena, *f.*, sand.

arenal, *m.*, sandy spot.

Arias, *pr. n. m.*

Arlanzón, *pr. n.* (*a small
stream flowing through Burgos; a town upon the stream,
east of Burgos*).

arma, *f.*, weapon, arm, arms;
hombre de —, *see* hombre.

armada, *f.*, navy, fleet.

armar, to arm, equip; to
draw, cock; to erect, set up;
refl., to be arranged, take
place.

Arnaldos, *pr. n. m.*, Arnold.

arnés, *m.*, armor.

arrancar, to pull out, tear
away.

arras, *f. pl.*, thirteen gold
coins given by the bride-
groom to the bride at the
wedding; dowry.

arrastrar, to drag.

arrecoger, *arch. for* recoger.

arreglado á, conformably to.

arremeter, *tr.*, to urge on;
intr., to hasten, spur; —
con, to attack.

arreo, *m.*, adornment, decora-
tion, dress.

arrepentirse, to repent, regret.

arriba, up, upward, up-stairs.

arrimarse á, to lean against,
approach.

arrojar, to hurl, throw, spit
out.

arroyo, *m.*, rivulet, stream.

artero, cunning, artful.

artillería, *f.*, artillery.

arzobispo, *m.*, archbishop.

asaz, *arch.*, enough, much,
greatly.

asegurar, to make certain, re-
assure.

asemejarse, to resemble.

asentar, to seat, fix, pitch
(*camp*).

asestar, to aim, strike with a
weapon.

así, thus, so; also.

asir, to seize.

asomar, to appear, come into
view.

asosegar, *arch. for* sosegar.

asta, *f.*, shaft, shank.

astroso, vile, despicable.

astucia, *f.*, cunning.

Asturias, *pr. n. f. pl.* (*a province of Spain, on the Bay of
Biscay*).

atal, *arch. for* tal.

atar, to tie.

atender, to await, wait for.

atento, attentive.

atestar, to cram, stuff.

atrás, behind, backward.

atravesar, to traverse, go
through.

atreverse, to venture, dare.

atronar (*arch. for* tronar), to thunder, resound.

aullido, *m.*, howl.

aun, aún, yet, still; even; also, too.

aunque, although.

ave, *f.*, bird.

avecica, avecilla, *f.*, little bird.

Ave María, *m.*, Hail Mary (*a short prayer of the Catholic Church*).

avenirse (con), to settle (with), make peace (with).

aventajado, excellent, surpassing.

avezado, accustomed.

avisar, to notify, warn; — de, warn against.

¡ay! ah! alas!; ¡—de! alas for!

ayer, yesterday.

ayo, *m.*, tutor, governor.

ayuda, *f.*, assistance, aid.

ayudar, to help, aid, assist.

Azoguejo, *pr. n.* (*dim. of* azogue = *Arabic* es-sôq, *market-place*).

azor, *m.*, goshawk.

B

babieca, *m.*, idiot, numskull.

Babieca, *pr. n. m.*

bailar, to dance.

Baldovinos, *pr. n. m.*, Baldwin.

ballesta, *f.*, crossbow; stave (*of a bow*).

ballestero, *m.*, crossbowman.

banco, *m.*, bank, shoal.

banda, *f.*, band.

bandera, *f.*, banner.

banquete, *m.*, banquet, feast.

bañar, to bathe.

baptizar (*arch. for* bautizar), to baptize; to act as godfather to (V, 36).

baraja, *f.*, pack (*of cards*).

barba, *f.*, beard; *pl.*, beard.

barca, *f.*, boat, skiff.

barquero, *m.*, boatman.

barragán, –na, *arch.*, strong, brave.

barrio, *m.*, quarter (*of a city*).

basca, *f.*; hacer —s, *arch.*, to pant with rage.

Basco, *pr. n. m.*

bastante, quite, sufficiently.

bastar, to suffice, be enough.

bastecer (*arch. for* abastecer), to supply, provision.

batalla, *f.*, battle; (*arch.*) division of an army, army; *pl.*, combat, thick of the fight.

bayo, *adj.*, bay.

beber, to drink.

bel, *arch. for* bello.

Belerma, *pr. n. f.*

Beltrán, *pr. n. m.*, Bertram.

bello, beautiful, fair.

Bencerraje, *pr. n.*, Abencer-
rage.
bendición, *f.*, blessing.
bendito, blessed.
bermejo, bright red; Torres
Bermejas, Vermilion Tow-
ers.
Bernaldo, *pr. n. m.*, Bernard.
besar, to kiss.
bestia, *f.*, beast; (*fig.*) dunce,
blockhead.
bien, *m.*, good, property; wel-
fare, blessing, happiness.
bien, well, finely; indeed.
Biscaya, *pr. n. f.* (*now spelled*
Vizcaya), Biscay.
blanco, white.
blando, soft.
blanquito (*dim. of* blanco),
very white.
boca, *f.*, mouth, lips; (*fig.*)
tongue.
bocado, *m.*, mouthful, bite;
bit (*of a bridle*).
boda, *f.*, wedding; *pl.*, marriage, wedding.
bofetón, *m.*, cuff, buffet, blow
with the hand upon the
face.
bolsillo, *m.*, purse.
bondad, *f.*, goodness, kindli-
ness.
bonete, *m.*, cap.
bordón, *m.*, staff; bass string
(*of a musical instrument*);
bowstring ? (LVIII, 55).

borla, *f.*, tassel.
borracho, *m.*, drinker, drunk-
ard.
borzeguí, *m.* (*mod.* borceguí),
buskin, half-boot.
Boyso, *pr. n. m.*
bracero, *m.*, one with a stout
arm for throwing (*as a
lance*). *See* ventaja.
brasa, *f.*, red-hot coal.
bravata, *f.*, insulting threat,
bravado.
braveza, *f.*, courage, valor;
cristianos de —, gallant
Christians.
bravo, rough, wild, savage.
brazo, *m.*, arm.
brial, *m.*, silk skirt.
brincar, to skip, hop.
brindar, to invite.
brioso, spirited, courageous.
brocado, *m.*, brocade, cloth
embroidered with gold or
silver.
bueno, good, kind; brave;
pleasing, agreeable.
buey, *m.*, ox.
Burgos, *pr. n.* (*city of* 30,000;
capital of Old Castile).
burla, *f.*, jest.
burlar, to jest; no son burlas
de —, are no jesting matter.
burro, -a, *m. and f.*, donkey
ass.
busca, *f.*, search, pursuit.
buscar, to seek, search for.

C

cábala, *f.*, divínation.

cabalgar, to ride (*horseback*); (*arch.*) to mount.

caballería, *f.*, cavalry, company of horsemen; knighthood; á fe de —, on my knightly honor.

caballeriza, *f.*, stable.

caballero, *adj.*, riding (*a horse*), astride.

caballero, *m.*, knight, gentleman, horseman.

caballo, *m.*, horse.

cabe, *prep.*, beside.

cabello, *m.*, hair (*of the head*).

caber, to fall to the share of; to touch, reach, belong to.

cabeza, *f.*, head.

cabo, *m.*, end, extremity, bottom; de — á —, completely, all.

cabriola, *f.*, gambol.

cabriolar, to caper, frisk.

cacha, *f.*, handle.

cachicuerno, with a horn handle.

cada, each.

cadena, *f.*, chain.

cadencia, *f.*, cadence.

caer, to fall, fall out.

caja, *f.*, box; drum; coffin.

Calahorra, *pr. n.* (*an ancient town 75 miles northwest of Saragossa*).

calandria, *f.*, calendar lark.

calma, *f.*, calm; en —, calm.

calor, *m.* (*and arch. f.*), heat, warmth.

calzada, *f.*, paved road, road, highway.

calzar, to put on, wear (*shoes or spurs*); (*as noun*) footwear, shoes (XXXIX, 3).

callar, *tr.*, to hush, silence; *intr.*, to keep silence, be still.

calle, *f.*, street.

cama, *f.*, bed, couch.

camarera, *f.*, chambermaid; keeper of the wardrobe.

caminar, to travel, journey, march, proceed.

camino, *m.*, road; ir —, to go on the way (XXXVI, 33).

camisón, *m.*, long shirt.

campal, *adj.*; batalla —, pitched battle.

campo, *m.*, field, battle-field, dueling-ground; camp.

Campos, *pr. n.*

Campo-Viejo, *pr. n.*, Campo Vecchio.

canal, *f.*, drinking trough.

canción, *f.*, song.

cano, hoary, white, with white hair.

cansado, weary, tired.

cantar, to sing, chant, crow.

cantar, *m.*, song.

Cantaranas, *pr. n.*

cantarcillo, *dim. of* cantar.

capa, *f.*, cloak.

capitán, *m.*, captain.

captivar (*arch. for* cautivar), to capture, take prisoner.

captividad, *f.* (*arch. for* cautividad), captivity.

captivo, *arch. for* cautivo.

Capuana, *pr. n. f.*

cara, *f.*, face.

cárcel, *f.*, prison, jail.

carcelero, *m.*, jailer.

cardenal, *m.*, cardinal.

cargo, *m.*, dignity, office.

caridad, *f.*, charity.

carillo, *m.*, dear friend.

Carlos, *pr. n. m.*, Charles.

carne, *f.*, flesh, meat; beast (IX, 9).

caro, dear.

Carpio, El, *pr. n. m.*

carretón, *m.*, cart.

carrillo, *m.*, cheek.

Carrión, *pr. n.*

carta, *f.*, letter.

casa, *f.*, house, household, family.

casamiento, *m.*, marriage.

casar, to give in marriage; —se con — con, to marry.

casco *m.*, helmet; hoof (*of a horse*).

Castel Novo, *pr. n. m.* (*Italian*, New Castle).

castellano, Castilian.

castidad, *f.*, chastity.

castigar, to punish, chastise.

castigo, *m.*, punishment.

Castilla, *pr. n. f.*, Castile.

castillo, *m.*, castle, fortress.

Castroviejo, *pr. n.* (*a small town in the province of Logroño*).

catar, to look at, see, consider; (*as noun*) appearance.

cativo, *arch. for* cautivo.

caudal, *adj.*, copious, of much water; *m.*, fortune, wealth.

causa, *f.*, cause, reason, account.

causar, to cause, bring about.

cautivo, captive.

Cava, *pr. n. f.*

caviloso, worrying, pondering.

caza, *f.*, hunt, chase, hunting, fowling; game (*that which is hunted*).

cazador, *m.*, hunter, huntsman.

cazar, to hunt, go fowling.

cebar, to feed.

cebra, *f.*, zebra.

Cebrián, *pr. n. m.* (*arch. for* Cipriano), Cyprian.

cenar, to sup, take supper.

cendal, *m.*, silk gauze, sendal.

centella, *f.*, flash.

ceñir, to gird on, attach by a belt.

cerca, *adv.*, near; — de, near, close to.

cercado, surrounded by defenses, walled in.

cercar, to besiege, lay siege to.

cerco, *m.*, siege, blockade; **poner** —, to besiege, surround.

cerrar, to shut, close.

cerro, *m.*, hill.

cerrojo, *m.*, bolt.

certificar, to assure, inform.

cesar, to çease, stop.

cetro, *m.*, scepter.

Ceupta, *pr. n., mod.* Ceuta (*a Spanish fort on the African coast, nearly opposite Gibraltar*).

cibdad, *arch. for* ciudad.

Cid, El, *pr. n. m.* (*Arabic* sîdî, *my lord*).

cielo, *m.*, heaven, sky.

ciento, cien, one hundred.

cierto, *adj.*, certain, sure; *adv.*, certainly.

cima, *f.*, top, summit; **por — de**, at the highest part of.

cinco, five.

cinto, *m.*, belt.

citar, to make appointment with, summon.

ciudad, *f.*, city. *See* **villa**.

clarín, *m.*, bugle, clarion.

claro, bright, clear, pure.

clemencia, *f.*, mercy.

cobardía, *f.*, cowardice.

cobrar, to recover.

cobrir, *arch. for* **cubrir**.

cocina, *f.*, kitchen.

cocinero, *m.*, cook.

cogedor, *m.*, collector, tax-gatherer.

coger, to catch, seize; to gather, pick; (*arch.*) to receive, shelter.

Coímbra, *pr. n.*

colgar, *tr.*, to hang; *intr.*, to hang, be suspended.

colodrillo, *m.*, back of the head.

color, *m. and f.* (*to-day always m.*), color.

colorado, red.

combate, *m.*, combat, fight.

comenzar, to begin.

comer, to eat, consume, devour; to dine.

cometer, to commit.

comida, *f.*, meal, food; dinner.

como, *adv.*, as, like; *conj.*, how, since, as, when; — **que**, since; **cómo** (*interr. or interj.*), how, why.

compadre, *m.*, friend, comrade.

compaña, *f.* (*arch. for* **compañía**), company, society, escort.

compañía, *f.*, company, society.

comparecencia, *f.*, appearance (*before a judge in response to a summons*).

complacencia, *f.*, satisfaction.

completo, complete.

componer, to amount to.

comprar, to buy, purchase.

con, *prep.*, with.

conceder, to grant.

concejo, *m.*, city government, (*hence*) city (*with all its inhabitants*).

concertar, to arrange, agree upon.

concierto, *m.*, agreement.

concluir, to conclude, end.

concurrencia, *f.*, assembly.

condado, *m.*, earldom, county (*territory ruled by a count, or the dignity and title of count*).

conde, *m.*, count.

condena, *f.*, sentence.

condenado, confounded.

condesa, *f.*, countess.

confesar, to confess.

conforme, *prep.*, according to, according as.

conjurar, to conjure, urge.

conocer, to know, recognize, be *or* become acquainted with.

conosco, *arch. for* conozco.

conquistar, to conquer, subdue.

conseja, *f.*, story.

consejar, *arch. for* aconsejar.

consejero, *m.*, counselor.

consejo, *m.*, counsel, advice.

consentir (en), to consent (to), connive (at).

conservar, to keep.

consolación, *f.*, consolation, comfort.

consolar, to console, comfort.

consonancia, *f.*, harmony.

Consuegra, *pr. n.*

consuno, *adv.*; de —, in league with, in agreement with.

contado, few, scarce; jornadas contadas, marches laid out in advance, (*hence*) forced marches.

contar, to tell, relate; to reckon, count.

contener, to contain.

contentarse, to be contented.

contento, *adj.*, satisfied, contented; *m.*, contentment.

contino, *adj.* (*arch. for* continuo); ropas continas, ordinary dress, every-day clothes.

contra, *prep.*, against.

contray, *m.*, fine woolen cloth (*made in Courtray, Belgium*).

convidar, *tr.*, to invite; *intr.*, to issue invitations.

convite, *m.*, invitation; banquet.

coraje, *m.*, valor; anger; *pl.*, fit of passion.

corazón, *m.*, heart; courage; de —, heartily, lovingly.

cordal, *m.*, wisdom-tooth; (XXV, 4) rope?; (*cf. Libro*

de Alexandre, Janer, copla 1347*b*; Morel-Fatio, copla 1489*b*).

cordel, *m.*, cord, small rope.

Córdoba, *pr. n.*, Cordova (*city of Andalusia with 57,000 inhabitants*).

corona, *f.*, crown.

corredor, -ra, running, galloping.

correo, *m.*, mail.

correr, *tr.*, to pursue, chase; to travel over; *intr.*, to run, flow; to drip (*arch. meaning*).

corrido, ashamed.

cortador, -ra, sharp.

cortar, to cut, cut off, cut down.

corte, *f.*, court; *pl.*, Cortes, parliament; court (XLIV, 24).

cortés, courteous, gracious, gentle.

cortesía, *f.*, civility, courtesy; favor.

corvejón, *m.*, hock, bend of the knee.

corveta, *f.*, curvet, bound.

cosa, *f.*, thing; es — de los mirar, they are a sight to see.

cosque, *m.*; tomar el — (LVIII, 30; *unknown expression; apparently*, to set out).

costado, *m.*, side.

costar, to cost.

costoso, costly, dear.

crecer, to increase; (*of tide*) to flow.

crecido, full-grown, great, extreme; full (*of the moon*); long (*of the hair and beard*).

creer, to believe, think.

criado, *m.*, servant.

criar, to bring up, educate, rear; to nurse, suckle.

cristiano, Christian.

crudo, rough.

cruzado, *m.*, crusader.

cuadrillo, *m.*, bolt, quarrel.

Cuadros, *pr. n. m.*

cual, which; what, of what sort; cada —, every one.

cual, *adv.*, like, as.

cualquier, —ra, *adj.*, whatever, any.

cualquiera, *pron.*, any one.

¡cuán! *interr. and interj.*, how.

cuando, when.

cuanto, as many, how many.

cuanto, *pron.*; en —, as soon as; en — á, as for.

cuarenta, forty.

cuarto, *adj.*, fourth; *m.*, room.

cuatro, four.

cuatrocientos, -as, four hundred.

cubrir (*p. p.* cubierto), to cover.

cuchillo, *m.*, knife, dagger.

Cuenca, *pr. n. (a mountain town* 85 *miles east of Madrid).*

cuenta, *f.,* account; *pl.,* beads; **no tiene —,** it can't be counted.

cuento, *m.,* story, relation; **sin — ni par** (*arch. phrase*), beyond all reckoning.

cuerda, *f.,* string; rope, halter.

cuerno, *m.,* horn.

cuero, *m.,* rawhide, leather.

cuerpo, *m.,* body.

cuidado, *m.,* care, anxiety.

cuidar, to believe (*arch. meaning*).

cuidoso (*arch. for* **cuidadoso**), attentive, solicitous.

cuita, *f.,* affliction, sorrow, anxiety.

cuitado, sad, miserable, unhappy.

culebra, *f.,* snake.

culpa, *f.,* blame; fault; guilt; **por nuestra —,** as a punishment to us.

culpado, guilty.

cumplido, full, complete.

cumplir, *tr.,* to carry out, fulfil, keep; **— 21 años,** to be 21 years of age; *impers.,* to behoove, be fitting; *refl.,* to expire, be ended (*of time*).

cuñado, *m.,* brother-in-law.

curar, to care for, minister to;

— de, to care about, be anxious about; to care for, take care of (*arch. meaning*).

Ch

chico, little, small.

chico, –a, *m. and f.,* boy, girl.

chiquito (*dim. of* **chico**), small, tiny.

chusco, funny; rascally.

D

dádiva, *f.,* gift.

daga, *f.,* dagger.

dama, *f.,* lady.

danzar, to dance.

dar, to give, render; to strike; **—á,** to hit, strike, fall upon; **—en,** to strike upon; **—por,** to proclaim; *refl.,* to give oneself up, surrender.

dardo, *m.,* dart, light lance.

de, *prep.,* of, from, to, in, as, by; than; **— que** (*arch.*), as soon as, when.

debajo, *adv.,* beneath, under; *arch. as prep. for* **debajo de**; **— de,** underneath, beneath.

deber, to be under obligation, have to, must, ought; to owe.

decidor, –ra, witty.

decir, to tell, speak, say, call.

decir, *m.,* opinion, saying.

decretar, to decree, give (*sentence*).

dedo, *m.*, finger.

defender, to defend; to prevent.

defensar (*arch.*), to defend.

degollar, to behead.

dejar, to let, allow; to leave, desert; to cease; to put off.

delante, *adv.*, before (me, *etc.*), in (my) presence; — de, before.

delantero, foremost, first.

delgado, slender.

demanda, *f.*, request, petition; search, inquiry.

demandar, to ask, ask for, demand; to woo; to accuse one of something, make accusation (*arch. meaning*); —lo, to demand satisfaction for something.

demonio, *m.*, devil.

demostrar, to show.

demudado, altered, changed.

dende (*arch. for* desde), from that time.

dentro, *adv.*, within; de —, inside; — de, within.

derecho, *adj.*, right; straight.

derramar, to shed, lose.

derredor; al — de, around, round about.

derribar, to cast down, knock down, overthrow, unhorse.

derrocar, to overthrow, un-

horse (*in this sense, arch. for* derribar).

desacatar, to treat with disrespect, insult.

desafiar, to challenge, defy.

desaguisado, *m.*, injury, offense.

desaparecer (*also refl.*), to disappear.

descabalgar, to dismount.

descalzo, unshod, bare.

descansar, to rest.

descanso, *m.*, rest, repose.

descender, to descend, get down.

desceñir, to ungird.

descolorido, pale.

descomunal, monstrous, huge.

desconsolado, disconsolate.

descontento, discontented, dissatisfied.

descortesía, *f.*, incivility, rudeness.

descubrir, to discover; *refl.*, to reveal one's thoughts.

desde, *prep.*, from, since, after; — chicos, from their childhood.

desdicha, *f.*, misfortune.

desdichado, unlucky, unfortunate, wretched, unhappy.

desear, to desire.

deseo, *m.*, wish.

desgarrar, to rend, tear.

desgracia, *f.*, misfortune; en mi —, to my sorrow.

deshacer, to tear to pieces.

deshonra, *f.*, dishonor.

deshonrado, dishonored.

desierto, deserted.

desligar, to unbind, undo.

desmayar, to become discouraged, disheartened; to faint.

desmesurado, disrespectful, impudent.

desnudar, to strip off; *refl.*, to undress.

desollar, to flay; to fleece.

despavorido, terrified.

despedida, *f.*, parting, farewell, leave-taking.

despedir, to dismiss, escort to the door; *refl. with* de, to take leave of.

despegar, to separate; — la lengua (*for* despegar los labios), to speak.

despertar, *intr.*, to awake.

desplumar, to pluck, strip off feathers.

después, *adv.*, afterwards; — de, — que, after.

desque, *conj.* (*arch.*), as soon as.

desterrar, to exile, banish.

destigar, ? *See note to* LV, 12.

destino, *m.*, destination.

destreza, *f.*, dexterity.

destrozar, to break to pieces, wear out.

destruir, to destroy.

desventurado, unfortunate, wretched.

desviar, to avert.

detener, to hold, detain; *refl.*, to stop, tarry.

determinar, to determine, decide.

dexar, *arch. for* dejar.

día, *m.*, day; de —, by day, day; medio —, noon.

diablo, *m.*, devil.

dicha, *f.*, happiness, good fortune.

dichoso, happy, fortunate.

Diego, *pr. n. m.*, James.

diente, *m.*, tooth.

diez, ten.

diligente, diligent; prompt, quick.

dinero, *m.*, money.

Dios, *m.*, God; id con —, depart in peace.

dirección, *f.*, direction.

discrepar, to be at variance with.

discreto, prudent.

disculpa, *f.*, excuse.

disimulado, secret, disguised.

disparate, *m.*, nonsense, blunder.

distinto, different.

divertir, to amuse.

división, *f.*, difference.

dixe, dixo, *arch. for* dije, dijo.

do, *adv.* (*arch. for* donde, de donde), where, on which,

whence; **por** —, through which.

dó, *arch. for* **doy** *and* **dónde**.

dobla, *f.*, ancient Spanish gold coin, worth about ten pesetas ($2.00).

doblado, increased, heavy.

doblar, to double.

doble, double; thick, heavy.

doce, twelve.

doler, to grieve, cause sorrow.

Dolfos, *pr. n.*

dolor, *m.*, pain, grief, sorrow; **con** —, grieving.

domeñar, to subdue, be master of.

domingo, *m.*, Sunday.

don, don (*gentleman's title, used only before the Christian name*).

don, *m.*, gift.

donaire, *m.*, grace, elegance; witticism.

doncella, *f.*, girl, maiden.

donde, *adv.*, where, whither; *arch. for* **de donde**; — **quiera**, wherever.

donoso, amusing.

doña, lady (*lady's title, see* **don**).

dorado, gilded.

dormir, to sleep.

dos, two.

doscientos, **-as**, two hundred.

dotar, to endow.

dote, *m. and f.*, dowry.

dragón, *m.*, dragon.

duelo, *m.*, lament, mourning.

dueña, *f.*, lady.

Duero, *pr. n.* (*one of the great rivers of Spain and Portugal, flowing west into the Atlantic from Old Castile*).

dulce, sweet; **agua** —, fresh water.

duque, *m.*, duke.

Durandarte, *pr. n. m.*

durar, to last, continue.

duro, hard.

E

é, *for* **y** *before* **i** *and* **hi**; *and arch. for* **y** *in all cases.*

eco, *m.*, echo.

echar, to throw, cast, throw on; to put on; to emit, shed, shoot; — **á**, to begin to; — **mano á**, to seize.

edad, *f.*, age.

ejercia, *f.* (*arch. for* **jarcia**), rigging, shrouds.

Elvira, *pr. n. f.*

embajada, *f.*, embassy, message; business, errand.

embarcar, to embark.

embelesar, to charm, ravish.

empanada, *f.*, meat pie, patty.

empecer, to hurt, injure.

emperador, *m.*, emperor.

empezar, to begin.

emplear, to spend, pass; **bien se te emplea**, thou hast thy deserts, it serves thee right.

en, *prep.*, in, on, upon, at; as.

enamorada, *f.*, lover, mistress, sweetheart.

enamorado, *m.*, lover, dear one.

enamorarse (de), to become enamored (of), fall in love (with).

enano, *m.*, dwarf.

enantes, *adv.*, *arch. for* **antes.**

encanecer, to turn white *or* gray; to see grow gray.

encantar, to charm, enchant.

encima, *adv.*, above; *arch. as prep. for* **encima de;** — **de,** on, on top of, upon.

Encinal, El, *pr. n.*

encomendar, to entrust, commend.

encontrar, to meet, find; *refl. with* **con,** to meet.

encubrir, to hide, conceal.

encuentro, *m.*, encounter, shock.

enemigo, *m.*, enemy.

engañador, *m.*, deceiver, impostor.

engañar, to deceive, impose upon.

engaño, *m.*, deceit; stratagem.

engañoso, deceitful.

engendrar, to beget, create.

enjugarse, to dry.

enojado, angered, angry.

enojar, to vex, anger; *refl.*, to become angry.

enojo, *m.*, vexation, anger; trouble.

ensalpicar, to spatter.

ensangrentar, to stain with blood.

enseñar, to show, display.

ensillar, to saddle.

ensoñar (*arch. for* **soñar**), to dream.

entender, to intend; to understand; to know how to; — **en,** to be occupied with.

entereza, *f.*, firmness.

enternecer, to affect, move to pity.

enterrar, to bury.

entonces, then.

entrada, *f.*, entrance.

entrambos, –as, both.

entrar, to enter.

entre, *prep.*, among, between; by means of (XL, 37); — **sí,** to himself, herself; — **que,** while.

entregar, to hand over, give up.

entrugar (*Asturian word, from Latin* **interrogare**), to ask, inquire.

enviar, to send.

envolver, to wrap.

escaño, *m.*, bench.

escapar, *tr.*, to enable to es-

cape, free from (*danger*);
intr., to escape.

esclarecido, illustrious, noble.

esclavina, *f.*, pilgrim's cloak.

escrebir, *arch. for* escribir.

escribano, *m.*, notary.

escribir (*p. p.* escrito), to
write.

escripto, *arch. for* escrito.

escuchar, to listen to, over-
hear, hear.

escudero, *m.*, young gentleman, young sir, squire.

escudilla, *f.*, bowl.

escudo, *m.*, crown (*coin varying in value;* 50 *or* 75 *cents*).

escupir, to spit.

escuro (*arch. for* oscuro),
dark, gloomy.

ese, –a, –o, *demonstrative adj.*,
that; *often used instead of
the definite article.*

esforzado, strong, valiant.

esforzar, *tr.*, to encourage;
intr. (*arch.*), to redouble
one's efforts; *refl.*, to exert
oneself.

esfuerzo, *m.*, courage, spirit.

esotro, *pron.*, that other, that.

espada, *f.*, sword.

espalda, *f.*, shoulder; *pl.*, back.

espantar, to frighten.

espanto, *m.*, fright; poner —,
to frighten.

España, *pr. n. f.*, Spain.

espera, *f.*, respite.

esperar, *tr.*, to await, wait for;
to give respite; *intr.*, to hope,
expect.

espeso, thick.

espía, *m. and f.*, spy.

espín; puerco —, porcupine.

espinilla, *f.*, shin-bone.

espino, *m.*, hawthorn.

esposa, *f.*, wife, spouse.

espuela, *f.*, spur.

espuma, *f.*, foam, froth.

estaca, *f.*, stake.

estado, *m.*, rank.

estandarte, *m.*, standard.

estar, to be (*temporarily*),
stand, remain; — bien á,
to suit, become.

este, –a, –o, *demonstrative adj.*,
this; en esto, at this point,
juncture.

estilo, *m.*, custom, fashion.

estimar, to respect, honor.

estopa, *f.*, burlap.

estoque, *m.*, rapier.

estorbar, to hinder, interfere
with.

estrado, *m.*, low carpeted
platform, stand.

estrecho, *m.*, strait.

estrella, *f.*, star.

estribo, *m.*, stirrup.

estruendo, *m.*, clash, noise.

evangelio, *m.*, gospel.

evidencia, *f.*, certainty.

experimentar, to experience.

exponer, to lay open, explain.

expresar, to express.

extender, to extend; *refl.*, to go far; to be liberal.

extranjero, foreign.

extraño, strange.

extremado, important, large; excelling.

extremo, extreme; por —, extremely; *m.*, extremities.

F

fablar, *arch. for* hablar.

facer, *arch. for* hacer.

fada, *f.*, fairy, enchantress.

fadar (*arch. for* hadar), to enchant, bewitch.

Fadrique, *pr. n. m.*, Frederick.

Fajardo, *pr. n.*

falagar, *arch. for* halagar.

falcón, *m.*, *arch. for* halcón.

falsedad, *f.*, falsity; false deed, treason.

falsía, *f.*, falseness, untruth.

falso, false.

faltar, to be lacking, be missing; to stay away, fail to appear; to fail, fall short.

faltriquera, *f.*, pocket.

fallar, to decree.

fallar, *arch. for* hallar.

fallecer, to die.

fama, *f.*, fame, reputation; report; echar —, to spread the report.

fantasía, *f.*, fancy, idea.

fasta, *arch. for* hasta.

fatigar, to tire, weary; **to** vex.

favor, *m.*, favor.

faz, *f.*, face.

faz, *arch. for* hace.

fe, *f.*, faith; promise, troth.

fementido, false, faithless.

feridor, *m.* (*arch. for* **heridor**), striker, wielder.

ferir, *arch. for* herir.

fermoso, *arch. for* hermoso.

Fernán, Fernando, *pr. n. m.*, Ferdinand.

feudo, *m.*, fief; fealty.

fiar, to trust; to give surety for, back; **como hombre de** —, like a man true to his trust; *refl. with* de, to trust.

fiesta, *f.*, festivity, merriment; holiday.

figura, *f.*, form, figure; disguise.

fijo, –a, *arch. for* hijo, –a.

filo, *m.* (*arch. for* hilo), thread, edge; **media noche por** —, exactly midnight, the stroke of midnight.

fin, *m. and f.* (*to-day always m.*), end; al —, at last; **en** —, in short.

finado, *m.*, dead man.

finar, to die; *refl.* (*arch.*), to die.

fincar (*arch.*), to remain.

fino, fine.

firmeza, *f.*, firmness, constancy.

fita, *f.* (*arch. for* hita), a small headless nail.

Flandes, *pr. n.*, Flanders.

flema, *f.*, coolness, motionlessness.

flor, *f.*, flower; prime, bloom.

florido, flowery, of flowers; elegant, choice.

florín, *m.*, a silver coin (*equal to the* escudo *in value*).

fogueado, *p. p.*, fired. *See note to* XXXVIII, 13.

fonte-frida,*f.* (*arch. for* fuentefría), cold spring.

fortuna, *f.*, fortune, fate.

forzado, compulsory.

fraile, *m.*, friar.

francés, –sa, French.

Francia, *pr. n. f.*, France.

franco, frank, liberal; Frankish.

franqueza, *f.*, generosity.

freno, *m.*, bridle.

frente, *f.*, forehead.

frío, cold, cool.

frisado, *m.*, silk fabric with a long nap.

fuego, *m.*, fire.

fuente, *f.*, spring.

fuera, *adv.*, outside, without; de —, outside, on the outside; from abroad.

fuerte, strong.

fuerza, *f.*, strength, force,

power; por —, violently; necessarily, perforce.

fuir, *arch. for* huir.

fumador, *m.*, smoker.

furia, *f.*, fury, rage.

furto (*arch. for* hurto); á — de, without the knowledge of.

G

gabela, *f.*, tax, levy.

Gadea, *pr. n. f.*, Agatha.

gafo, *m.*, leper.

Gaiferos, *pr. n. m.*

gala, *f.*, ornament.

galán, *m.*, gallant, lover.

galán, —no, gallant, splendid.

galardón, *m.*, reward, recompense.

galera, *f.*, galley.

Galván, *pr. n. m.*, Gawain.

gallardo, graceful, gallant.

gallo, *m.*, cock; leader.

gana, *f.*, desire; muy de —, diligently; de buena —, gladly, at his *or* her pleasure; de mala —, against (my) will, in spite of (my)-self.

ganado, *m.*, herd of cattle.

ganancia, *f.*, gain, spoils.

ganar, to gain, win, capture, earn.

gañán, *m.*, laborer.

García, *pr. n.*

gargajo, *m.*, phlegm.

garganta, *f.*, throat.

gavilán, *m.*, sparrow-hawk.

gemir, to groan, moan.

Generalife, *pr. n.*

gente, *f.*, people, folk; servants, retinue; grandes —s, great numbers of men; — de poco, mean folk.

gentil, elegant, of good manners; — hombre, fine fellow, gentleman.

gesto, *m.*, countenance, expression of face; face.

Gibraltar, *pr. n.*

Ginebra, *pr. n.*, Geneva.

ginebrino, native of Geneva, Genevan.

gineta, *f.* (*now spelled* jineta); á la —, (riding) with very short stirrup-leathers.

ginete, *m.* (*now spelled* jinete), horseman, rider.

glera, *f.*, gravelly spot.

gloria, *f.*, glory; blessedness, bliss.

golfo, *m.*, gulf.

golpe, *m.*, blow.

Gómez, *pr. n.*

Gonzales, González, *pr. n.* (=son of Gonzalo).

Gonzalo, Gonzalvo, *pr. n. m.*

Gonzalvico, *pr. n. m., dim. of* Gonzalvo.

gorra, *f.*, cap.

gota, *f.*, drop.

gracia, *f.*, divine grace, kindness; favor; gracefulness; (*in familiar use*) name; *pl.*, thanks.

grado, *m.*, degree; de —, de buen —, gladly.

grana, *f.*, scarlet.

Granada, *pr. n. f.*

grande, great, large; loud; los —s y los chicos, both great and small, grown persons and children.

grande, *m.*, noble, grandee (*nobleman of the first rank, who may wear his hat in the king's presence*).

grave, great, serious.

gresca, *f.*, uproar, stir.

grima, *f.*, horror, astonishment.

gritar, to cry, shout.

grito, *m.*, cry, shout; dar —s, to shout, shriek.

grueso, fat, plump.

gualardón, *arch. for* galardón.

guante, *m.*, glove, gauntlet.

guarda, *f.*, custody, guardianship, ward; su — seguían, accompanied them.

guarda, *m. and f.*, guard, sentinel.

guardar, to guard, keep, preserve.

guarir (*arch.*), to be cured, recover.

guarnecer, to garrison.

guerra, *f.*, war; de —, on war-
like errand.

guerrero, *m.*, warrior, soldier.

guisa, *f.* (*arch.*), way, manner.

gusto, *m.*, pleasure.

Gustos, Gústioz, *pr. n.*

H

haber, to have (*often used as
arch. for* tener); — de, to be
about to, be to, intend to,
must (*often used without
special force*); ¿qué habéis?
what is the matter?; *impers.*
(hay, etc.), to be, exist; ha
siete años, 7 years ago, for
7 years.

haber, *m.*, property.

hablador, -ra, speaking, talk-
ing; *m.*, speaker.

hablar, to speak, talk, say;
(*arch.*) to tell.

hacer, to make, do; commit,
perform; cause; — viento,
to blow; hace siete años, 7
years ago, for 7 years; *refl.*,
to be held, be done, take
place; be sent (III, 43).

halagar, to cajole, talk softly
to.

halcón, *m.*, falcon.

hallar, to find; *refl.*, to be
present.

hambre, *f.*, hunger.

harina, *f.*, flour.

Haro, *pr. n.*

hasta, *prep.*, until, up to, to;
— que, until.

hay, *from* haber, there is,
there are.

haya, *f.*, beech-tree.

haz, *m.*, rank (*of soldiers*).

he, *interj.*, behold.

hecho, *m.*, act, deed.

hender, to split.

heredad, *f.* (*arch. for* heren-
cia), inheritance.

heredar, to inherit, inherit
the estate of.

herida, *f.*, wound.

herir, to wound; to strike.

hermana, *f.*, sister.

hermano, *m.*, brother.

hermoso, beautiful.

hermosura, *f.*, beauty.

Hernán, Hernando, *pr. n.*,
Ferdinand.

hidalgo, *m.*, nobleman.

hi-de-perro, *m.*, dog (*insult
applied to Moors*).

hi-de-puta, *m.*, ill-born person.

hierro, *m.*, iron; head, tip (*of
an arrow or lance*); *pl.*, fetters.

higo, *m.*, fig.

hija, *f.*, daughter.

hijadalgo, *f.* (*arch.*), noble-
woman, lady of noble fam-
ily.

hijo, *m.*, son; *pl.*, children.

hijodalgo (*arch. for* **hidalgo**), *m.*, *pl.* **hijosdalgo**, nobleman, noble.

hilar, to spin.

hincar; — **de la rodilla**, to bend the knee, kneel.

hinchar, to swell.

hinojo, *m.*, knee; **de —s**, on his knees.

hito, *m.*; **en —**, fixedly; **de — en —**, fixedly, attentively.

hiz, *arch. for* **hice**.

hobo, *arch. for* **hubo**.

holanda, *f.*, fine linen, cambric.

holgar, *tr.* (*arch.*), to divert, amuse; *intr.*, to take pleasure, recreation; to be glad, rejoice; *refl.*, *same as intr.*

hombre, *m.*, man; — **de armas**, man-at-arms (*mounted*).

hombro, *m.*, shoulder.

homenaje, *m.*, homage, act of fealty.

hondo, *m.*, bottom, deep.

honor, *m.*, honor.

honra, *f.*, honor.

honrado, honorable, of honor.

honrar, to honor.

hora, *f.*, hour; **mal —**, **mala — (for en mal —)**, in an evil hour; **mal — vengáis**, ill betide you.

horca, *f.*, gallows.

hospital, *m.*, almshouse, hospital.

hoy, to-day.

huérfano, bereaved; *m.*, orphan.

huerta, *f.*, pleasure-garden, summer-house.

huerto, *m.*, orchard, garden.

hueste, *f.*, army, division of an army; host.

huir, to flee; — **el campo**, to abandon the field.

humildemente, humbly.

humillarse, to bow, kneel.

hundir, to sink, crush down.

Hungría, *pr. n.*, Hungary.

I

idea, *f.*, idea, fancy.

ides, *arch. for* **vais**.

iglesia, *f.*, church.

igual, *adj.*, equal; *m. and f.*, equal, peer; (*hence*) husband, wife.

igualar, to make equal.

imagen, *f.*, image.

imaginar, to imagine, conceive.

imitar, to imitate.

impuesto, imposed.

inconveniente, *m.*, objection, drawback.

indicio, *m.*, trace, sign; *pl.*, description.

infanta, *f.*, maiden of noble blood (*arch. meaning*); princess.

infante, *m.*, youth of noble blood (*arch.* *meaning*); prince, infante. (*It really is not known why the Infantes de Lara received this title; see* RMP, *Inf. de Lara, glosario.*)

infantina, *f.*, little princess.

infinito, infinite.

ingenuo, ingenuous.

inmenso, immense.

instante, *m.*, instant.

instrumento, *m.*, instrument.

intención, *f.*, intention.

inventar, to invent, concoct.

ir, to go; to concern, be at stake; **más me va que la vida**, more than my life is at stake; **— á**, to go to (*do*), begin to (*often merely redundant*); *refl.*, to depart, go away, escape.

ira, *f.*, anger, fury.

J

Jacobillo, *pr. n. m.* (*dim. of* Jacobo), little James.

jaque, *m.*, check (*in the game of chess*).

jara, *f.*, cistus, rock-rose; field planted with cistus.

jaral, *m.*, field of cistus, rough land, brake.

jardín, *m.*, garden.

jilguero, *m.*, linnet.

Jimena, Ximena, *pr. n. f.* (*French* Chimène).

Joan = Juan.

Jordán, *pr. n.*, Jordan.

jornada, *f.*, day, day's work, (*day's*) march.

joven, young.

Juan, *pr. n. m.*, John.

jubón, *m.*, sleeve-waistcoat, jerkin; waist.

judío, Jewish; *m. and f.*, Jew, Jewess.

juego, *m.*, game, materials of a game (*as board and men*).

juez, *m.*, judge, justice.

jugador, *m.*, player, gambler.

jugar, *tr.*, to stake; *intr.*, to play, be at play.

juicio, *m.*, judgment, trial.

Julián, *pr. n. m.*, Julian.

juntar, to unite; *refl.*, to meet, assemble, join.

junto, *adj.*, together; *adv.*, near (*when used as prep. it should properly be followed by á*).

jura, *f.*, oath.

juramento, *m.*, oath.

jurar, to swear.

juro, *m.*, right of perpetual ownership.

justicia, *f.*, justice; court of justice, judge; officers (*of the law*).

justicia, *m.*; **— mayor**, chief

justice (an important judicial and executive officer in Castile).

justiciar (arch. for ajusticiar), to execute.

justo, just.

juzgar, to judge.

L

labio, m., lip.

labrador, m., farmer, peasant.

labrar, to construct; to carve (stone), embroider (cloth).

lado, m., side.

ladrillado, brick-paved.

lagarto, m., lizard.

lágrima, f., tear.

Laínez, pr. n. (= son of Laín).

Lambra, pr. n. f.

lance, m., crisis, peril; incident, adventure.

lanza, f., lance.

lanzada, f., lance-thrust; lance-wound.

Lara, pr. n.

lasamente, wearily, weakly.

lástima, f., pity.

lavar, to wash.

Lázaro, pr. n. m., Lazarus.

lazo, m., knot; lacing.

leal, loyal.

legua, f., league (nearly four miles).

lejos, adv., far, far away.

lengua, f., tongue.

León, pr. n. m., Leon (a former province in the northwest of Spain; also a city, capital of the province, with 15,000 inhabitants); golfo de —, gulf of Lyons.

leonés, –esa, Leonese.

Leonor, pr. n. f., Eleanor.

letra, f., letter (of a word); letter (= epistle, arch. meaning).

Letrán, pr. n., Lateran.

levantar, to raise; refl., to arise, get up.

libertad, f., liberty, freedom.

libertar, to liberate, set free.

librar, to free; to preserve.

libre, free.

licencia, f., permission, leave.

lid, f., fight, combat.

lidiar, to fight.

ligereza, f., swiftness.

ligero, light, active, lively, swift.

lima, f., file; — sorda, file blunted with lead so as to make its action noiseless.

limosna, f., alms.

limpiar, to clean; to wipe away.

linaje, m., lineage, family.

lindo, fair, pretty.

loco, mad, crazy.

Lombardía, pr. n., Lombardy.

Lorca, pr. n. (city of 60,000 inhabitants in the province

of *Murcia, formerly an important fortress*).

lotero, *m.*, lottery-player.

lozanía, *f.*, vigor, spirit, pride.

lozano, robust, vigorous; healthy, blooming.

Lozano, *pr. n. m.*

luego, in a short time, presently, soon, then, at once.

lugar, *m.*, spot, place; stead.

lugués, −esa, Lucchese, of Lucca. *See note to* XXVIII, 14.

lumbre, *f.*, light.

luna, *f.*, moon.

lunar, *m.*, mole, birthmark.

luto, *m.*, mourning; de —, dressed in mourning.

Ll

llamada, *f.*, summons.

llamar, to call, summon; *refl.*, to be named.

llano, flat, smooth; *m.*, plain.

llanto, *m.*, weeping, lamentation.

llegada, *f.*, arrival.

llegar, to arrive; — á, to reach.

lleno, full, filled; de —, squarely.

llevar, to carry, carry away, take, take in company; to wear; to have; *as auxiliary sometimes equals* tener.

llorar, *tr.*, to bewail, lament, mourn; *intr.*, to weep.

lloroso, weeping, tearful.

M

Macarena, *pr. n. (a quarter of Seville)*.

macho, *m.*, he-mule.

madre, *f.*, mother.

madrugar, to rise early.

maestre, *m.*, grand master.

maestro, *m.*, expert; *(arch.)* surgeon.

magüer, −ra, *conj. (arch.)*, although.

Mahoma, *pr. n. m.*, Muhammed, Mahomet.

mal, *adv.*, badly, ill, with evil fortune; severely, hard.

mal, *m.*, evil, harm; disease; por mi —, to my sorrow; hacer — á, to harm, hurt, punish; — haya, woe betide.

malamente, badly, with evil intent; extremely.

maldad, *f.*, wickedness.

maldecir, to curse.

maldito, cursed, accursed; maldita la cosa, not a thing.

malenconía, *f. (arch. for* melancolía), melancholy, despondency.

maleza, *f.*, underbrush, thicket.

malicia, *f.*, malice, cunning.

malo, bad, evil, wicked, cowardly; mal hora, *see* hora.

malvado, wicked, cruel.

mallado, of mail.

mamar, to suck, be nursed.

mamparar (*arch. for* amparar), to protect, guard.

mancebo, *m.*, youth, young man.

mancilla, *f.*, dishonor, disgrace; (*arch.*) pity, grief.

manchego, of La Mancha (*the southeast portion of New Castile*).

mandado, *m.*, command.

mandar, to order, command, rule over; to offer; to send.

mandato, *m.*, command.

manejar, to wield, handle, manage.

manera, *f.*, way, manner; sobre —, excessive, extreme.

mano, *f.*, hand.

manteca, *f.*, lard, butter.

mantel, *m.*, table-cloth.

mantener, to keep, preserve.

manto, *m.*, cloak.

mantón, *m.*, cloak.

maña, *f.*, habit, custom (*arch. meaning*).

mañana, *f.*, morning; morrow; otro día de —, on the morning of the next day; *adv.*, to-morrow.

mañanica, mañanita, *f.* (*dim. of* mañana), early morning, dawn.

mar, *m. and f.*, sea.

maravedí, *m.*, Spanish coin no longer in use. Its value varied at different times from 4 cents to ½ of a cent.

maravilla, *f.*, wonder, marvel; á —, wonderfully.

maravillarse, to wonder, marvel.

marcha, *f.*, progress; á poco rato de —, after walking a little while.

marfil, *m.*, ivory.

María, *pr. n. f.*, Mary.

Mariana, *pr. n. f.*, Marian.

marido, *m.*, husband.

marinero, *m.*, sailor, mariner.

marroquí, Moroccan.

Marsín, *pr. n. m.* (*French* Marsilie).

Marte, *pr. n. m.*, Mars.

Martín, *pr. n. m.*, Martin.

mas, but.

más, more, most; no . . . —, no longer, not . . . again.

mástel, *m.* (*arch. for* mastelero), topmast.

matador, *m.*, slayer, killer.

Mataleona, *pr. n. f.*

matanza, *f.*, slaughter, massacre.

matar, to kill, slay; to destroy; *refl. with* con, to fight with.

Maynés, *pr. n. m.*

mayo, *m.*, May.

mayor, greater, greatest, very great; older, oldest.

mayoral, *m. and f.*, leader, master, mistress.

Mazote, *pr. n. m.*

medio, half, mid-; — día, noon; media noche, midnight; *m.*, midst, middle.

mediodía, *m.*, midday, noon.

mejor, *adj. and adv.*, better, best.

Melchor, *pr. n. m.*, Melchior.

melena, *f.*, long locks, mane.

memoria, *f.*, memory.

menear, to stir, bestir, move.

menester, *m.*, necessity, need; ser —, haber —, to be necessary.

mengua, *f.*, lack, want.

menguar, to diminish, ebb.

menor, younger, youngest, smaller, smallest.

menos, less, least; ni —, nor still less.

mensajero, *m.*, messenger.

mentir, to lie, deceive.

mentira, *f.*, lie, falsehood.

menudico, small, tiny.

menudo, minute; common.

mercadería, *f.*, merchandise, trade.

merecer, to deserve.

Mérida, *pr. n. (city in Estre-*

madura, with 10,000 *inhabitants).*

mes, *m.*, month.

mesa, *f.*, table.

mesmo, *arch. for* mismo.

mesón, *m.*, inn, tavern.

mesurado, self-controlled, temperate, modest.

metal, *m.*, metal.

meter, to put, place, drive in; *refl. with* por, to enter by.

mezclar, to mix; *refl.*, to mingle.

mezquino, wretched, unhappy (*arch. meaning*).

mezquita, *f.*, mosque.

miedo, *m.*, fear.

mientra, *arch. for* mientras.

mientras, — que, while.

mil, one thousand.

milagro, *m.*, miracle.

mío, *pron.*, mine, my; los —s, my friends, followers, family.

mirar, to gaze, gaze at, look at, observe, watch, consider; —lo mal, not to consider duly, act rashly.

mirlo, *m.*, blackbird.

misa, *f.*, mass.

miseria, *f.*, poverty; misery.

mismo, same, very, self.

mocho, flat-topped (*without a spire*).

mojón, *m.*, boundary stone.

moler, to grind, pulverize.

momento, *m.*, moment, instant.

moneda, *f.*, coin.

monje, *m.*, monk.

montaña, *f.*, mountain.

montar, to raise, set up; — en, —se en, to mount (*a horse*).

monte, *m.*, mountain.

Montesinos, *pr. n. m.*

montiña, *f.*, *arch. for* montaña.

monumento, *m.*, bier, catafalque.

Morayma, *pr. n. f.*

morcillo, glossy-black.

moreno, brown, dark.

morería, *f.*, Moorish quarter of a city; horde of Moors.

Morián, *pr. n. m.*

Moriana, *pr. n. f.*

morico, –a, morillo, –a, *m. and f.*, little Moor, Moorish boy, girl.

morir, to die.

morisma, *f.*, Moors (*collectively*).

Mormojón, *pr. n.*

moro, Moorish; *m. and f.*, Moor.

mostrar, to show, display.

mover, to move, stir; to begin.

mozo, young; *m.*, lad, young fellow.

mozuela, *f.*, young girl.

muchacho, *m.*, boy, lad.

mucho, much, many; tener en —, to esteem highly.

mucho, *adv.*, much; *used archaically for* muy.

mudarse, to change position, stir.

Mudarra, *pr. n. m.* (*Arabic* Mutarraf).

Mudarrillo, *dim. of* Mudarra.

muermo, *m.*, glanders.

mudo, dumb.

muerte, *f.*, death; herida de —, mortal wound.

muerto, dead; killed; *m.*, dead man, dead body.

mujer, *f.*, woman, wife.

muladar, *m.*, dunghill.

mulo, –a, *m. and f.*, mule.

mundo, *m.*, world; todo el —, everyone.

muralla, *f.*, rampart, wall.

músico, *m.*, musician.

muy, *adv.*, very, much; *used archaically for* mucho; — mucho, *arch. for* muchísimo.

N

nacer, to be born; to be found; to start, begin to grow, spring up; mal nacido, ill bred, of low birth.

nada, nothing, anything.

nadie, no one, any one.

naipe, *m.*, playing-card.

nao, *f.*, ship, vessel.

Nápoles, *pr. n.*, Naples.

nascer, *arch. for* nacer.

natural, natural, usual; own, lawful; Francia la —, their native France.

Navarra, *pr. n.*, Navarre.

Navas, *pr. n. f. pl.* (nava, *a plain surrounded by mountains*).

necesario, necessary, needful.

necesitado, needy, in straits.

negar, to deny, refuse.

negro, black, gloomy, wretched.

nel, 'nel, *arch. form for* en el.

ni, neither, nor.

nin, *arch. for* ni.

ninguno, *adj.*, not . . . any, no; *pron.*, no one.

niño, -a, *m. and f.*, child, boy, girl.

no, not, no.

noche, *f.*, night; de —, by night.

nombrado, renowned.

nombre, *m.*, name.

non, *arch. for* no.

nora = en hora; — buena estéis, good fortune attend you.

notar, to dictate.

noticiar, to make known.

noventa, ninety.

nuera, *f.*, daughter-in-law.

nueva, *f.*, news, tidings; *pl.*, news.

nueve, nine.

nuevo, new.

nunca, never, ever.

Nuño, *pr. n. m.*

O

ó, or.

obediencia, *f.*, obedience.

obispo, *m.*, bishop.

objeto, *m.*, object.

obligar, to oblige, put under obligation; to earn one's regard.

obra, *f.*, work, deed.

octavo, eighth.

ocupado, occupied, busy.

ocurrencia, *f.*, occasion.

ocho, eight.

oferta, *f.*, offer.

oficiar, to officiate at, celebrate, aid in singing.

ofrecer, to offer, present.

ogaño, *adv.*, this year, at present.

oir, to hear.

ojo, *m.*, eye.

Olinos, *pr. n. m.* (*The Portuguese form of the name is* Nillo; *Wolf* [*Proben, p.* 94, *note* 1] *says it is the Germanic* Nilaus, Niels, = Nicholas.)

oliva, *f.*, olive-tree; olive-wood.

olivar, *m.*, olive-grove.

Oliveros, *pr. n. m.*, Oliver.

oloroso, perfumed.

olvidar, to forget; *refl. with* de, to forget.

onza, *f.*, ounce.

oponerse, to object, protest.

ora, now.

oración, *f.*, prayer.

ordenado, *m.*; — de evangelio, gospeler, cleric ordained to chant the gospels. *See note to* XIV, 14.

ordenar, to arrange.

Ordóñez, *pr. n.* (=son of Ordoño).

oreja, *f.*, ear.

origen, *m.*, origin.

orilla, *f.*, border, shore; —s de, á —s de, on the shore of.

oro, *m.*, gold.

Orpas, *pr. n. m.*

osado, bold.

usar, to dare.

otorgar, to grant, concede; to agree to.

otro, another, other; — día de mañana, the morning of the next day.

Oviedo, *pr. n.* (*city of 50,000, capital of the former province of the Asturias*).

P

Pablo, *pr. n. m.*, Paul.

Padilla, *pr. n.*

padre, *m.*, father; *pl.*, parents.

padrino, *m.*, godfather.

paga, *f.*, payment; sum.

pagar, to pay, repay; to pay for, atone for.

pago, *m.*, payment; reward.

pájaro, *m.*, bird.

paje, *m.*, page.

palabra, *f.*, word.

palacio, *m.*, palace.

paladín, *m.*, paladin (*one of Charlemagne's Twelve Peers*).

Palencia, *pr. n.*

Palenzuela, *pr. n.*

paleto, *m.*, rustic, hayseed.

palmerico, *m.*, little pilgrim.

palmero, *m.*, pilgrim, palmer.

palmo, *m.*, span (*eight inches*).

palo, *m.*, wood.

paloma, *f.*, pigeon, dove.

palomar, *m.*, pigeon-house, dove-cote.

palomita, *f.*, little dove.

pan, *m.*, bread, loaf of bread; wheat.

pandectas, *f. pl.*, pandects (*code of laws compiled by the Emperor Justinian*).

paniaguado, *m.*, intimate friend, comrade.

paño, *m.*, cloth; *pl.*, clothes.

par, *m.*, equal, peer; en — de (*arch.*), beside; de — en —, wide open; — y —, through and through, side by side; sin cuento ni —, *see* cuento.

para, *prep.*, to, in order to, for,

toward; ¿— qué? why? for what purpose?

parar, to stop; *refl.*, to stop, stand.

parecer, to appear, be in sight; to seem; to seem right.

parescer, *arch. for* **parecer.**

parias, *f. pl.*, tribute.

parida, *f.*, woman who has recently given birth to a child.

pariente, -a, *m. and f.*, relative, kinsman, kinswoman.

parir, to bring forth, bear.

París, *pr. n.,* Paris.

parte, *f.*, part, share; side; *pl.*, talents, qualities; **de — á —,** through and through; **de mi —, de — mía,** from me, for me.

partida, *f.*, departure; part, place (*arch. meaning*); **de —,** about to leave.

partir, *tr.*, to split, divide, break in two; *intr. and refl.*, to set forth, depart.

pasa, *f.*, raisin.

pasada, *f.*, passage, passing.

pasado, *adj. and m.*, past.

pasar, to pass; to carry over, across; to pierce.

pascua, *f.*, Easter; **Pascua de Flores,** Easter; **ropas de —,** festal garments, best dress.

pasear, —se, to walk about.

paso, *m.*, step, pace.

pastor, *m.*, shepherd.

pata, *f.* (*foot and leg of lower animals*), foot, hoof, forefoot.

patada, *f.*, tread, hoof-beat.

patán, *m.*, churl, rustic.

pavor, *m.*, fear, dread.

pecado, *m.*, sin; devil.

pecar, to sin, commit an offense.

pechar, to pay a tax of.

pecho, *m.*, breast; tax.

pedazo, *m.*, piece.

pedir, to ask, ask for; to call for, require.

pedrería, *f.*, precious stones; **de gran —,** richly studded with gems.

Pedro, *pr. n. m.,* Peter.

peinar, to comb.

peine, *m.*, comb.

pelear, to fight, combat.

peligrar, to be in danger.

peligro, *m.*, peril; **á — de,** in peril from.

pena, *f.*, penalty, punishment.

penado, sorrowful; suffering.

penar, to suffer.

pendón, *m.*, pennant, banner.

pensamiento, *m.*, thought.

pensar, to think, deem; **á mi —,** in my opinion.

peña, *f.*, rock, (*large*) stone.

peón, *m.*, foot-soldier.

peor, *adj. and adv.*, worse, worst.

pequeño, little, small; *m.*, child.

pera, *f.*, pear.

peral, *m.*, pear-tree.

perder, to lose, forfeit; to ruin.

pérdida,*f.*, loss, thing lost; **perder una —**, to suffer a loss.

perdón, *m.*, pardon, forgiveness.

perdonar, to pardon, forgive.

perecer, to perish; to suffer.

perfilar, to hold so as to show the outline. *See note to* XXIII, 9.

permitir, to permit.

pero, but.

perrita, *f.* (*dim. of* **perra**), little dog.

perro, *m.*, dog.

persona, *f.*, person.

pertenecer, to belong; to concern; to befit.

perverso, wicked, malignant.

pesar, *tr.*, to weigh; **á oro te le —án**, you shall be paid his weight in gold for him; *intr.*, to weigh; to cause regret, sorrow; **pésete**, confound you; **pese á mis moros**, woe betide my Moors; **me pesa de ello**, I am sorry for it.

pesar, *m.*, sorrow, grief, regret; indignation; scruple; **á — de**, in spite of.

pescado, *m.*, fish (*after it is caught*).

petición, *f.*, request.

pez, *m.*, fish (*in the water*).

pícaro, rascally, crafty.

pico, *m.*, pick; beak.

pie, *m.*, foot, hoof, hind foot (*of animals*); **de —s**, standing.

piedad, *f.*, pity.

piedra, *f.*, stone.

piel, *f.*, skin.

pierna, *f.*, leg.

pieza, *f.*, piece; *pl.*, armor.

pino, *m.*, pine-tree, pine.

pío, piebald.

pisar, to trample, tread under foot.

placentero, joyful, contented.

placer, to please, suit.

placer, *m.*, pleasure, joy.

plantar, to plant.

plañir, to sob, lament, whine.

plata, *f.*, silver.

plato, *m.*, plate, dish.

plaza,*f.*, square, market-place.

poblado, *m.*, village.

poblar, to people.

pobre, poor, sorry.

pobreza, *f.*, poverty.

poco, *adj.*, small, little, petty, few; **gente de —**, worthless folk, common people; *adv.*, little.

poder, to be able; to have power.

poder, *m.*, power, force; en —
de, in the hands of.

poderoso, powerful.

po'l, *colloquial for* por el.

polvo, *m.*, dust.

poner, to place, put, set, set
up; to send; to spread; to
impose, enjoin; — nombre
á, to name; —se á, to begin
to.

por, *prep.*, to, in order to; in,
at, by; for; along, through,
throughout; on account of;
instead of; — eso, on that
account; — tanto, there-
fore.

porfía, *f.*, persistence, insistence (*in dispute*); dispute,
discussion.

porque, because, in order that.

portero, *m.*, porter, door-
keeper, mace-bearer.

portillo, *m.*, breach.

posada, *f.*, lodging; inn.

posar, to rest, lodge; to perch,
alight.

poseer, to possess.

posible, possible.

posponer (*p. p.* pospuesto),
to lay aside.

postigo, *m.*, postern-gate
(*small gate in or beside a
large one*).

postrero, last.

potencia, *f.*, faculty.

pradal, *m.* (*arch.*), field.

prado, *m.*, field, meadow.

preciar, to value, prize, esteem.

precio, *m.*, price.

precisamente, precisely, exactly.

preguntar, to ask.

premio, *m.*, reward.

prenda, *f.*, security, satisfaction for an injury; dear one.

prender, to seize, imprison,
capture.

preparar, to prepare.

presentar, to present, make a
gift of; *refl.*, to appear.

presente, *adj.*, present.

preso, *m.*, captive, prisoner.

prestar, to lend.

preste, *m.*, priest (*arch. meaning*).

presteza, *f.*, speed, haste.

presto, soon, quickly.

presumir, to be conceited.

priesa, *f.*, haste.

prieto, black.

primero, *adj.*, first; *adv.*, first,
sooner, before.

primo, *m.*, cousin.

primoroso, fine, elegant.

principal, important, chief,
foremost.

príncipe, *m.*, prince.

prior, *m.*, prior (*head of a
monastery, or, sometimes,
next in authority to the
abbot*).

prisa, *f.*, haste, hurry, speed;
darse —, to make haste;
traer —, to be in haste.
prisión, *f.*, prison; imprisonment; *pl.*, imprisonment;
chains, fetters.
privado, privileged, favorite,
in favor.
probar, to prove.
procedencia, *f.*, source.
proceder, to conduct.
pródigo, prodigal, free.
proeza, *f.*, valor, prowess.
promesa, *f.*, promise.
prometer, to promise.
proposición, *f.*, proposition;
member.
pueblo, *m.*, town, village; people, nation.
puerco, -a, *m. and f.*, pig, hog,
sow; wild boar.
puerta, *f.*, door, gate.
puerto, *m.*, pass (*through the
mountains*).
pues, then, since, accordingly;
well; — que, although, because, since.
punta, *f.*, point.
puntapié, *m.*, kick.
punto, *m.*, point, moment; al
—, immediately; subir los
—s, to increase the pace.
puntualidad, *f.*, punctuality.
puñada, *f.*, blow with the fist,
cuff.
puñal, *m.*, dagger, poniard.

puño, *m.*, fist, grasp.
puridad; en — (*arch.*), secretly, in private.

Q

que, *pron.*, who, which, that;
(*followed by infinitive*) anything; *conj.*, that, for, since,
and; *adv.*, than, as.
¡qué! ¿qué? what, what a,
how.
quebrar, to break.
quedar, to remain, be left.
quedo, quiet; de —, softly, in
a low voice.
queja, *f.*, complaint.
quejarse (de), to complain
(of), find fault (with).
quemar, to burn.
querella, *f.*, complaint, reproach.
querer, to wish, desire (*often
used in rs. without addi-
tional force*); — á, to love;
quiera . . . quiera, either
. . . or.
querido, beloved, dear; *m.*,
loved one, lover.
quien, *pron.*, who, he who;
— quiera, any one.
¿quién? *pron.*, who?
quieto, still.
quince, fifteen.
quistión, *f.* (*arch. for* cues-
tión), dispute, quarrel.

quitar, to take away, remove, release; to deprive; — **el cerco,** to raise the siege; **quítate allá,** get away from here.

quizá, perhaps.

R

rabia, *f.,* rage, madness; **si mala — vos mate,** a murrain on you.

rajar, to cleave.

rama, *f.,* branch, bough, limb.

ramo, *m.,* bough.

raro, unusual.

rato, *m.,* while, short space of time.

razón, *f.,* reason, reasoning; speech, words; **dar —,** to inform, give an account.

razonar, to talk, discourse, converse.

real, royal.

real, *m.,* tent of the king *or* general of an army; camp; coin (*to-day equal to about 5 cents*).

recado; á buen —, under safe guard.

recaudo, *m.,* precaution, care; surety, bail.

recebir, *arch. for* **recibir.**

recelarse, to fear, suspect.

reciamente, stoutly, hard, vigorously; loudly.

recibir, to receive.

recio, *adj.,* strong, hard; *adv.,* vigorously, stoutly, hard.

reclamar, to claim, demand.

recoger, to keep, put away; to pick up.

recompensa, *f.,* reward, recompense.

recordar, to awake from sleep.

rededor; al —, round about.

referir, to relate.

regalar, to favor, pet.

regir, to manage, wield.

reina, *f.,* queen.

reinado, *m.,* reign; kingdom (*arch. meaning*).

reinar, to reign.

reino, *m.,* kingdom.

reir (*also refl.*), to laugh.

relación, *f.,* narrative, tale.

religión, *f.,* religion; **entrar en —,** to take the veil

relincho, *m.,* neigh, neighing.

relucir, to shine, glow, glitter.

relumbrar, to shine, glow.

remediar, to remedy, alter for the better.

remedio, *m.,* remedy.

Renaldo, —s, *pr. n. m.,* Reynold.

renegada, *f.,* renegade, Christian woman converted to Mohammedanism.

renegar (de), to deny, give up a religion, abjure.

renovar, to renew.

repartidor, –ra, free-handed, generous.

repecho, *m.*, slope.

repetir, to repeat.

replicar, to reply; to repeat (*arch. meaning*).

reprender, to reprove.

reptar (*arch. for* retar), to challenge, defy.

rescatar, to ransom.

resguardar, to defend.

resollar, to breathe, take breath.

respingo, *m.*, kick, jerk.

resplandecer, to gleam, shine.

responder, to answer, reply.

responso, *m.*, responsory for the dead.

respuesta, *f.*, answer, reply.

restregar, to rub.

resuelto, *p. p.*, resolved, determined.

reto, *m.*, challenge.

retornar; — en sí, to come to oneself (*arch. use*).

retraer; —lo á alguien, to reproach one with it, blame one for it.

retraído, *p. p.*, in retirement, in seclusion.

reventar, to burst; to die (*suddenly or of exertion*).

revolver, to turn about, wrap about; to foment disturbances in.

revuelta, *f.*, second turn *or* whirl; vueltas y —s, struggling back and forth.

revuelto, *p. p.*; — en sangre, dripping with blood.

rey, *m.*, king; Día de los Reyes, Epiphany (*January sixth*).

rezar, to pray.

ribera, *f.*, bank, shore.

riberica, *dim. of* ribera.

rico, rich, costly.

Rico Franco, *pr. n. m.*

ricohombre, *m.*, noble (*of the highest rank*).

rienda, *f.*, rein; restraint.

riguroso, severe, harsh.

río, *m.*, river.

riqueza, *f.*, riches.

risueño, smiling, merry.

robar, to steal, rob; to deprive; to carry off, abduct.

roble, *m.*, oak-tree.

robo, *m.*, theft.

rocín, *m.*, nag, work horse.

rodado, with dark spots.

rodar, to spin.

rodear, to pass around; to drive around; to roll over.

rodilla, *f.*, knee.

Rodrigo, *pr. n. m.*, Roderick.

rogar, to ask, request, entreat, beg.

Roldán, *pr. n. m.*, Roland.

Roma, *pr. n.*, Rome.

romance, *m.*, ballad, *romance*.

romería, *f.*, pilgrimage.
romero, *m.*, pilgrim, palmer.
romper, to break; to tear.
Roncesvalles, *pr. n.* (*French* Roncesvaux*).
ropa, *f.*, clothes; *pl.*, clothes, garments.
roque, *m.*, rook, castle (*at chess*).
rosa, *f.*, rose.
rosal, *m.*, rose-bush.
Rosalinda, *pr. n. f.*, Rosalind.
rostro, *m.*, face.
roto, *p. p.*, torn, ragged.
roznar, to bray.
ruán, –na, roan.
rubio, blonde, fair.
rucio, light gray.
ruiseñor, *m.*, nightingale.
Ruy = Rodrigo.

S

saber, to know, know how, learn.
sacar, to take out, pluck out, help out; to draw; to derive; to bring away, lead away; — la lengua, to stick out the tongue.
saeta, *f.*, arrow.
sagaz, sagacious, far-sighted.
sagrado, *m.*, place of refuge, sanctuary.
sala, *f.*, hall.
salario, *m.*, salary, wages.

Salas, *pr. n.*
Salido, *pr. n.*
salir, to go out, come out, depart; to go out to meet; to appear; salga lo que saliere, come what may.
salmón, *m.*, salmon.
saltar, to leap.
salvar, to save, bless.
salvo, safe; á su —, without danger; en —, safe, in safety.
sanar, to cure, heal.
sancto, *arch. for* santo.
Sancha, *pr. n. f.*
Sancho, *pr. n. m.*
sangre, *f.*, blood; race, lineage; de —, bloody.
sangriento, bloody.
San Juan, *pr. n. m.*, Saint John; Saint John's Day (*June* 24).
sano, sound, healthy; alive (XIV, 42).
Sansueña, *pr. n.*, Saxony; Saragossa. *See note on* XXII, 39.
sant, *arch. for* san.
Santelmo, *pr. n. m.*, Saint Elmo.
Santiago, *pr. n. m.*, Saint James the Greater (*patron saint of Spain*).
Santiago, *pr. n.*, Santiago de Compostela (*city of* 25,000, *capital of Galicia*).

santo, *abbreviated to* sant, san, holy, saint.

saña, *f.*, anger, passion.

sapo, *m.*, toad.

sastre, *m.*, tailor.

saya, *f.*, (*outer*) skirt.

sayal, *m.*, sackcloth.

sayo, *m.*, long loose cloak without buttons.

secar, to dry; *refl.*, to dry up.

secreto, *m.*, secret.

sed, *f.*, thirst.

seda, *f.*, silk.

sedes, *arch. for* sois.

segador, *m.*, reaper.

seguir, *tr.*, to follow, pursue; *intr.*, to continue; *refl.*, to continue.

según, *prep. and conj.*, according to, as.

segundo, second.

seguridad, *f.*, safety.

seguro, safe, sure, certain.

seis, six.

selva, *f.*, wood.

semana, *f.*, week.

semejante, such, similar.

semejar (á), to resemble.

senda, *f.*, path.

sendos, –as, one for each, respective.

sentar, to seat; *refl.*, to sit down.

sentencia, *f.*, sentence, decree.

sentido, *m.*, feeling, con-sciousness; sense, senses; understanding.

sentimiento, *m.*, sorrow.

sentir, to feel, perceive.

seña, *f.*, mark, sign for identification; (*arch.*) banner; *pl.*, description.

señal, *f.*, sign, token, portent; mark, scar.

señalado, noted, famous.

señor, *m.*, sir, gentleman; noble; lord, master.

señora, *f.*, lady, mistress.

señorear, to rule, be lord of.

señoría, *f.*, dominion.

separarse, to part.

sepultura, *f.*, grave, tomb.

ser, to be (*permanently*).

servicio, *m.*, service.

servidor, *m.*, servant, wooer, lover.

servir, to serve, pursue.

sesenta, sixty.

seso, *m.*, brains, understanding.

Sevilla, *pr. n.*, Seville (*capital of Andalusia, with* 150,000 *inhabitants*).

si, *conj.*, if, whether; as, so (*in exhortations, when it is derived from Latin* sic).

siempre, always, ever.

sierra, *f.*, saw; mountain range.

Sierra Morena, *pr. n.* (*the low ridge of mountains sep-*

218 VOCABULARY

*arating Andalusia from Es-
stremadura).*
siesta, *f.*, siesta, rest taken
during the heat of the day;
con la gran — que hace, on
account of the great heat.
siete, seven.
signo, *m.*, sign, symbol; sign
of the zodiac.
silla, *f.*, chair; saddle.
simplón, *m.*, simpleton.
sin, without; besides.
siniestro, left.
sino, but, except, unless; **no
hace —**, he does nothing
but; **— que**, except that.
sinon, *arch. for* **sino**.
siquiera, whether.
sirena, *f.*, siren, mermaid.
sirviente, *m.*, servant.
so, *prep.*, under, below.
so, *arch. for* **soy**.
sobarbada, *f.*, sharp reproof,
blame.
soberbia, *f.*, pride, arrogance.
soberbio, proud, haughty, in-
solent.
sobra, *f.*; *pl.*, leavings, crumbs.
sobre, above, on, upon; concerning; near, in front of
(*a city*).
sobredorar, to gild.
sobrino, *m.*, nephew.
socorrer, to help, aid, succor.
socorro, *m.*, aid, succor.
sol, *m.*, sun.

solamente, *adv.*, only, merely.
soldada, *f.*, pay, wages.
soldado, *m.*, soldier.
soler (*impers.*), to be wont,
use.
solimán, *m.*, corrosive subli-
mate.
Solisa, *pr. n. f.*
solo, alone, single, only.
sólo, *adv.*, only, merely; **tan
—**, only.
soltar, to let go; to solve, explain.
sombrero, *m.*, hat.
son, *m.*, sound; tune.
sonada, *f.* (*arch.*), sound,
noise (*of instruments*).
sonar (**á**), to be reported (to),
reach the ears (of).
soñar, to dream.
sopa, *f.*, sop of bread; **— en
vino**, bread dipped in wine.
soplo, *m.*, puff; **dar un —
(por)**, to blow (upon).
sordo, deaf; noiseless; **lima
sorda**, *see* **lima**.
sosegar, to calm, quiet.
sospirar (*arch. for* **suspirar**),
to sigh.
subir, *tr.*, to raise, lift up;
intr., to go up, come up,
mount, rise.
suceso, *m.*, event.
sudar, to sweat, perspire.
suegra, *f.*, mother-in-law.
sueldo, *m.*, pay, wages.

suelo, *m.*, floor, ground.

sueño, *m.*, sleep; dream, vision.

Suero, *pr. n. m.*

suerte, *f.*, manner; lot, fate; echar —s, to draw *or* cast lots.

sufrir, to permit; to suffer, endure.

suma, *f.*, sum.

suplicar, to entreat.

suplicio, *m.*, place of punishment.

suponer, to suppose.

suspender, to suspend, stop.

sustentar, to maintain, keep up; to endure.

suyo, *pron.*, his; los —s, his followers.

T

taberna, *f.*, tavern, drinking house, barroom.

tabla, *f.*, table; *pl.*, backgammon.

tablado, *m.*, platform; staging, scaffold.

tajador, –ra, sharp.

tal, such, so, a certain, the following; con — que, provided that; *pron.*, such a thing.

tamaño, so great.

también, also.

tampoco, neither, (not) either.

tan, so; á — bien, exceedingly well.

tanto, so many, as many, so much, as much; otros —s, an equal number, as many again.

tañer, to play (*an instrument*), sound.

tardar, to delay.

tarde, *adv.*, late.

Tarfe, *pr. n. m.*

¡tate! *interj.*, stop! take care!

tejer, to weave.

tela, *f.*, cloth; lists (*enclosed space for a tournament or celebration*).

temblar, to tremble, shake, quiver.

temer, to fear.

temor, *m.*, fear.

templar, to temper.

temprano, early.

tender, to spread, unfold, unfurl; to hold out.

tenencia, *f.*, occupation; en —, in fief.

tener, to have, hold, keep, possess, maintain; — en mucho, to esteem; — por, to consider as; no — que dar, to have nothing to give; — que hacer, to have to do, must do (*archaically* tener de hacer *and* tener hacer *are used in the same sense. Cf.* XLIV, 94; XLIV, 172).

teñir, to dye, stain.

tercero, third.

ternía, *arch. for* tendría.

terno, *m.*, tern, "gig" (*com-bination of three numbers in a lottery*).

testamento, *m.*, last will, tes-tament.

teta, *f.*, breast, nipple; niño de —, suckling child.

tía, *f.*, aunt.

tiempo, *m.*, time.

tienda, *f.*, tent.

tierra, *f.*, land, earth, ground; estate, native place.

tinta, *f.*, ink.

tinto, *p. p.*, dyed.

tío, *m.*, uncle.

tirar, to throw, hurl; (*with* á) to throw at, aim at.

tiserica, *f.* (*dim. of* tisera, *arch. for* tijera), scissors.

toca, *f.*, any head-dress of thin cloth, kerchief; —s de caminar, traveling ker-chief.

tocar, to touch; to sound, play, blow (*trumpet*), beat (*drum*); — en, to affect, move.

todavía, yet, however.

todito (*dim. of* todo), every single one.

todo, all, every.

Toledo, *pr. n.* (*city of* 25,000, *formerly capital of kingdom of Castile*).

tomar, to take, get; to accept,

receive; to seize; to ad-minister (*an oath*).

topar, to meet by chance, happen upon.

torcer, to twist, wind, wring out.

tordico, *m.* (*dim. of* tordo), thrush.

tornaboda, *f.*, the day after a wedding; the festivities held on that day.

tornadizo, *m.*, turncoat, de-serter.

tornar, *tr.*, to return, give back; to take back (XXXVII, 41); *intr.*, to return; — en sí, to come to oneself, re-cover consciousness; — á hacer, to do again; *refl.*, to return.

tornasol, *m.*, changeable color.

torneo, *m.*, tournament.

Toro, *pr. n.* (*town of Old Cas-tile,* 20 *miles east of Za-mora*).

torpeza, *f.*, clumsiness.

Torquemada, *pr. n.*

torre, *f.*, tower.

tortolica, *f.* (*dim. of* tórtola), turtle-dove.

trabajar, to work.

trabajo, *m.*, labor, toil.

traer, to bring, bear, carry, wear; cansado traigo el ca-ballo, my horse is tired.

traición, *f.*, treachery, treason.

traidor, *m.*, traitor.

tranzado, cut off, short.

tras; — de, behind, after.

traslado, *m.*, notification (*to a party sued*).

traspasar, *tr.*, to transfer; *intr.*, to faint, lose consciousness.

tratar, to treat; to talk; to arrange; — de, to discuss; *refl.*, to be arranged.

trayo, *arch. for* traigo.

trece, thirteen.

tregua, *f.*; *pl.*, truce.

treinta, thirty.

treinteno, thirtieth.

tremedal, *m.*, quagmire.

trémulo, shaking.

trenza, *f.*, lock, braid.

tres, three.

trescientos, –as, three hundred.

tributario, tributary, tax-paying.

tributo, *m.*, tribute, tax.

trigo, *m.*, wheat.

triste, sad, wretched; — del caballero, alas for the knight; — de mí, woe is me.

tristeza, *f.*, grief, sorrow.

trompeta, *f.*, trumpet, bugle.

trompo, *m.*, top.

trucha, *f.*, trout.

trujeron, *arch. for* trajeron.

tullido, crippled, maimed.

turbante, *m.*, turban.

turbar, to trouble, alarm, confuse.

turbio, muddy, turbid.

Turpín, *pr. n. m.*, Turpin.

U

ufano, proud, glad.

último, last.

ultrajar, to insult, despise.

uno, a, one, the same; á una, together; *pl.*, some; *pron.*, one; — á —, one by one.

uña, *f.*, nail, claw, talon.

urdirse, to arise, occur.

Urraca, *pr. n. f.* (*dim. of* María).

Urueña, *pr. n.*

usar (*with or without* de), to use.

usurero, *m.*, money lender, usurer.

V

vado, *m.*, ford.

vaivén, *m.*, swinging, swaying.

val, *m.*, vale, valley.

Valencia, *pr. n.* (*city on the Mediterranean, with* 200,000 *inhabitants*).

valentía, *f.*, valor, courage.

valer, *tr.*, to defend, protect, avail; *intr.*, to be worth; más vale, it is better.

valía, *f.*, worth, excellence.

valiente, valiant, brave.

valor, *m.*, courage.

Valladolid, *pr. n.* (*city of Old Castile, 76 miles southwest of Burgos, population 70,000*).

vano, vain.

vara, *f.*, javelin, lance (*not for use in war*); wand, staff of office.

varica, *f.* (*dim. of* vara), little rod, staff.

varón, *m.*, male, man.

vasallo, *m.*, vassal, follower.

vaso, *m.*, glass.

vaticinio, *m.*, prophecy, prediction.

vees, *arch. for* ves.

vega, *f.*, meadow, plain.

veinte, twenty.

vela, *f.*, vigil, watch; sail.

velador, *m.*, watcher, watchman, sentinel.

velar, *tr.*, to veil (*a bride and groom at the nuptial mass*); *intr.*, to watch, keep vigil, be awake.

Velázquez, *pr. n.*

Vellido, *pr. n. m.*

venablo, *m.*, javelin.

vencedor, *m.*, conqueror.

vencer, to conquer.

vender, to sell; to betray.

Venecia, *pr. n.* Venice.

veneno, *m.*, poison.

vengador, –ra, avenging.

vengar, to avenge, take revenge for; *refl. with* de, to take revenge on.

venida, *f.*, coming, arrival.

venir, to come; ¡bien vengáis! welcome!; *refl.*, to come away, escape.

ventaja, *f.*, advantage; muy buen bracero á —, excelling all in hurling a lance.

ventana, *f.*, window.

ventura, *f.*, fate, fortune, good fortune, luck, happiness.

venturoso, fortunate.

ver, to see.

veras; de —, in earnest.

veraz, veracious, true.

verdad, *f.*, truth; ser —, to be true.

verdadero, true, real.

verde, green.

verdugo, *m.*, hangman.

vergüenza, *f.*, shame.

verná, *arch. for* vendrá.

vernía, *arch. for* vendría.

verter, to pour.

vestido, *m.*, dress, garment; *pl.*, clothes, garments.

vestir, to wear, put on; bien vestido, well dressed.

vez, *f.*, time; stead; una —, once; otra —, again.

vía, *f.*, way, road, route.

vianda, *f.*; *pl.*, victuals, food.

vida, *f.*, life; á —, with life, alive; mi —, my dear; prados de mi —, my well-loved meadows.

vide, *arch. for* vi.

vido, *arch. for* vió.

viejo, old.

viento, *m.*, wind.

vigor, *m.*, energy.

villa, *f.*, city *or* town (*which was granted special privileges by royal charter, but less important than those held by a* ciudad).

villanesco, rustic.

villanía, *f.*, meanness, base deed, villainy.

villano, *m.*, churl, peasant.

vino, *m.*, wine.

violento, violent.

violín, *m.*, violin.

vira, *f.*, dart, arrow.

visera, *f.*, vizor.

visitar, to visit.

víspera, *f.*, evening before.

vista, *f.*, sight, view.

viuda, *f.*, widow.

Vivar, *pr. n.* (=Bivar, *a village* 6 *miles north of Burgos*).

Vivarambla, *pr. n., mod.* Bibarrambla (*from Arabic* Bab-ar-rambla, *Gate of the sandy plain*).

vivir, to live.

vivo, alive, living.

volar, to fly; (*as noun*) flight.

voluntad, *f.*, will.

volver, to turn, return; — á

hacer, to do again; *refl.*, to turn, return; to be disturbed, rebellious.

vos, *pron., arch. for* vosotros, os, *and* usted.

voz, *f.*, voice; shout; word; á voces, loudly; dar voces, to shout, cry out.

vuelta, *f.*, turn, circuit; return; —, —, turn back, turn back.

vueso, *arch. for* vuestro.

Y

y, and.

ya, already, now; — que, since.

yacer, to lie.

yantar (*arch.*), to dine, eat.

yegua, *f.*, mare.

yerba, *f.*, grass, plant, herb.

Z

Zacatín, *pr. n.* (*Arabic* as-saq-qâtîn, *old-clothes dealers*).

zagaya, *f.* (=azagaya), assagai, javelin.

Zaida, *pr. n. f.*

Zaide, *pr. n. m.*

Zamora, *pr. n.* (*city of León, on the river Duero, population* 15,000).

zamorano, *m.*, inhabitant of Zamora.

zapateta, *f.*, caper.

zapato, *m.*, shoe.

INDEX TO FIRST LINES